Day Hikes
in the Pacific
Northwest

90 favorite trails, loops, and
summit scrambles within a few
hours of Portland and Seattle

Don J. Scarmuzzi

WESTWINDS
PRESS®

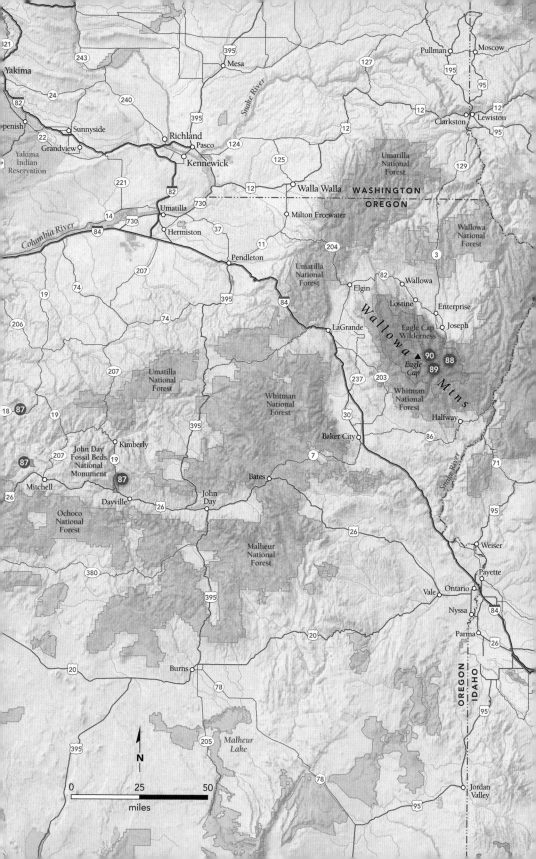

CONTENTS

Overview Map 2
Preface 7

MOUNT ST. HELENS–INDIAN HEAVEN WILDERNESS–GIFFORD PINCHOT NATIONAL FOREST

1 Lewis River Falls 11
2 Lemei Rock Loop 16
3 Falls Creek Falls 20
4 Soda Peaks Lake to West Soda Peak 22
5 Observation Peak to Sister Rocks 26
6 Siouxon Peak to Huffman Peak 28
7 Ape Cave Loop 31
8 Goat Mountain...................................34
9 Sheep Canyon Loop 37
10 Coldwater Peak 40
11 Norway Pass and Harmony Falls 43
12 Mount Margaret 46
13 Mount Whittier 49
14 Mount St. Helens 50

MOUNT ADAMS–GOAT ROCKS WILDERNESS

15 Johnson Peak 57
16 Hogback Mountain 61
17 Bear Creek Mountain 65
18 Nannie Ridge to Cispus Pass...........68
19 Goat Lake Loop to Hawkeye Point...72
20 Old Snowy Mountain........................75
21 Hellroaring Canyon Viewpoint to Iceberg Lake Overlook 77
22 Stagman Ridge Loop.......................80
23 High Camp/Adams Glacier Meadows to Equestria Lake 83
24 Mount Adams 86

MOUNT HOOD–SALMON-HUCKLEBERRY WILDERNESS

25 Wildcat Mountain 91
26 Salmon Butte 94
27 Hunchback Mountain 97
28 Devil's Peak Lookout 99

29 Tom Dick and Harry Mountain 101

30 Trillium Lake Snowshoe Loop 104

31 Palmateer Point 106

32 Lookout Mountain 108

33 Tamanawas Falls 110

34 Tilly Jane Snowshoe Loop 112

35 Cooper Spur 115

36 Lamberson Butte to
Newton Creek Canyon Loop 118

37 Little Zigzag Canyon Loop 121

38 Paradise Park to
Mississippi Head Loop 125

39 Illumination Saddle 128

40 Ramona Falls Loop 131

41 Yocum Ridge 134

42 Lost Lake Butte 137

43 Buck Peak 139

44 McNeil Point 142

45 Vista Ridge to Cairn Basin Loop 146

46 Barrett Spur Summit 148

**MOUNT JEFFERSON–OPAL
CREEK–BULL OF THE WOODS
WILDERNESS**

47 Silver Falls State Park 151

48 Butte Creek Falls to Abiqua Falls ... 155

49 Table Rock 158

50 Rooster Rock to
Pechuck Lookout 160

51 Little North Santiam Loop to
Three Pools 163

52 Henline Mountain and
Henline Falls 167

53 Opal Creek 170

54 Whetstone Mountain 173

55 Dome Rock 177

56 Big Slide Mountain to Bull of the
Woods Loop 180

57 Lower Soda Creek Falls 183

58 Iron Mountain Lookout to
Cone Peak Loop 185

59 Maxwell Butte 189

60 Three Fingered Jack Loop 190

61 Porcupine Rock to
Cirque Lake Loop 194

62 Upper Downing Creek Falls 197

63 Grizzly Peak 199

64 Triangulation Peak 201

65 Bear Point 202

66 Pacific Crest Trail to
Park Ridge Summit 204

67 Jefferson Park to
Park Ridge Summit 207

**THREE SISTERS WILDERNESS
AND SOUTH**

68 Mount Washington 211

69 Sahalie–Koosah Falls Loop 214

70 Tamolitch (Blue) Pool 216

71 Belknap Crater 219

72 Black Crater 221

73 No Name Lake to
Broken Saddle 223

74 Broken Top 226

75 South Sister 230

76 Mount Thielsen 232

77 Crater Lake, Watchman Peak Lookout,
and Garfield Peak 234

**OREGON NORTHERN COASTAL
RANGE**

78 Clatsop Spit Loop 241

79 Saddle Mountain 243

80 Clark's Mountain
(Tillamook Head Summit) 245

81 Cannon Beach to Silver Point 248

82 Neahkahnie Mountain 250

83 Rogers Peak 253

84 Kings Mountain Loop 256

85 Elk Mountain 260

86 Marys Peak 262

EASTERN OREGON–WALLOWAS

87 Painted Hills 267

88 Aneroid Mountain 273

89 Glacier Lake 276

90 Eagle Cap 279

Index 284

Acknowledgments 291

PREFACE

The superbly magnificent Pacific Northwest is forever an outdoor treasure of indescribable value. This guidebook covers the South Cascades in Washington through Oregon, including the North Coastal Range all the way to the Wallowas in the northeast part of the state. Simply put, *Day Hikes in the Pacific Northwest* is a day hiker's dream in print. It's written solely with the hiker in mind so jaunts are easily followed with colorful pictures and detailed maps. Concise directions with road conditions from Portland (or Seattle, in a few cases) to each trailhead are given (where online map services fail at times), along with what pass is needed to park at the trailhead or on the hike if any, and whether or not a restroom is present at the trailhead. For each hike, the mileage, compass directional, landmarks, and suggested routes for loops are described meticulously. Many people by habit hardly ever drive more than an hour or two from the house to the trailhead, but for that extra hour or so most avid hikers and locals have known for a long time their efforts are well rewarded! The hikes with drives longer than 4 hours are better enjoyed when camping or seeking accommodations near the trailheads.

For parking, many trailheads require a day use fee, which can be covered by a Northwest Forest Pass in Oregon or a Northwest Forest Pass or Discover Pass in Washington. Both passes are good for one day ($5 to around $12 per vehicle) or one year ($30 to $35) and are available online (www.fs.usda.gov/detail/r6/passes-permits/recreation/?cid=fsbdev2_027010, or discoverpass.wa.gov), at ranger stations, and at many retail outlets. It's always helpful to look up your hike online for particulars on payment at the trailhead and to make sure trails are open. At times a trail may be inaccessible due to rock- or landslides, flooding, road closures, fires, snow, or for wildlife protection. I also highly recommend glancing over the hike before leaving home for vital info including what else to bring.

Each hike begins with essential information about elevation, distance, duration (includes short breaks), difficulty level, and trip reports that point out any noteworthy and important tidbits. Elevation information includes the highest point (or points) and destination of a hike as well as the maximum vertical gains you will experience along the trail. Difficulty level is broken up into five categories: **easiest** (short hike, little to no elevation change, sometimes paved, ideal for families and novices), **moderate** (brief hike, more elevation change but easier than most), **strenuous** (longer hike, some steeps, trail-locating, use of hands for balance possible), **very challenging** (fairly long hike, sustained steeps for thousands of feet, bushwhacking, scrambling, GPS device helpful, use of hands necessary), and **expert only** (very long hike, punishing steeps, overgrown paths, exposed cliffs, climbing-type moves possible though no climbing gear mandatory, traction devices at times, route-finding).

For the sake of brevity, I use the abbreviations **TH** (trailhead), **FR** (Forest Road), **ft** (feet), **mi** (mile), **AWD** (all-wheel drive/4WD). Likewise I refer to Pacific Crest Trail 2000 (also known as the Pacific Crest National Scenic Trail or Crest Trail) as the **PCT**. A switchback is a spot in a trail that zigzags sharply, whether once or fifty times. A shoulder is a rise or small ridge. "Exposure" refers to an individual's level of risk of falling where a tumble would be fatal. A trail section described as "airy" is exposed to some degree, with drop-offs. Exercise extreme caution in such areas. "Gendarmes" refer to spiked pinnacles or spires blocking a ridgeline, borrowing its meaning from medieval French soldiers standing at guard. The maps are tracked correctly even when USGS trails are slightly off. Distances on the maps given are approximate but easy to follow.

Again, this is a hiking guidebook for hikers who love to hike! There are no token hikes or fluff sections about how to hike, who to bring, or how to make trail mix! We cut to the chase and get to the goods here! Presented with originality are many popular hikes and several you may have never heard of. Most have other options and loops within them as well, more than doubling the actual number of total hikes listed. Colorful topographic maps and pictures help tie in the text, making each hike perfectly straightforward to follow.

A dry, warm hiker is a happy hiker! Bring some if not all of the following on your day hike: your experience, a friend, lots of layers (synthetic or not) including backup rain gear and dry socks, sunscreen, water or purifier, food, flashlight or headlamp, map or GPS or compass, fresh batteries, smartphone backup battery/charger, first aid kit with an emergency blanket, lighters, knife, insect repellent, whistle—and a sense of humor.

MAP LEGEND

North indicator

LEWIS RIVER TRAIL 31
Trail & place name label

Trailhead marker & name label

Viewpoint marker

MOUNT ST. HELENS

INDIAN HEAVEN WILDERNESS

GIFFORD PINCHOT NATIONAL FOREST

1 Lewis River Falls 11

2 Lemei Rock Loop 16

3 Falls Creek Falls 20

4 Soda Peaks Lake to
West Soda Peak 22

5 Observation Peak to
Sister Rocks.................................. 26

6 Siouxon Peak to
Huffman Peak 28

7 Ape Cave Loop 31

8 Goat Mountain............................. 34

9 Sheep Canyon Loop 37

10 Coldwater Peak 40

11 Norway Pass and
Harmony Falls 43

12 Mount Margaret 46

13 Mount Whittier 49

14 Mount St. Helens 50

1   LEWIS RIVER FALLS

ELEVATION: 1740 ft, with about 500 ft vertical gain total taking the same trail each way with ups/downs

DISTANCE: 3½ mi up, 6½ mi round-trip; 3¾ mi one way to Quartz Creek TH from Lower Falls Recreation Area

DURATION: 2 hours one way Lower Falls Recreation Area to Quart Creek TH, 3–4 hours round-trip for all of the local waterfalls

DIFFICULTY: Moderate. Wide, rolling trails, not long, tree roots, drop-offs, steeper past base of Upper Lewis River Falls, narrowing

---

TRIP REPORT: Even though the regions between Mount St. Helens and Mount Adams are in Washington, they are much closer to Portland than Seattle for hiking and are covered here in the first two sections. This stroll is perfect on a warm spring day after the roads and trails are all clear of snow and the river is raging with several quality drops and many side streams nearby that give birth to several smaller but interesting waterfalls. Great for the whole family and reminiscent of Eagle Creek in the Columbia River Gorge, only much briefer. If you are swimming to cool off, don't wander under any of the cascades because of falling rocks and a strong undertow. If you came from Curly Creek Road, you should stop near the top of Oldman Pass on the curve-riddled road at McClellan Viewpoint (with restroom) for a great look at Mount St. Helens with Goat Rocks to the right of the volcano and more surprises farther right (NE) as well. And a must-stop from both THs off FR-90 near milepost 20½ is Curly Creek Falls with a natural rock arch between two cascades. See below for that nonhiking option to visit before they dry up completely in summer. No fee required, and restrooms are present.

TRAILHEAD: Lower Falls Recreation Area. For the fastest drive from Portland with less traffic (90 mi, less than 2 hours), take I-84 E to exit 44 (Cascade Locks), continue under Bridge of the Gods and turn right up the circle to cross over it into Washington after paying the toll, turn right on WA-14 E 5¾ mi, turn left (N) through Carson on Wind River Road (FR-30) 14 mi NW (¼ mi past National Fish Hatchery), turn right to stay on FR-30 for 12¾ mi (toward Ape Cave), turn left on Curly Creek Road almost 5 mi, turn right on rougher FR-90 about 9½ mi (at 7¾ mi the road turns to gravel with many potholes but not bad for only ½ mi), turn right into the day use area at Lower Falls Recreation Area and right again into the loop to park near the restrooms. Quartz Creek (Lewis River) TH is 2¾ mi farther on FR-90. Alternately from Portland

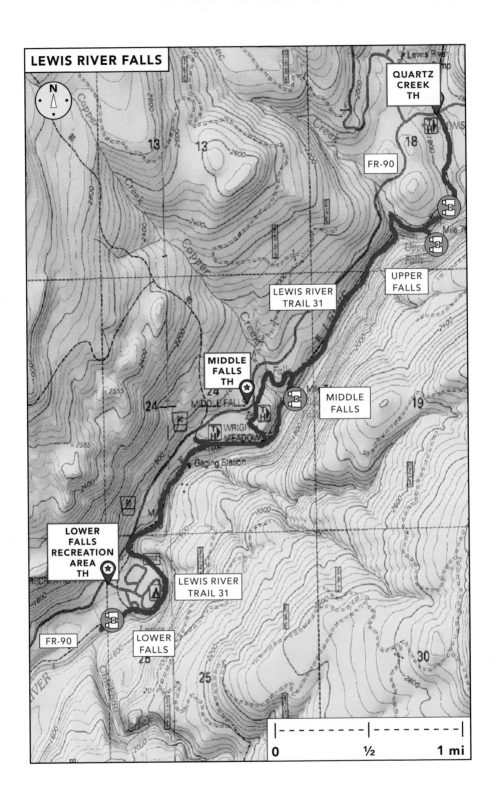

LEWIS RIVER FALLS

QUARTZ CREEK TH

FR-90

UPPER FALLS

LEWIS RIVER TRAIL 31

MIDDLE FALLS TH

MIDDLE FALLS

LOWER FALLS RECREATION AREA TH

LEWIS RIVER TRAIL 31

FR-90

LOWER FALLS

0   ½   1 mi

Smaller cascades on mossy Alec Creek rushing toward the Lewis River.

take I-5 N to exit 21 (Woodland/Mount St. Helens), turn right on Lewis River Road (WA-503) 28 mi to Cougar, then into rougher FR-90 E, less than 20 mi along the third consecutive large reservoir (Lake Merwin, Yale Lake, and Swift Reservoir in that order), turn right after the last one (just past Pine Creek Information Center) to stay on FR-90 E (toward Carson, opposite FR-25, watching for deer) crossing the bridge at the E end of the reservoirs and continue almost 14 mi (½ mi of rougher gravel road with potholes near end), turn right into Lower Falls Recreation Area and right again into the loop to park near the restrooms (92 mi, 2½ hours from Portland). Bring a shuttle bike or vehicle for a one-way hike to/from Quartz Creek (Lewis River) TH.

ROUTE: Take the main signed Lewis River Trail 31 left of the restroom or any one of the trails past the restroom only 50–100 ft to a couple great official overlooks of Lower Lewis River Falls (43 ft high, up to 200 ft wide). These are one of the most dramatic falls right off the bat and look brilliant regardless of the water flow, just like most of the neighboring falls. You can walk right on the main trail a few feet and hike down one of the super-steep bushwhack paths closer to the river for other angles if you desire, but none are too great. Try the one opposite a short spur path to the right which leads toward a small waterfall off a nearby creek, if any.

Frozen in time are Upper Lewis River Falls from the highest viewpoint.

Follow Lewis River Trail 31 N near the edge of the bluff and stay to the right, along the river with more views of the waterfall. Other paths join from the campground on the left near another outhouse as you ascend the hill gently E of the campground and parallel closer to FR-90 for a bit. Then head downhill past huge Douglas firs and cross one creek and a small bridge to a larger footbridge with a thin little waterfall just below it at 1 mi from the campground. Ignore other trails coming down from FR-90 and from Middle Falls TH for now. Copper Creek Falls (26-ft plunge) is on the Middle Falls loop, a possible variation on the return to add almost a mile mostly for exercise. You may also be rerouted toward Middle Falls TH on the up and down loop back to Trail 31 in case of slides lower on Copper Creek.

For an interesting waterfall excursion with very little effort, try Curly Creek Falls from milepost 20½ off FR-90 onto FR-9039 for exactly 1 mi W to signed parking on the left. Walk left of the vault toilet, turning right at the immediate fork 100 ft to the log pole fenced viewing area of the splendid 86-ft falls in two drops. Then continue briefly to another viewing area and, bonus, this one for the narrower Miller Creek Falls plunging 66 ft into a pool (less than ½ mi and 20 minutes round-trip; flat, wide path).

At more than 1½ mi from the TH on Trail 31 arrive at another decent footbridge, this one over Copper Creek. Lower Copper Creek Falls cascades as a washboard directly below the bridge in a couple tiers (more than 32 ft total) with the lower one almost out of sight; an easy bushwhack path between the tiers lies 75 ft farther if you wish. Follow the clear river briefly to Middle Lewis River Falls (33 ft high, up to 300 ft wide, gentle sliding cascade) visible from a tough angle. The trail soon turns under a wall of tears as the overhanging cliff drips (or pours) onto you and the moss-covered steep forest.

It's ¾ mi from the Middle Falls TH as you pass another waterfall very similar to Middle Lewis River Falls on the trail to Upper Lewis River Falls (58 ft high, 175 ft wide). These are the tallest of the area's falls with a few amazing angles, the worst through the trees and brush covering part of a rocky beach as you first see the waterfall. Work to the river's edge with some difficulty for that faraway shot or simply continue over another bridge to a switchback near the base of the falls where you can scramble down the larger rocks 30 ft to the shore for the best look across the beautiful water. During low flow the curtain is reduced to streaming cascade on the far left.

Continue to hike steeper less than ½ mi up to Taitnapum Falls (16 ft high, 60 ft wide) before you call it a day with one worthwhile bushwhack path down to the top of Upper Lewis River Falls along the way. Take the spur easily 100 ft to the old log pole "fencing" or better yet move to the space between two fallen trees down to the left being very cautious near the edge. The larger of those trees works great to steady your camera if you don't mind the carpenter ants. While being only a few feet away from the very top of the cascade the falls feel more powerful here than at any other point on the hike! The final waterfall is easy to see from a signed perch above them 10 ft off the main trail to the right. Quartz Creek TH on FR-90 is about ¾ mi farther so return back 3 mi and an hour W the same route to the day use area main TH on Trail 31 when you are ready.

2 LEMEI ROCK LOOP

ELEVATION: 5926 ft on top of Lemei Rock; 5685 ft at Lake Wapiki overlook; 5237 ft at the saddle N of Bird Mountain; with vertical gains of 1925 ft, plus 100 ft for Lake Wapiki overlook; 1235 ft for Bird Mountain loop without Lemei Rock (plus 400 ft for Junction Lake loop)

DISTANCE: 3½ mi one way to Lemei Rock with Lake Wapiki overlook, 7½ mi round-trip no loops; more than 9½ mi round-trip including Bird Mountain loop (6¾ mi Bird Mountain loop alone); 10 mi round-trip Junction Lake loop and Bird Mountain loop without Lemei Rock and Lake Wapiki overlook

DURATION: 3–5 hours round-trip for all routes

DIFFICULTY: Mix of moderate for most routes (steeps near TH and on Trail 108, wide trails, well-traveled, mosquitoes, GPS device helpful) and strenuous for Lemei Rock (scrambling, mostly stable rock, route-finding, very steep, narrow ridgetop, some exposure)

TRIP REPORT: This listing encompasses several hike and loop options within one, the most popular being a trek up Lemei Rock (pronounced LEM-ee-eye), a break at Lake Wapiki overlook, then a loop around Bird Mountain to the same TH. You can also omit Bird Mountain or Lemei Rock and the overlook and venture farther past several more excellent lakes on a Junction Lake loop, then finish directly or add Bird Mountain or Lemei Rock and the overlook. There are around 175 lakes total (when the snow finally melts off by July) in Indian Heaven Wilderness (southernmost Cascades in Washington) worth revisiting many times, but remember to bring bug spray through August as swarms of mosquitoes will make you wish you came later when the huckleberries are ripe and the air is crisp. There's a price to pay to catch the wildflowers in full bloom. Either way the views and experience are very much worthwhile. Be prepared for rapidly changing weather at all times. Closed late October through June. Northwest Forest Pass required, and a vault toilet is present.

TRAILHEAD: Cultus Creek Campground. Take I-84 E from Portland to exit 44 (Cascade Locks), continue under Bridge of the Gods and turn right up the circle to cross over it into Washington after paying the toll, turn right on WA-14 E 5¾ mi, turn left (N) through Carson on Wind River Road (FR-30) 14 mi NW (¼ mi past National Fish Hatchery), turn right to stay on FR-30 for 15 mi (with 5 mi of gravel road in the middle), turn right to stay on FR-30 (Lone Butte Road, Sawtooth Berry Fields) 8 mi, turn right on FR-24 (gravel, rougher for 2WD) 4¼ mi, park at the end of the

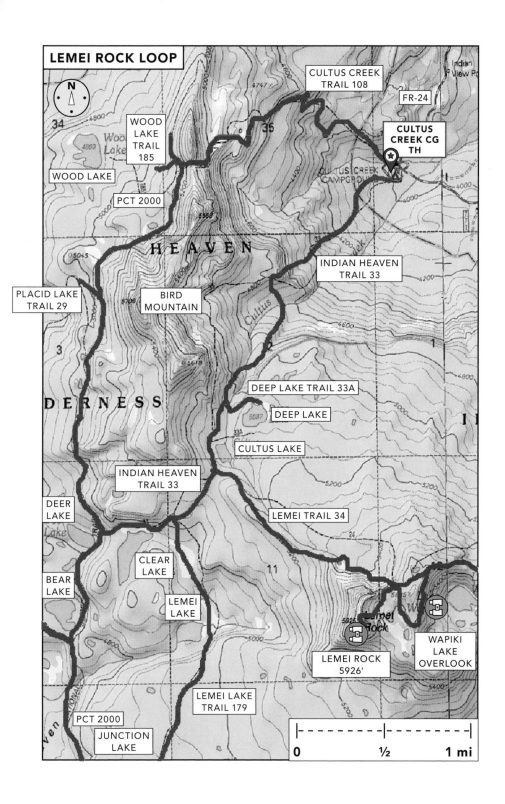

LEMEI ROCK LOOP

N

CULTUS CREEK
TRAIL 108

FR-24

CULTUS
CREEK CG
TH

WOOD
LAKE
TRAIL
185

WOOD LAKE

PCT 2000

H E A V E N

INDIAN HEAVEN
TRAIL 33

PLACID LAKE
TRAIL 29

BIRD
MOUNTAIN

D E R N E S S

DEEP LAKE TRAIL 33A

DEEP LAKE

CULTUS LAKE

INDIAN HEAVEN
TRAIL 33

DEER
LAKE

LEMEI TRAIL 34

BEAR
LAKE

CLEAR
LAKE

LEMEI
LAKE

WAPIKI
LAKE
OVERLOOK

LEMEI ROCK
5926'

PCT 2000

LEMEI LAKE
TRAIL 179

JUNCTION
LAKE

0   ½   1 mi

campground loop near the Indian Heaven Trail sign (90 mi, 2 hours from Portland).

ROUTE: The steeper trail on the right (N) leaving the campground is the return for the clockwise loop around Bird Mountain with or without Lemei Rock on Cultus Creek Trail 108. Avoid it to begin up Indian Heaven Trail 33 (W briefly, then SW) steadily with a decent pitch through the big firs a mile to the first great views breaking out of the woods. See nearby Sawtooth Mountain and Mount Rainier behind to the N with the Goat Rocks area panning right to Mount Adams.

Continue a bit easier another mile through trees and meadows with shots up to Bird Mountain's E-facing cliff band. Deep Lake Trail 33A on the left (and other spurs nearby) moves about ¼ mi down to Deep Lake, but stay right on Indian Heaven Trail 33 and you will start to see beautiful Cultus Lake through the thinning woods to the next intersection. The loops continue S (or soon W), but for Lemei Rock and/or the overlook turn left (SE) past Cultus Lake on Lemei Trail 34 after getting a good look at the steep but flat-topped Lemei Rock across the clear lake (surrounded by lupine and others late June into September).

Hike SE on Trail 34 up through lush heather meadows for about a mile before the route becomes steeper and narrower ¼ mi to the base of Lemei Rock near a large open meadow on its NE flank. The summit is the highest point in the Indian Heaven Wilderness and may not be doable for most weekend warriors, but more experienced day hikers generally have no problem and the payoff is unbeatable. To skip the summit or head to the overlook first, follow one of the spur trails from the main trail only a couple hundred yards farther to a little high point and clearing out of the trees on the rim of an ancient crater 500 ft directly above Lake Wapiki to the E. You come around the corner and are suddenly greeted with the sizable, colorful lake and Mount Adams looming. Return down to the Cultus Lake intersection after deciding whether or not you are summiting Lemei Rock.

The panorama is already incredible before you sneak up to the Lake Wapiki overlook where the bright lake explodes into view.

For Lemei Rock (more than ¼ mi spur to the peak, easy Class 3, gloves may help) begin SW on the solid path in the grassy flats directly toward the peak. The path fades to the larger rocks and a much steeper scree field that you must traverse. Climb SW steeply up the gully to a weakness in the narrow ridgeline near the top (look for cairns). From there it's a short scramble S to the summit with fairly solid rock and definite drop-offs but with the best views in the region of four big Cascade volcanoes and a whole lot more! Be mindful of lingering ice and gusting winds from the high ridge.

From the Cultus Lake intersection, turn right (NE) from Trail 34 to walk directly back to the TH on Trail 33 in a little more than 2¼ mi. Alternatively, turn left (SW) from the intersection for the loops on Trail 33 away from Cultus Lake for less than ½ mi easily down to the next confluence. For the Junction Lake loop you would turn left (S) on Lemei Lake Trail 179 close to 2 mi and a few hundred feet down to PCT 2000 as the path widens through the meadows, passing Lemei Lake to the left (E) en route to Junction Lake (appearing on your left), which is just N of East Crater (one of many shield volcanoes in the area). Turn right (N) after Junction Lake at the end of the trail onto the PCT for 1½ mi with a pleasant grade up a couple hundred feet past several more quality waters including Elk Lake (more than ½ mi spur Trail 176 heads left, NW), Bear Lake, and Deer Lake (nearest the juncture with Indian Heaven Trail 33 on the right moving E). Stay on the PCT for Bird Mountain loop; directions follow in next paragraph. It's a pretty easy walk on Trail 33 without Bird Mountain loop up more than ¼ mi passing Clear Lake (one of many great picnic spots) to the end of the Junction Lake loop at Trail 179, where you continue left on Trail 33 less than ½ mi up to Lemei Trail 34 (on the right) at Cultus Lake. Finish left on Trail 33 to the TH.

From Lemei Rock across Indian Heaven Wilderness to Mount Adams.

For the Bird Mountain loop near Deer Lake, stay on the PCT (at about 4900 ft) to the N as you only gain 300 ft in 1¾ mi through the woods (ignoring Placid Lake Trail 29 on the left at 1 mi up) with smaller ponds scattered on the traverse to your exit on the right (E) just past Wood Lake Trail 185 (heads down to the left, W, for ½ mi). Leave the PCT to walk right (E) on Cultus Creek Trail 108 up less than ¼ mi to a major saddle on Bird Mountain. You can bushwhack spur paths very briefly left (N) or fairly briefly right (S) from the saddle that will take you to outstanding vistas on the ridge crest. Bird Mountain's steep summit scramble however is not recommended with much overgrowth and no better views.

Hike down Trail 108 to the NE, then SE quite steeply at times 1½ mi to the TH with smaller trees and wide-open views to Mount Adams and Mount Rainier most of the route. There are more than a half-dozen switchbacks to the campground and end of the clockwise loop. Voilà!

3 FALLS CREEK FALLS

ELEVATION: 2375 ft, with 950 ft vertical gain to the top of the falls

DISTANCE: 2¼ mi directly to the falls on Lower Trail, 4½ mi round-trip; 6¼ mi round-trip loop with Upper Trail

DURATION: 2-3 hours round-trip

DIFFICULTY: Moderate. Steeper at times, uneven wet trails, well signed, humid in summer, a few drop-offs from Upper Trail

TRIP REPORT: Bring the family, possibly swim in the chilly creek, and enjoy a mostly laid-back walk with great benefits and options. Road may be gated 1½ mi from TH December through March. No fee required, and a restroom is present.

TRAILHEAD: Falls Creek Falls TH. Take I-84 E from Portland to exit 44 (Cascade Locks), continue under Bridge of the Gods and turn right up the circle to cross over it into Washington after paying the toll, turn right on WA-14 E 5¾ mi, turn left through Carson on Wind River Road (FR-30) 14 mi NW (¼ mi past National Fish Hatchery), turn right to stay on Wind River Road (FR-30) ¾ mi, take the first right on gravel FR-3062 for 2 mi, fork right on FR-057 almost ½ mi to the end at a large gravel lot (65 mi, 1½ hours from Portland).

Mossy boulders line the path the final feet to Falls Creek Falls.

ROUTE: Start a hundred yards past the sign, walking right (ENE) on Trail 152A at the juncture (opposite the return loop on Trail 152B) for 1 mi staying S of and close to Falls Creek with chances to work down to the water. You will rise up gradually and cross over a solid suspension bridge to the N side. Continue another mile steadily through big, old fir and cedar to the next signed intersection. Turn right more than ¼ mi SE to the Falls Creek Falls viewing area around the corner as you begin to hear the roar of the thunderous four-tiered waterfall.

There is a 30-ft mini falls (difficult to see) below the 60-ft drop into a moss-

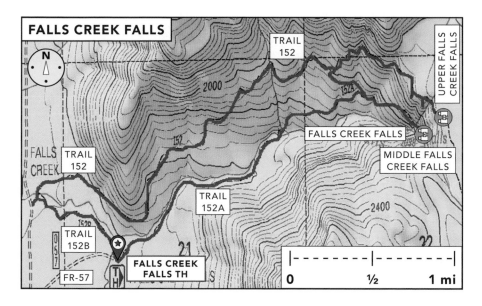

FALLS CREEK FALLS

TRAIL 152

UPPER FALLS CREEK FALLS

2000

FALLS CREEK FALLS

MIDDLE FALLS CREEK FALLS

FALLS CREEK

TRAIL 152

TRAIL 152A

2400

TRAIL 152B

FALLS CREEK FALLS TH

FR-57

0   ½   1 mi

lined pool directly in front of you, and the spread-out Middle Falls Creek Falls (90 ft high) is topped with yet another waterfall (60 ft high) just out of sight above. Watch for spray and return NW more than ¼ mi on Trail 152A. Turn right (N) to work steeper from the signage up to the return loop Trail 152 in ½ mi, but head right (SE) a mile to the top of the falls for a slight detour. The brief spur paths to the right from the detour give you good shots of Upper Falls Creek Falls but please use caution near the steeps close to the viewpoints of the waterfall, the valley, and the mountains W in Trapper Creek Wilderness.

Return on the Upper Trail 1 mi to the juncture for the counterclockwise loop, then walk 1¾ mi W down an easy grade on Trail 152 to a faint trail on the left that leads S immediately to a third footbridge. Cross it and fork left (ESE) instead of right (toward Fall Creek TH) on Trail 152B ½ mi along the creek through the forest and past a safe beach area to the end of the loop at a spur just a few feet to your vehicle.

The wider curtain of Middle Falls Creek Falls above the lower drops and just below the narrowest uppermost drop.

4 SODA PEAKS LAKE TO WEST SODA PEAK

ELEVATION: 3750 ft at Soda Peaks Lake; 4550 ft on West Soda Peak; 4450 ft on East Soda Peak; with vertical gains of 2600 ft from Trapper Creek TH to Soda Peaks Lake (3400 ft with West Soda Peak); 2300 ft from Soda Peaks TH (2425 ft with West Soda Peak); and 1150 ft for both summits without visiting the lake from Soda Peaks TH

DISTANCE: 4½ mi to the lake from Trapper Creek TH, 9½ mi round-trip; 5¾ mi to West Soda Peak, 11½ mi round-trip; 2¼ mi to the lake from Soda Peaks TH, 4½ mi round-trip (5 mi round-trip with West Soda Peak); 3½ mi round-trip to both summits without the lake from Soda Peaks TH

DURATION: 3 hours to the lake from Trapper Creek TH, 5–6 hours round-trip with short breaks; 4 hours to West Soda Peak, 6–8 hours round-trip; 3–4 hours round-trip with both summits and the lake from Soda Peaks TH (2 hours round-trip without the lake)

DIFFICULTY: Strenuous. Many steep switchbacks from Trapper Creek TH, wide, tacky and smooth trail with pine needles, decent signage; brief, but ups/downs to lake from Soda Peaks TH; steep but straightforward bushwhack last ¼ mi to peaks; noticeable absence of crowds

---

TRIP REPORT: Visit the highest point (or both summits) of an old volcano crater and/or a beautiful little subalpine lake in the Trapper Creek Wilderness. The Soda Peaks TH with its longer and slightly more difficult drive but much shorter hike (with a few options) is listed below. But the super easygoing drive and hike from Trapper Creek (lower) TH with abundant exercise through a dreamlike ancient forest to Soda Peaks Lake is described first. And truthfully it's just fun to say Soda Peaks Lake! Northwest Forest Pass required only at Trapper Creek TH, and a vault toilet is present only at the lower TH as well.

TRAILHEAD: Trapper Creek TH (1150 ft) or Soda Peaks TH (3675 ft). For Trapper Creek (lower) TH, take I-84 E from Portland to exit 44 (Cascade Locks), continue under Bridge of the Gods and turn right up the circle to cross over it into Washington after paying the toll, turn right on WA-14 E 5¾ mi, turn left (N) through Carson on Wind River Road (FR-30, see next paragraph for Soda Peaks TH) 14 mi NW (¼ mi past National Fish Hatchery), stay straight on Mineral Springs Road less than ½ mi, turn right on Little Soda Springs Road (FR-5401) over gravel more than ¼ mi to the end at a large dirt parking circle for Trapper Creek Wilderness.

Last of the ice and snow melting off Soda Peaks Lake in late May.

For Soda Peaks (upper) TH, take Wind River Road 8½ mi NW, turn left on Hemlock Road ¼ mi, turn right on Szydlo Road 3½ mi into one lane (FR-54) at least 2½ mi, stay right at fork (left is gravel) 6¾ mi roughly paved (with ¼ mi washboard gravel) to a three-way intersection. Turn right 50 ft into gravel to the small pullout on the left opposite the overgrown trail before the old green gate (around 66 mi, less than 2 hours from Portland).

ROUTE: From the Trapper Creek (lower) TH, begin N past the signs (free self-issue Wilderness Permit) to an immediate juncture, staying left on Trapper Creek Trail 192 almost 2 mi heading WNW before you cross Trapper Creek over a very solid bridge that may still smell of fresh cut wood. In between, the wide smooth trail ambles up and down minimally with some massive Douglas fir, hemlock, and cedar. The lively forest floor with huckleberry, Oregon grape, and other low flora keeps your eyes and senses stimulated throughout the old growth woods.

Less than a mile from the juncture is Observation Peak Trail 132 taking off to the right. Continue straight on Trapper Creek Trail 192 crossing a creek without difficulty and contour up where the views open up slightly before reaching a larger creek, this one with a flat log to cross over to the next immediate intersection. Turn hard left (S) on Trail 133 by the big sign next to the creek for Soda Peaks Lake and walk down past moss-covered fallen trees through the emerald forest more than ¼ mi to the bridge over Trapper Creek (less than 1 hour from the TH).

Just to the left of the bridge and creek heading back SE is an optional bailout or return loop route on Mineral Springs Road (FR-5401, partially overgrown to begin). It's ¼ mi shorter, wide, flat, gravel, less intense, and filled with private rental cabins on Trapper Creek until the big orange gate blocking the road a hundred yards or so from the main TH.

To bypass the optional bailout and continue on to the lake or summits, follow Trail 133 past the Trapper Creek footbridge easily for ¼ mi S before the composure of the day's leisurely pace changes abruptly at the first switchback marked by a huge Doug fir blocking any other would-be trails. Hike steeply (but thankfully not too agonizingly) more than a mile W for 16 switchbacks before you reach a high spot on the ridgetop. Traverse easier slightly below the ridgeline on the left (S) and then back to the ridge again seeing Mount Hood along the way.

After walking down to a saddle begin to climb steeper up 16 more switchbacks. See Observation Peak through the big trees to the right (E), then West Soda Peak (W) after crossing the ridge on a traverse S around a rocky section. Continue back to the ridge for an easier time. Begin to ascend steeper again traversing the right side of the ridge crest the final ¾ mi W to the lake with a couple longer switchbacks along the way.

Soda Peaks Lake can be explored on both sides of the big "no camping" sign near the lake's outlet from thin bushwhack paths. Large trees nearly surround Soda Peaks Lake providing little more view than of the small, clear lake itself, usually stocked with brook trout. One exception is the large scree field left (S) of the lake under East Soda Peak that can be ascended a hundred vertical feet or so, with no trail, to a truncated shot of nearby Mount St. Helens and also Mount Adams and Mount Rainier on a clear day! Return the same way or continue to the high ridge from the main trail or even West Soda Peak for the best views all day.

To continue to the high ridge for the summits, cross the stream from the outlet N of Soda Peaks Lake at a wider expanse over branches and where possible, and continue ¾ mi up the solid trail to the ridge and saddle between peaks. Walk across a slide path en route, and then ascend a couple steeper switchbacks near the saddle. Snow melts off slowly on this section and the lake (sometimes into late June or even July). If it's icy it will be tough to cross the slide path and stay near the trail with the steep pitch. From the high ridge right to West Soda Peak lingering snow dissipates quickly. See the end of this hike for the description left to East Soda Peak. Turn right (NW) up the ridge saddle (4300 ft); remember the switchback, as on the return you will turn sharply left here to go back down to the lake. You can see Mount Adams, Mount St. Helens, Mount Rainier, Goat Rocks, and Mount Hood through the trees from near the saddle or above.

In more than ¼ mi break off from the trail as it begins to descend left (at a sign for Trapper Creek Wilderness posted high on a tree) around a mile NW to Soda Peaks TH. The hidden route to West Soda Peak begins only about 6 ft left (S) of the ridgeline (with views down to Soda Peaks Lake and East Soda Peak). For the summit, bushwhack to the right off the main trail and straight up the ridgeline or slightly left of it passing over larger trees and debris. Climb past smaller pines into a very steep grassy meadow dotted with wildflowers and great shots of Mount Adams, Soda Peaks Lake, East Soda Peak, and others. Work up to the top left of the meadow and return to the woods up a steep elk path a bit easier using route-finding skills to the nearby tree-covered tiny

peak with only a few vistas discernible through the trees. See below for the less-traveled East Soda Peak, or return the same way past the lake to Trapper Creek TH.

From Soda Peaks (upper) TH at the pullout before the gate, take the path across the road 50 ft past brush to a free self-issue Wilderness Permit kiosk with a map. Then continue S on Soda Peaks Lake Trail 133. The path widens nicely through large cedars and then becomes a bit overgrown again near the W ridge of Soda Peaks at less than ½ mi from the TH. Drop down left a few feet over the widening trail then work steeper up through the beautiful forest (with only occasional looks out) to the ridge again. Hike fairly steeply up the narrowing ridge crest over a few tree roots and rocks and then traverse E under West Soda Peak. Head up steadily across a scree field and through the woods before easing to the high ridge just E of West Soda Peak (around 1 mi from the TH). See tree-covered East Soda Peak above Soda Peaks Lake and much more.

For West Soda Peak begin about 6 ft left (S) of the ridge and follow the brief description above, but to get more out of the hike feel free to visit the lake and/or East Soda Peak first and finish with West Soda Peak if coming from Soda Peaks TH. For these continue down the high ridge between summits about ¼ mi without difficulty to a vague juncture with a rock cairn against a tree in the middle of the trail and stacked old logs across the trail. Turn left down the switchback with a couple more switchbacks ¾ mi down 500 ft to Soda Peaks Lake. Check out views from the large scree field S of the lake (see above) and return the same way.

For East Soda Peak (more than ¼ mi away) from the vague juncture at the saddle on the high ridge (4300 ft) continue E past small trees on the overgrown ridge section as the path reveals itself quickly and opens up pleasantly with little vegetation. There are many small logs, branches, and sticks to cross without any trouble as the path disappears. Bushwhack up the left side of the wide ridgeline or wherever possible as the route steepens somewhat past a small bump with many good-sized mossy cedars to the rounded large summit area. There you find fewer trees, not enough to see views out from, but just enough to create a cool echo effect with your voice; try it! Return SW down to the juncture on the high ridge (4300 ft) and continue to Trapper Creek TH or the much closer Soda Peaks TH.

ELEVATION: 4207 ft; 4268 ft for Sister Rocks; with 1600 ft vertical gain including both summits

DISTANCE: 7 mi round-trip for all the high points and spur paths from the uppermost TH

DURATION: 4 hours round-trip

DIFFICULTY: Moderate. Signed, ups/downs okay, multiple summits, scrambling, narrow, steeper on Sister Rocks, bugs in late June through July

---

TRIP REPORT: Begin at the highest of many THs for this lovely brief day hike in Trapper Creek Wilderness suitable for hiking aficionados of all ages. Most people settle for the fascinating Sister Rocks area but it is possible to sneak in another quick summit with views of many high Cascade volcanoes. No fee or restroom.

The landmark from Sister Rocks across Trapper Creek Wilderness to Soda Peaks and Mount Hood.

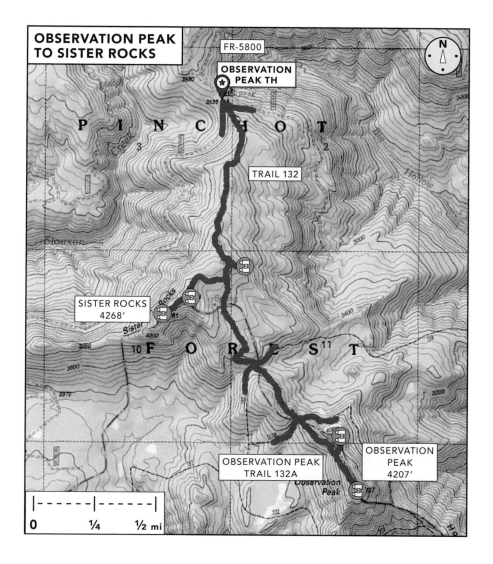

OBSERVATION PEAK
TO SISTER ROCKS

FR-5800

OBSERVATION
PEAK TH

PINCHOT

TRAIL 132

SISTER ROCKS
4268'

FOREST

OBSERVATION PEAK
TRAIL 132A

OBSERVATION
PEAK
4207'

0   ¼   ½ mi

TRAILHEAD: Observation Peak TH. Take I-84 E from Portland to exit 44 (Cascade Locks), continue under Bridge of the Gods and turn right up the circle to cross over it into Washington after paying the toll, turn right on WA-14 E 5¾ mi, turn left (N) through Carson on Wind River Road (FR-30) 14 mi NW (¼ mi past National Fish Hatchery), turn right to stay on FR-30 for 2 mi, fork left on narrower Dry Creek Road (FR-64, signed) 4 mi into gravel 2 mi, fork left on FR-5800 SSW steadily with some potholes 2 mi to signed parking on the left for Observation Trail 132 (73 mi, 1½ hours from Portland).

ROUTE: Hike S up the slender forested ridge trail with some fairly large Douglas firs around a mile without difficulty to a soft junction while crossing over the ridge. At this junction, there are two very short spur paths that head left (E) to a scree field with an unobstructed shot of nearby Mount Adams from the top of a rock pile past the brush. Rather than taking these short spurs, wait for the second path signed Sister Rock Trail just a few feet farther to the right from the main trail. Observation Peak is slightly anti-climactic compared to the more stimulating Sister Rocks summit area so we'll save the best for last.

Continue SSE on Trail 132 down about 400 ft and ¾ mi gradually (to regain later) to a saddle with two signed junctures that you pass, the first for Big Hollow Trail 158 on the left (E) near a campsite, then Trapper Creek Trail 192 on the right (W). In less than ½ mi is another saddle with two more trails taking off for the Trapper Creek TH several miles away; pass Trail 132B on the right, then you fork right at the next nearby juncture (opposite Trail 132) on signed Observation Peak Trail 132A for ½ mi SE with wildflowers to the old lookout site. See Mount Hood and perchance the top of Mount Jefferson.

About ¼ mi down from the very top is another short spur on the right to a lesser summit a couple hundred yards N up to mediocre views of Mount Adams and Mount Rainier over rock fins near the top of the ridge. Back on the main trail work NW past the two saddles and intersections up the hill to the Sister Rocks junction. Turn left (SW) ½ mi steeper and narrower up the solid ridge path to the viewpoint, first passing the high point over a bump in the woods, then down briefly to Sister Rocks (marked with a steel pole). The panorama includes Mount Hood, Mount Adams, Mount St. Helens, and much more within Gifford Pinchot National Forest.

6 SIOUXON PEAK TO HUFFMAN PEAK

ELEVATION: 4169 ft; 4106 ft; with vertical gains of about 1300 ft for Siouxon Peak alone, 2200 ft for both summits from the highest TH

DISTANCE: 5 mi one way for both peaks, 9½ mi round-trip

DURATION: 2 hours to Huffman Peak hiking Siouxon Peak first, 4 hours round-trip

DIFFICULTY: Strenuous. Solid trails, steeper at times, no signs, ups/downs, scrambling, GPS device helpful

TRIP REPORT: This sweet double-peak hike has many redeeming qualities, including great views of four large Cascade volcanoes and plenty of exercise while exploring a long ridgeline most of the day. The least redeeming quality is the drive up the final 6 mi to the highest TH as it's actually rougher than the hike itself. It is, however, perfect if you are upset with your vehicle! The pothole-ridden dirt road has awkward drainage gullies to cross and narrows briefly, allowing overgrown branches to perhaps scratch your vehicle. The beauty is that you can accomplish both summits fairly easily in one day. Other starting points make the hike twice as long and difficult, and mandatory creek fords and are usually not mentioned. Check ahead to be certain all roads to the TH are open, especially near winter. Also beware of bee swarms in June and July on the final miles of the drive, but thankfully they don't seem to follow you on the hike. No fee or restroom.

TRAILHEAD: Siouxon Peak TH. Take I-84 E from Portland to exit 44 (Cascade Locks), continue under Bridge of the Gods and turn right up the circle to cross over it into Washington after paying the toll, turn right on WA-14 E 5¾ mi, turn left through Carson on Wind River Road (FR-30) 14 mi NW (¼ mi past National Fish Hatchery), turn right to stay on Wind River Road (FR-30) 2 mi, fork left onto narrow Dry Creek Road (FR-64, signed) 4 mi rougher. Continue into unpaved on FR-64 for 2 mi, fork right to stay on FR-64/Dry Creek Road (no more signs, FR-58 is the left fork) less than ½ mi, fork left on FR-64 for 3½ mi, fork right on Siouxon Road (FR-6403) 3 mi to the end of the drivable road with plenty of parking on the sides. High-clearance 2WD or AWD recommended (75 mi, 2 hours from Portland).

ROUTE: There is no water along these trails far above Siouxon and Wildcat Creeks. Walk up the continuation of the old road (Huffman Peak Trail 129, no sign) W from the TH at 2868 ft. Ascend steadily about an hour and 2¼ mi through open areas and trees finishing with 3 steeper switchbacks before the trail levels a bit. You'll have views not far from the TH of nearby Mount St. Helens and Swift Reservoir with Mount Rainier far to the NNE, and above that you'll see Mount Adams and Mount Hood on a clear day. Mount Adams gets even bigger from the top of the switchbacks briefly to the summit trail on the left. Take Trail 129B ¼ mi S to the Siouxon Peak (old lookout

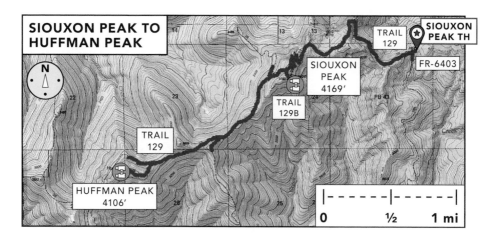

From Siouxon Peak on a bluebird day across part of Swift Reservoir to Mount St. Helens and Mount Rainier.

site) by following the rocky ridge crest without difficulty. Keep an eye on a solid E-facing cliff band to the top. There are plenty of wildflowers en route; some trees obscure the view of Mount St. Helens, but Huffman Peak is visible SW.

Backtrack to the summit spur trail and proceed left (SW) down the narrower Trail 129 for about 500 vertical ft and 1 mi to a low point in the ridge saddle at the next juncture. Wildcat Trail 156 (signed) takes off left (S) very steeply, but continue SW instead ¾ mi on Trail 129 to the spur paths leading ½ mi up to Huffman Peak. Leave Trail 129 heading right to the N of Huffman Peak and choose a spur, as you begin to bushwhack W, mostly through the woods nearest the ridge. The route quickly becomes a very steep scramble. Finish over rocks on the right past a fake little high point to another decommissioned lookout site in the clearing. See nearby SW Huffman Peak and others, Mount St. Helens, Mount Adams, Mount Rainier, and Mount Hood. Return the same way for a delightful day!

ELEVATION: 2480 ft, with 400 ft vertical gain plus 200 ft more for the lower cave

DISTANCE: 4¼ mi round-trip loop including the lower cave spur

DURATION: 2½ hours round-trip

DIFFICULTY: Mix of easiest (gentle slope and wide trails at ground level, obvious route in/out of caves, wide mellow lower cave, headlamp required) and moderate for the upper cave alone (sharp volcanic rock, steep navigating, brief rope support provided, narrow at times, multiple lights recommended)

TRIP REPORT: Spelunking for miles through an underground lava tube near the climber's TH for Mount St. Helens is certainly not your average day hike! The very best time is on the hottest summer days as the temperature stays a constant 42 degrees Fahrenheit year-round in the tube! Remember to bring a jacket, hat, and gloves. Also bring solid hiking shoes for the magma and multiple flashlights per person including a headlamp. If it's raining outside, then it may also be raining within the tube. The upper cave, although rated as moderate, is not for people with a fear of enclosed places, the elderly, babies, and very small children.

Most folks, however, have no problem with the lower cave and the trail that follows the entire tube above ground. No dogs either way. Ape Headquarters is the TH located between the upper and lower caves. The only other entrance into the tube is from the top and so it makes for a great loop in either direction. Here we descend the tube from the top as it seems a touch easier and with better anticipation! The tube is open year-round, but a closed gate in winter moves the TH back almost a mile on the road to Trail of Two Forests TH (Washington Sno-Park Pass and snowshoes required). Ape Headquarters is open mid-June through Labor Day (10 a.m.–5 p.m.), then weekends through September; guided tours and lanterns are offered for a fee. One more noteworthy option from Ape Headquarters TH is Volcano View Trail heading NW from the parking lot ¾ mi up 400 ft through woods (for shade) to a paved viewpoint (also accessible from farther up FR-8303). Northwest Forest Pass required, and restrooms are present.

TRAILHEAD: Ape Headquarters. Take I-5 N from Portland to exit 21 (Woodland/Mount St. Helens), turn right on Lewis River Road (WA-503) 28 mi to Cougar, then into rougher FR-90 at exactly 31 mi from I-5. Continue 3½ mi more (1 mi past seeing

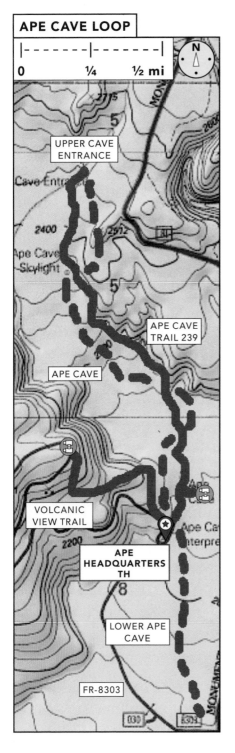

APE CAVE LOOP

|- - - - - - -|- - - - - -| N

0   ¼   ½ mi

2775

5

UPPER CAVE
ENTRANCE

Cave Entr

2400   2972

Ape Cave
Skylight

5

APE CAVE
TRAIL 239

APE CAVE

VOLCANIC
VIEW TRAIL

2200   Ape Ca
                 terpre

APE
HEADQUARTERS
TH

8

LOWER APE
CAVE

FR-8303

030   830

Swift Dam from the highway and third consecutive reservoir passed). Turn left on signed FR-83 N for 1¾ mi. Turn left on FR-8303 (small brown sign) for 1 mi to the large parking lot on the right (65 mi, 1½ hours from Portland).

ROUTE: Walk the main trail a hundred yards to the information kiosk at the lower entrance to the lava tube. Continue to the right on Ape Cave Trail 239 aboveground to warm up with a brief hike before cooling off. Travel the wide trail N through trees and sizable openings crossing magma fields a bit steeper at times. One short spur path around a lava field early on will provide a great shot of the top of Mount St. Helens in the same direction (N). Enjoy the unusual landscape with more surprises and after around 1¼ mi and 30 minutes you'll reach the upper cave entrance with less fanfare. In fact, you will barely notice the opening except for a sign and the steel ladder.

After a nice picnic, layer up for your subterranean trek and begin down the steep ladder into the darkness of the upper cave. Unlike what many people may think, the lava tube was formed almost 2000 years ago and was not at all affected by the explosion on Mount St. Helens in 1980. Although Ape Cave is impressive, the longest lava tube in the world is the Kazumura Cave in Hawaii at almost 41 mi! Walk S as you immediately realize this is no ordinary cave. It's 1½ mi and about 45 minutes to the main cave entrance, so take your time. After more than ¼ mi you pass the only skylight (besides the cave entrances) far too high

Meatball in the lower cave is simple to reach but only with abundant lighting!

to escape, but notice how the moss and ferns grow into the cave only as far as the light penetrates.

The ceiling appears white for a ways, then the walls, too, as the tube narrows for a few feet. The cave widens again and the floor might be wet for a bit as you also must work down magma boulders (hiking gloves help) over a couple sets of steep lava falls. It does in fact funnel down quite narrowly with help from a fixed rope on one little 8-ft section. Then you hike over a few sets of rock piles where ceiling collapses have occurred and end up in a large section that's very wide and tall just before the metal staircase and sign at the main entrance juncture.

The lower cave is very easy and only ¾ mi long with gradual elevation change as you notice the interesting formations including a large boulder, known as the "meatball," wedged in a narrow section about halfway. For the most part, the floor is much smoother than the upper cave and it stays fairly spacious until the tube tapers down to the end where you must crawl if you wish to explore the last few feet. Return the same way and ascend the metal staircase that turns to stone near the entrance at the information kiosk.

8 | GOAT MOUNTAIN

ELEVATION: 4965 ft, with vertical gains of 1540 ft from the upper TH; 2915 ft from the primary TH

DISTANCE: 1 mi up from the upper TH, 2 mi round-trip; 3¼ mi up from the primary TH, 6½ mi round-trip; 7½ mi round-trip counterclockwise loop

DURATION: 1-plus hour up, 2 hours round-trip; 2½ hours up, 5–6 hours round-trip loop

DIFFICULTY: Strenuous. Very steep final mile, narrow, bushwhacking, trail-finding, not possible when wet, more difficult bushwhack for loop

TRIP REPORT: So many Goat Mountains, so much time! So let's hike this rarely climbed highest point (itself a small lava dome volcano) in Cowlitz County with little pomp only 5 mi SW of Mount St. Helens. No fee or restroom at either TH.

TRAILHEAD: Kalama Horse Camp or the upper TH. For Kalama Horse Camp TH, take I-5 N from Portland to exit 21 (Woodland/Mount St. Helens), turn right on Lewis River Road (WA-503) 26½ mi toward Cougar, turn left (N) on Merrill Lake Road (FR-81, Kalama Recreation Area, milepost 35½) 8¼ mi to a juncture with the left fork on FR-030 heading to the upper TH. For the Kalama Horse Camp (primary) TH, continue ¼ mi on paved FR-81 to the fork at Kalama Horse Camp, then either proceed straight ¼ mi more past the green gate to a tiny pullout on the left (milepost 9) next to the Fossil Trail sign or take a right at the fork to much more parking at the horse camp. Park in the day use area gravel lot to the right in front of signs for Toutle Trail 238 (65 mi, less than 1½ hours easily to the primary TH from Portland).

For the more difficult and longer drive to the upper TH, follow gravel FR-030 for ¼ mi, turn right on FR-8117 for 3 mi (unmarked, gravel, potholes) passing FR-040 on the right just past FR-030. Then briefly is a left turn, then quickly a right turn to stay on FR-8117. Fork right (at about 2700 ft) to stay on FR-8117 for 1¾ mi to the end (also unsigned), turn right on narrowing FR-470 almost ½ mi to a nondescript saddle before the road becomes completely overgrown (few parking spots but not much competition (72 mi, 1¾ hours from Portland). No fee at either TH, and there is an outhouse at the horse camp.

ROUTE: From the primary TH on the S side of the Kalama Horse Camp lot, find the narrow path only a few feet left of the wider Toutle Trail 238. Follow it a hundred yards then begin to work left (N) on any solid path briefly to FR-81. Cross the road to the TH and a small, old sign for Fossil Trail 242 and continue ½ mi NE on the narrow, but easy, path to an old closed roadway (FR-550). Take the wide gravel road left another ½ mi a bit steeper to a solid switchback. After a second turn you begin to see the sheer granite cliffs S of Goat Mountain through the trees. The view only improves as you ascend another turn, then take 3 easier switchbacks through the big, old noble and silver firs, western hemlock, and huckleberry patches to the thin saddle at a faint three-way intersection (2¼ mi from TH). To the left is the slightly overgrown path down the narrow rise SW 125 ft to the upper TH on FR-470.

From the quiet wildflower-surrounded upper TH and saddle (with a look down to part of Merrill Lake) the first feet of the trail are

Foxglove is brilliant with the goal in sight up the ridge and a corner of Merrill Lake coming into view.

nearly impossible to locate and there is no signage. When driving up you would look and then walk left (NE) at the saddle through a thicket of trees and bushes only a few feet before the more solid spur becomes discernible a hundred feet or so up to the Fossil Trail.

Turn left on Fossil Trail from the upper TH spur only 40 ft, or the same distance if you are coming from the primary TH to a faded path on the right. Leave Fossil Trail (continuing N around the base of the mountain) and take the bushwhack path a few feet to the nearby W ridge where the true scrambling begins. The super-steep yet surprisingly solid path has scant but very helpful flagging more than ½ mi E before the final ¼ mi or so N along the rocky and fairly slender high ridge (still tree-covered but less so). See Mount St. Helens instantly once you attain the high ridge. Steep ups and downs exist but are minimal, making you pay attention past pines and over the larger boulders comprising the summit block.

Be careful to the top where there is a USGS benchmark and a forested twin peak farther N. Even with a few trees, Mount St. Helens is in your face with Mount Adams behind to the right, and part of the reservoir system to the S can be seen as well as Mount Hood. On a clear day you see N of Mount St. Helens into the Mount Margaret Backcountry to the pointed Coldwater Peak with Mount Rainier in the background. Return mindfully down to the three-way intersection at the saddle

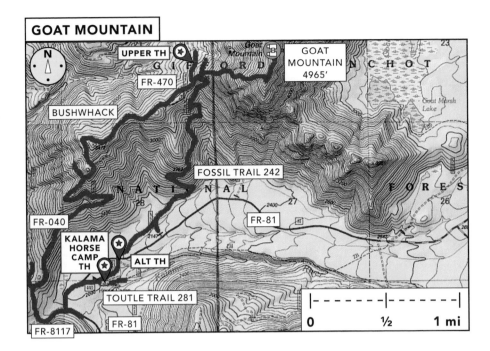

GOAT MOUNTAIN

N

UPPER TH

FR-470

BUSHWHACK

GOAT MOUNTAIN 4965'

Goat Marsh Lake

FOSSIL TRAIL 242

FR-040

FR-81

KALAMA HORSE CAMP TH

ALT TH

TOUTLE TRAIL 281

FR-8117

FR-81

0   ½   1 mi

above the upper TH on the Fossil Trail and fork to the left for the easiest descent by the same route to the horse camp as most people do. Fork to the right (down briefly) to the upper TH if you parked there or are hiking the counterclockwise loop to the Kalama Horse Camp TH area.

From the upper TH continue right (SW) along the overgrown narrowing road (FR-470) N of several little ridge bumps on a fairly level but tough traverse less than 1 mi. The road is badly overgrown in spots where it narrows too, but finally widens and eases to a vague flat area in the trees on a bend. Walk diagonally across the flats left finding the rough bushwhack path again left of a tiny bump (3200 ft) and continue SW down the rise steeply a couple hundred feet. The route tapers and becomes overgrown the final feet to dirt and gravel FR-040.

Follow the wide road down to the left as the remainder of the route is a cakewalk. There are two turns followed by an easy traverse as you look back through the trees NE to see Goat Mountain and the very top of Mount St. Helens behind to the right. Reach FR-8117 less than 2½ mi from the upper TH. Turn left (S) on FR-8117 then left (E) on FR-030, and finally turn left (NNE) again on paved FR-81 less than ½ mi to either TH near the horse camp.

ELEVATION: 4835 ft, with about 2150 ft vertical gain total

DISTANCE: 12 mi round-trip loop

DURATION: 5–7 hours round-trip loop

DIFFICULTY: Strenuous. Several trails, fairly accurate signage, never too steep, slightly overgrown at times, ups/downs, minimal poison oak, long

TRIP REPORT: Open late June through October, this is without a doubt one of the very best day hike loops on the volcano itself, here from the lower western slopes of Mount St. Helens. Check the websites for road and trail conditions (www.fs.usda.gov/alerts/giffordpinchot/alerts-notices, wsdot.wa.gov/traffic/trafficalerts/) as snow melts late and the region surrounding Mount St. Helens is continuously changing throughout our lifetimes. This will be abundantly clear even from the TH located SW of the summit, which gets moved farther S with every major rock- and mudslide. No fee or restroom.

TRAILHEAD: Blue Lake TH. Take I-5 N from Portland to exit 21 (Woodland/Mount St. Helens), turn right on Lewis River Road (WA-503) 27½ mi, turn left (N) on Merrill Lake Road (FR-81, Kalama Recreation Area, milepost 35½) 12 mi (gravel last miles) into FR-8123 for 1½ mi to the end with plenty of parking on the sides (75 mi, 1½ hours from Portland).

Upper Sheep Canyon Falls off the beaten path on another delightful day hike.

ROUTE: Walk past the sign a long ½ mi N to Blue Lake over the rocky Toutle Trail 238 through the slide area; try not to lose your way as the route meanders up the drainage then left (NW) toward Coldspring Creek just below Blue Lake without much elevation gain. Find a suitable log crossing before the lake as it can be a bit tricky to the more solid trail traversing a steeper hillside and ridge directly on the other side of

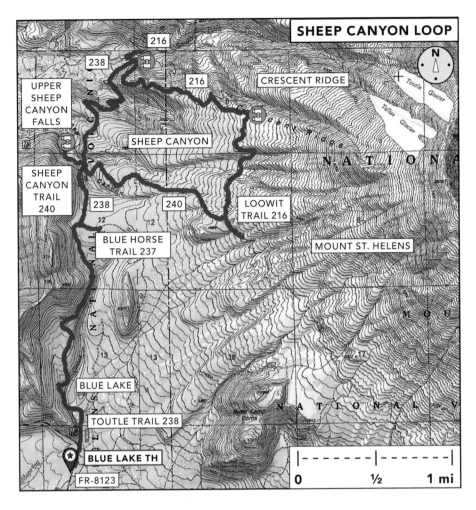

the creek. See Blue Lake through the woods from its left (W) side and continue 2 mi N without difficulty to a juncture with Blue Horse Trail 237 on the right (E). Stay N on Trail 238 as you continue to descend more than ½ mi to the next intersection at the beginning of the lollipop loop.

Turn right (ESE) on Sheep Canyon Trail 240 to take the loop counterclockwise and save the spur path to Upper Sheep Canyon Falls for the end of the loop for better lighting later in the day or visit them now if curiosity killed the cat. For the falls you would turn left (NW) on Trail 240 down a few hundred feet as the (main) Toutle Trail crosses the creek to the N over a bridge. The old road (Trail 240) opens up nicely to a great overlook of the 101-ft, two-tiered, thin waterfall in a narrow amphitheater. Be careful near the lip of the ravine.

Back to the four-way intersection, hike steadily steeper on Sheep Canyon Trail 1½ mi ESE to the end at the next juncture (Loowit Trail). You cross a cool creek over the bridge to begin up through several varieties of pine and fir. There are good shots of

Mount St. Helens through openings in the woods that drastically improve ahead. Turn left (N) on Loowit Trail 216 (encircles entire mountain for around 30 mi) 1 mi; the route dips down the first ½ mi crossing a small open gully near tree line then ascends to the high point of the day on Crescent Ridge. Begin to head down the ridge left (WNW) on the same trail as it narrows and is somewhat brushy but with the best views yet up the Toutle and Tallus Glaciers to Mount St. Helens, and N over toward the South Fork Toutle River. Easily and pleasantly descend about 1¾ mi from Loowit Trail to the next junction; you find yourself surrounded by multitudes of wildflowers including bear grass, lupine, and paintbrush late June through August.

You will need to turn right (SW) on Toutle Trail 238 to finish the loop but take Trail 216 right (W) instead a couple hundred yards toward the river to check out the canyon, stopping before the main trail continues down to cross the water. There's an open Indian paintbrush-covered meadow off-trail near the ledge with superb views up the South Fork Toutle River. Hike the last 1½ mi of the loop by staying right (SW) at the sign (for South Fork Toutle River, Toutle and Loowit Trails), soon crossing a small creek, then ascend the thin, uneven path as it winds up to the bridge near the Sheep Canyon Trail four-way intersection. Stay on Toutle Trail 238 for 3 mi S back to the TH without any trouble, the first mile being uphill.

Bear grass owns the steeper slopes up Crescent Ridge to Mount St. Helens in July.

ELEVATION: 5727 ft, with about 2000 ft vertical gain

DISTANCE: 6 mi one way, 12 mi round-trip

DURATION: 3–4 hours up, 6–8 hours round-trip

DIFFICULTY: Strenuous. Long, some steeps but not bad, rocky, drop-offs, narrow

TRIP REPORT: Fairly easy access to the goods for hiking within the Mount St. Helens volcanic blast zone is located at the Johnston Ridge Observatory (milepost 52 on State Road 504). David Johnston, who was the unfortunate volcanologist stationed N of the volcano that fateful day in May, was supposed to be out of harm's way when in fact the opposite was true. The summer crowds thin to the fork for Harry's Ridge, where even fewer hikers continue to Coldwater Peak or beyond. Bring plenty of water as the trails are dry. There are few services at the interesting interpretive center and little to no food options as is the case with all of the official viewpoints surrounding the mountain, which never received National Park status and kept the region rather wild without much infrastructure. A Monument Pass (day use fee per person over sixteen) is required for any of the viewpoints or trails from the observatory (open mid-May through October, 10 a.m.–6 p.m., restrooms inside), which is only 5 mi N of the crater in the center of the blast zone. You can always pay after if you get an early start hiking. The very best and free exhibits to be found for the volcano are at the Science and Learning Center back near milepost 43.

TRAILHEAD: Johnston Ridge Observatory. Take I-5 N from Portland and I-5 S from Seattle to exit 49 (Castle Rock/Toutle), turn toward Mount St. Helens Visitor Center on WA-504 E 50 mi to the end at a very large parking lot (110 mi, 2 hours from Portland; 155 mi, 3 hours from Seattle).

Spirit Lake and Mount St. Helens command your attention on the wildflower-covered trail near the summit of Coldwater Peak.

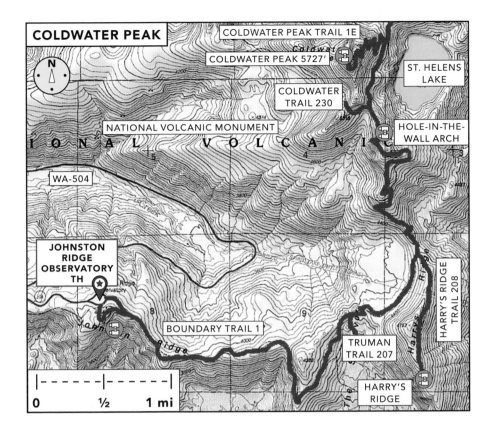

ROUTE: Begin up and over the hill on the trail past the first major viewpoint from the observatory, or better yet start the long hike from the far NE corner of the parking lot near another kiosk on the easier, paved Boundary Trail 1. The trail turns to dirt after the spur to the right (which leads up to the viewpoint and observatory). Follow great signage the entire way as Mount St. Helens is definitely the focus and there will be plenty of other eye candy to distract you as well. Bright red paintbrush and other wildflowers (late June into July) blanket the foreground as you work SE down and up the wide path past some scattered low flora.

Stay on the main trail as it narrows and requires your attention around a point to the junction with Truman Trail 207 (to Windy Ridge) at less than 2½ mi from the TH. Continue left (NE) up Boundary Trail 1 without difficulty less than a mile above the valley (possible elk or deer sightings) to the saddle and intersection with Harry's Ridge Trail 208, which heads to the right a mile to one of the better views above Spirit Lake. Hike left (N) instead from the wide saddle up the pumice path as the wind begins to pick up. See the sizable Spirit Lake coming into view with Mount Adams behind. Move up 2 switchbacks, then steeper and narrower on a steady traverse around left. After the third switchback, see Mount Hood above Harry's Ridge left of Mount St. Helens. After the seventh switchback, cross to the E side of the ridge passing old tree trunk bottoms with the tops completely missing or in the lakes. Soon you'll see St. Helens Lake (also partially covered with old trees floating since May 18, 1980), the top of Mount Rainier, and Coldwater Peak!

The famous eruption's landslide completely displaced all of the water from Spirit Lake in the form of a 600-ft wave that crashed onto the hillsides N, tearing all of the trees down then pulling them back into the lakes (including nearby Coldwater Lake) along with hundreds of feet of debris. This raised the water level 200 ft at Spirit Lake and created St. Helens Lake. Trees farther back were incinerated from the pyroclastic flow that followed.

Come down a fairly steep and slick switchback immediately and carefully to Hole-in-the-Wall Arch. Walk through the rocky doorway (with the only guaranteed shade of the day) to some of the best views on the hike! This arch and Coldwater Peak are both clearly visible from the TH area. Remain on the narrow, wildflower-surrounded trail down another steep switchback to better footing near another saddle and junction at 5 mi from the TH. Continue to the right on Trail 1 (opposite Coldwater Trail 230 heading NW) on an easier traverse above St. Helens Lake ½ mi N to the junction and signage for the summit to the left on Trail 1E.

Finish steadily on Trail 1E WSW up 13 switchbacks (only slightly overgrown at times) to the very top over the boulders near the last little old tower. If you frame Mount St. Helens correctly you can even hide the other seismic monitors on the summit area, which is covered with Western pasqueflower and others. See more of Goat Rocks to Mount Adams, Mount Rainier, and Mount Hood, with the continuation of the ridge leading to The Dome, Mount Margaret, and Mount Whittier. Return by the same route.

Trail to Coldwater Peak on the left under St. Helens Lake with the top of Mount Rainier barely discernible.

11 | NORWAY PASS AND HARMONY FALLS

ELEVATION: 4508 ft at Norway Pass (4640 ft on nearby highest point of trail); 3400 ft at Harmony Falls on Spirit Lake; with vertical gains of 950 ft for Norway Pass, 700 ft for Harmony Falls; 1650 ft for both plus more brief options

DISTANCE: 2¼ mi up, 4½ mi round-trip; 1 mi down, 2¼ mi round-trip; 6¾ mi for both

DURATION: 1 hour up, 2 hours round-trip; ¼ hour down, ½–1 hour round-trip for Harmony Falls plus more brief options

DIFFICULTY: Moderate for all. Steady grade, sometimes steeper, narrow, rocky

---

TRIP REPORT: The preeminent first-ever look directly to Mount St. Helens is from the hike to Norway Pass, followed by the separate short walk down to Spirit Lake at Harmony Falls. This is the only lakeside viewpoint, where Harmony Falls actually disappeared after the 1980 eruption when the lake level rose more than 200 ft. A small cascade above the lake is still present and known by the same name.

Independence Pass TH is in between these hikes and worth exploring ½ mi up steeper switchbacks to a high point (or continuing to more vistas), and the drive SW briefly to the end of FR-99 at Windy Ridge Viewpoint (with restroom and access trails, one with several hundred steps up to an expansive view) is a must if visiting the region. Northwest Forest Pass required at all THs, and vault toilets are present at Norway Pass TH and Windy Ridge Viewpoint.

TRAILHEAD: Norway Pass TH and Harmony Falls Viewpoint. Take I-5 N from Portland to exit 21 (Woodland/Mount St. Helens), turn right on Lewis River Road (WA-503) 28 mi to Cougar, then into rougher FR-90 at exactly 31 mi from I-5. Continue on FR-90 less than 20 mi along the third consecutive large reservoir (Lake Merwin, Yale Lake, and Swift Reservoir in that order), stay straight after the last one (just past Pine Creek Information Center) on winding FR-25 N (closed in winter) 25 mi, turn left (SW) on FR-99 for 9 mi, turn right on FR-26 steeper and slightly rougher 1 mi to the sizable parking lot at Norway Pass TH on the left. Harmony Falls Viewpoint is 5 mi farther S from FR-99 on the right, with Windy Ridge at the end of the drive 2 mi more. From Seattle, take I-5 S to exit 127 for WA-512 E to WA-7 S 52 mi, turn left in Morton on US-12 E 17 mi, turn right in Randle on WA-131 S 2¾ mi into FR-25 S (closed in winter) 17 mi, turn right on FR-99 and follow like above (110 mi, 2½–3 hours from Portland; 125 mi, 3-plus hours from Seattle).

NORWAY PASS AND HARMONY FALLS

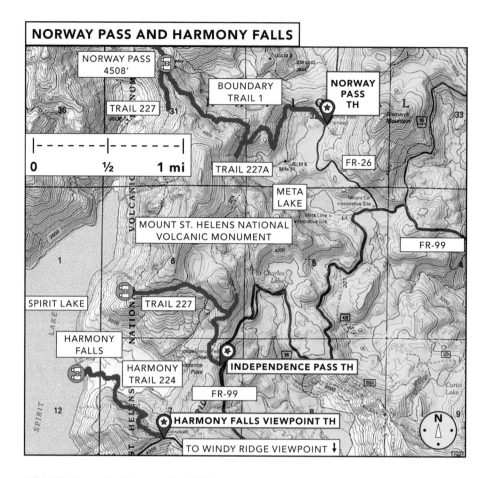

NORWAY PASS
4508'

BOUNDARY
TRAIL 1

NORWAY
PASS
TH

TRAIL 227

36

31

33

|- - - - - - -|- - - - - -|

0   ½   1 mi

TRAIL 227A

FR-26

META
LAKE

MOUNT ST. HELENS NATIONAL
VOLCANIC MONUMENT

FR-99

SPIRIT LAKE

TRAIL 227

HARMONY
FALLS

HARMONY
TRAIL 224

INDEPENDENCE PASS TH

FR-99

HARMONY FALLS VIEWPOINT TH

TO WINDY RIDGE VIEWPOINT ↓

N

ROUTE: From the Norway Pass TH begin N from the traffic circle at the end of the parking lot on Boundary Trail 1, then hike steadily up W and then S, traversing the slope well within the blast zone. Climb a few steeper turns, staying right on narrow Boundary Trail 1 after a mile from the TH instead of continuing S on Trail 227A. See tiny Meta Lake below across tons of bright wildflowers July into August as you undulate NW somewhat easier. Mount Rainier comes into view just before Norway Pass where mostly downed trees (without limbs or

The otherworldly landscape from Norway Pass to Mount St. Helens.

One of the floating fallen tree islands favoring the Harmony Falls area on Spirit Lake.

leaves), blanketing the surrounding hills and valleys, all lie in the same direction indicating the path of the pyroclastic blast!

Ignore old Trail 227 (usually closed due to slides) to the left (S) at the pass and also the continuation of Boundary Trail 1 to Mount Margaret, Coldwater Peak, or Mount Whittier to hang out near Norway Pass and return by the same route. Soak in the amazing shot across Spirit Lake (with many downed trees still floating as islands) to the volcanic pumice, rock, and debris up Mount St. Helens' open side of the crater!

From Harmony Falls Viewpoint begin NW gradually down Harmony Trail 224 with plenty of low shrubs, bushes, and trees making quite a comeback. Traverse an Indian paintbrush-covered plain (in late July) with Mount St. Helens coming into full view as you descend the creek with its many little cascades near Spirit Lake. Please remain on the trail at all times while enjoying the sights and do not contemplate stepping onto the logs floating since 1980. Return somewhat steeply the same way when you have had your fill.

12   MOUNT MARGARET

ELEVATION: 5858 ft, with 2300 ft vertical gain

DISTANCE: 5¾ mi, 11½ mi round-trip

DURATION: 2½ hours to the saddle (near 5600 ft) with Mount Whittier, up to another ½ hour to the summit, 5–6 hours round-trip

DIFFICULTY: Strenuous. Long, wide, gently graded, obvious, more difficult with snow covering steep slopes near saddle and top until late summer, traction devices necessary with snow

TRIP REPORT: After graduating from the previous hike (Norway Pass and Harmony Falls) this surprisingly sleepy summit is the next likely progression to get a bird's eye view, above St. Helens Lake and Spirit Lake, unobstructed to Mount St. Helens. For those with decent hiking skills, skipping ahead to attempt Mount Whittier (hike 13) and then finishing with Mount Margaret for dessert might make better sense. Northwest Forest Pass required, and an outhouse is present.

TRAILHEAD: Norway Pass TH. See hike 11 for directions.

ROUTE: See Norway Pass (hike 11) for further description taking Boundary Trail 1 WNW 2¼ mi fairly easily up to Norway Pass. Wildflowers surround you quickly July into August and a rather large and log-filled Spirit Lake below Mount St. Helens pops into view as you approach the pass. Magnificent perspective! Continue N near the juncture up the slope on Trail 1 a couple long turns toward Bear Pass steeper but without difficulty, then traverse almost 2 mi W with improving vistas. There are excellent

Early season trilliums line the path to Norway Pass.

views unfolding down right (NE) to Grizzly Lake and then we have Mount St. Helens behind Mount Margaret with Mount Rainier farther N behind Boot Lake en route to the intersection on the Mount Whittier-Mount Margaret saddle (5600 ft, 5 mi up).

At the saddle intersection, look to the right (N) for the faint route to the more difficult Mount Whittier, but for Mount Margaret you will head left (S) instead on a straightforward traverse path across somewhat steep and grassy and/or snowy slopes more than ½ mi to the right-hand turn onto Trail 1F off of Boundary Trail 1 (which continues past The Dome and Coldwater Peak 8 mi to the Johnston Observatory). You will finish ¼ mi NW then N steeper to the top of Mount Margaret.

For this in more detail you hike left (S) from the Mount Whittier-Mount Margaret saddle narrowly and well below (E) of the nearby large pillar to another saddle under Mount Margaret's steep and mostly open NE ridge. Without a ton of snow and ice remaining this area is quite colorful and easy to navigate around the summit block to the S. Take the narrow spur Trail 1F on the right traversing higher in the same direction (WNW). Even with some snow the final 200 ft of elevation gain should still be doable over the slope of least resistance winding up to the nearby high point (above most of the trees), finishing from the W with exquisite 360-degree views.

Be careful near the high boulders and return the same way when you are good and ready. More courageous types continue a bit more directly down the NE ridge super-steeply under various conditions bushwhacking to the main trail at the saddle before the main saddle and intersection. From there stay right (E) on Trail 1 down to Norway Pass TH.

Lingering snow on the summit block of Mount Margaret near Mount St. Helens.

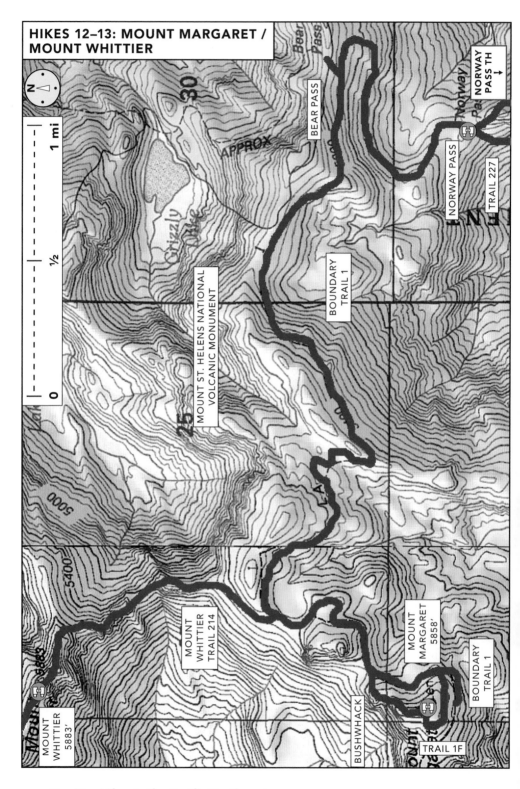

HIKES 12–13: MOUNT MARGARET / MOUNT WHITTIER

N

1 mi

½

0

BEAR PASS

NORWAY PASS TH

NORWAY PASS

TRAIL 227

Bear Pass

Norway

30

APPROX

Grizzly Lake

BOUNDARY TRAIL 1

MOUNT ST. HELENS NATIONAL VOLCANIC MONUMENT

25

5000

5400

5683

MOUNT WHITTIER TRAIL 214

MOUNT MARGARET 5858'

BOUNDARY TRAIL 1

MOUNT WHITTIER 5883'

BUSHWHACK

TRAIL 1F

13 MOUNT WHITTIER

ELEVATION: 5883 ft, with 2600 ft vertical gain plus 300 ft with Mount Margaret

DISTANCE: 5 mi to the Mount Whittier-Mount Margaret saddle; 6¼ mi to the summit 12½ mi round-trip; 14 mi round-trip with Mount Margaret

DURATION: 2½ hours to the Mount Whittier-Mount Margaret saddle, up to another hour to the summit, 5–7 hours round-trip; 6–8 hours round-trip with Mount Margaret

DIFFICULTY: Mix of strenuous for Mount Margaret (gently graded, obvious, more difficult with snow covering steeper slopes near saddle with Mount Whittier) and very challenging for Mount Whittier (nearly impossible with too much snow/ice covering a very thin section of trail along a cliff band under the summit block, ice axe and crampons recommended before late summer otherwise mostly navigable with care, narrow rocky ridgeline, steep, fairly solid, some exposure near peak, Class 3)

TRIP REPORT: Less frequented but wonderfully captivating to more advanced hikers, with its relatively easy late summer access and equally easy to access TH, is this prodigal summit. Check ahead as always for road and trail conditions (www.fs.usda.gov/detail/giffordpinchot/alerts-notices/?cid=fseprd492501). Northwest Forest Pass required, and an outhouse is present.

TRAILHEAD: Norway Pass TH. See hike 11 for directions.

ROUTE: See hikes 11 and 12 (Norway Pass and Mount Margaret) for the description to the Mount Whittier–Mount Margaret saddle (5600 ft, 5 mi up). Turn right (N) onto the faded Mount Whittier Trail 214 that soon descends a couple hundred feet over the thinning rocky ridge before rising very steeply NW with more surprises for the remainder of the route. One involves moving up a very thin ramp along a cliffy section blocking the ridge crest that presents problems when holding snow/ice. The boulders become larger and steeper the last ¼ mi or so and it's somewhat airy near the summit so use caution while admiring the sights and several neighboring lakes, perhaps not all unfrozen.

 Wildflowers exist all the way to the top as do many flying bugs during the peak of summer and the panorama with the active volcano highlighting the landscape is second to none! Return attentively back to the main saddle with Mount Margaret and turn left (E) 5 mi on Trail 1 down to the TH or tack on nearby Mount Margaret (hike 12, 1½ mi round-trip) to put the icing on the cake.

ELEVATION: 8330 ft; 8284 ft; with vertical gains of around 4700 ft for the summit, and 4570 ft for the rim viewpoint

DISTANCE: Almost 9 mi round-trip for the summit; 4 mi up, 8 mi round-trip for the rim viewpoint

DURATION: 4–6 hours to the summit, 3–5 hours to the rim viewpoint, 7–9 hours round-trip

DIFFICULTY: Mix of expert only for the summit (scrambling, steep, ups/downs, borders unstable cornices, drop-offs) and very challenging for the rim viewpoint (popular but regulated, bouldering, steady steep, rocky, blowing dust near rim, gaiters and goggles recommended, possible in snow with winter gear including traction devices)

TRIP REPORT: Many of our younger hikers were not around or can't remember May 18, 1980 when the 9677-ft volcano exploded violently, starting the world's largest landslide ever caught on video while spewing searing hot lava, rock, and dust

Rising above clouds hanging in the valley from the bottom of the famed route up Monitor Ridge.

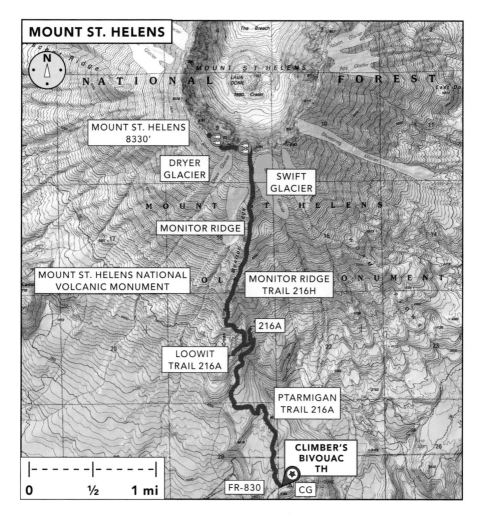

MOUNT ST. HELENS

MOUNT ST. HELENS
8330'

DRYER
GLACIER

SWIFT
GLACIER

MONITOR RIDGE

MOUNT ST. HELENS NATIONAL
VOLCANIC MONUMENT

MONITOR RIDGE
TRAIL 216H

216A

LOOWIT
TRAIL 216A

PTARMIGAN
TRAIL 216A

CLIMBER'S
BIVOUAC
TH

FR-830   CG

0   ½   1 mi

60,000 ft straight up into the atmosphere. Lakes disappeared, changed shape, or were born anew. The landscape forever changed and with blossoming new life over the decades the natural habitat and playground have also rebounded and expanded; for now, that is. Mount St. Helens is still more likely than most in the Cascade Range to erupt, but there are usually some pretty good warning signs before anything major ensues. Earthquakes on the other hand could happen at any time in the Pacific Northwest.

While most people stop at the rim itself or just right from the rim, the tiny mound to the left provides a much richer viewpoint. From there only more advanced hikers continue toward the actual summit, which has been eroding rapidly at almost an inch per year since 1980 (volcanoes.usgs.gov/volcanoes/st_helens/)!

Strictly limited by a purchased ($22) permit preprinted at home, only 100 climbers per day during prime-time months (May–October) are allowed above 4800 ft. Please remember permits sell out months in advance although winter and

snow travel is also permissible and enjoyable when safe (usually February–May when people ski, snowboard, and snowshoe, Sno-Park Pass required). A permit is required year-round and the number of climbers allowed increases for nonprime time. Keep in mind it may be 90 degrees at the TH in summer but 50 degrees with biting cold winds on the crater rim. Northwest Forest Pass required, and vault toilets are present at the TH and 2 mi up at the Loowit Trail intersection.

TRAILHEAD: Climber's Bivouac. Take I-5 N from Portland to exit 21 (Woodland/Mount St. Helens), turn right on Lewis River Road (WA-503) 28 mi to Cougar, then into rougher FR-90 at exactly 31 mi from I-5. Continue 3½ mi more (1 mi past seeing Swift Dam from the highway and third consecutive reservoir passed). Turn left (N) on FR-83 (small brown sign) 3 mi, turn left on FR-8100 (quickly notice a small brown sign for the Climber's Bivouac) 1½ mi. Turn right on steeper gravel FR-830 (okay for 2WD, slight washboard) to the end at a paved turnaround with ample parking and limited camping (bustling at all hours). From Seattle, take I-5 S 140 mi to exit 22 (Dike Access Road) driving left in the circle into Old Pacific Highway, turn slight left on E Scott Avenue, turn left in the roundabout on Lewis River Road (WA-503) and follow like above (75 mi, 1½ hours from Portland; 185 mi, 3½ hours from Seattle).

ROUTE: All hikers traveling over 4800 ft in elevation need to sign in and display their prepaid hangtag permit on their backpacks. Begin N up the wide Ptarmigan Trail 216A for a couple easy miles through the forest as you enter the National Volcanic Monument in Gifford Pinchot National Forest. Views of your soon-to-be nemesis in Monitor Ridge will come into view on the left after the first 1½ mi as the rocky moraine ridge defines itself to the intersection with Loowit Trail 216 that

Onlookers gaze to Spirit Lake as volcanic dust swirls from the rim of Mount St. Helens.

encircles the mountain. The last bit becomes steeper and rockier, mellows, then steepens again with a couple turns to the juncture. You see Mount Hood across the valley and Mount Adams much closer from the turns.

Head straight (N) on Monitor Ridge Trail 216H at the four-way signed intersection through the last of the trees. In 50 ft is a signed path right 40 ft to a visible outhouse. Walk out of the woods and move left directly toward the base of the lava-formed trail filled with rock and scree, as the true climb gets underway.

Past the nearby sign for Monitor Ridge (at less than 2½ mi from the TH) you see the crater rim and several more posts with blue markers denoting the trail's location through the boulder field. The hiking path between the rocks isn't difficult for a bit. Then the parallel moraine shoulder left (W) of the Swift Creek Flow joins Monitor Ridge (6500 ft, 3 mi from the TH) as the route becomes much steeper with bouldering involved ¼ mi more to a weather station (6850 ft). Gloves may help with sharp magma scrambling up the taxing, steep ridge. Continue quite steeply up the ridge with a few workable choices heading in the same direction N from the weather station.

Remember trail politeness and step aside for uphill traffic (while coming down) or those passing you as you ascend the progressively sandier, pumice-covered path (Trail 216H), with even more difficult footing close to the windy crater rim. The Swift Glacier appears to the right on the final grind as you notice the line of tiny people slogging up from thousands of feet down.

Once reaching the rim of the crater, you are instantly in awe of your locale in the universe as you catch your breath! Mount Rainier reigns to the N beyond tree-filled Spirit Lake, which leads up the blast zone past the actively steaming crater domes to the high rim of Mount St. Helens. Be especially cautious near the windy rim/high

ridge, not getting too close, as massive snow cornices exist year-round and are deceiving. Many people turn around in this general area and from a small bump to the right on the high ridge without ever reaching the true summit. Another mound just to the left is the true rim viewpoint. Some people wear goggles and masks to fend off the blowing dust at times. In winter or spring, glissading is a fun return option partway down from the rim near where the trail would be.

Turn left (WNW) 75 ft on Trail 216H from the rim, instead of stopping at the small bump to the right, up to a far superior rim viewpoint on one of several bumps along the rim. From there you clearly see the remainder of the more difficult route along the narrow ridge to the summit almost ½ mi (25–30 minutes) farther. Otherwise skip the top and enjoy a picnic (weather permitting) and break before the steep descent down Monitor Ridge to the TH.

For the true summit, navigate the faint, rocky path W a few feet just S of the ridgeline over then down steeply to a saddle under the peak. Beware of major overhanging cornices near the rim, keeping your distance, as you follow the route or

Mount Adams and hikers on the rim viewpoint from the summit of Mount St. Helens in late September.

snow tracks carefully past the top of the Dryer Glacier rising from the left (S). Finish to the steep, wider, open slope with more tiny scree and pumice before leveling out a few more feet to the top of the volcano.

Mount Jefferson is past Mount Hood to the S with Mount Adams behind some sweet angles over the rim much closer to the E. Mount Rainier commands respect to the NE behind Spirit Lake and the Mount Margaret Backcountry on a clear day. About 50 ft past the top is a cairn and boulder marking the end of the path. Return by the same route mindfully around the rim to the more popular smaller bumps, then hike much quicker S down Monitor Ridge with the spongy sand and dust helping you and your knees for the first stretch. After that you and your body are on your own!

MOUNT ADAMS

GOAT ROCKS WILDERNESS

15 Johnson Peak 57

16 Hogback Mountain 61

17 Bear Creek Mountain 65

18 Nannie Ridge to Cispus Pass......68

19 Goat Lake Loop to
Hawkeye Point 72

20 Old Snowy Mountain..................75

21 Hellroaring Canyon Viewpoint to
Iceberg Lake Overlook...............77

22 Stagman Ridge Loop 80

23 High Camp/Adams Glacier
Meadows to Equestria Lake.......83

24 Mount Adams 86

<table>
<tr><td>**15**</td><td>**JOHNSON PEAK**</td></tr>
</table>

ELEVATION: 7487 ft, with at least 3200 ft vertical gain from either TH; around 2000 ft vertical gain from a viewpoint without the summit

DISTANCE: 7 mi up, 14 mi round-trip; 12 mi round-trip without the summit

DURATION: 4–6 hours up, 8–10 hours round-trip; 3 hours up to the viewpoint

DIFFICULTY: Very challenging. Long, fairly steep summit bid, bushwhack, minimal scrambling, route-finding, steep slope difficult with snow to summit juncture or Heart Lake, ice axe and crampons required until late summer, rocky summit block, mountain goat encounters possible

---

TRIP REPORT: Undervalued is this lesser known summit on the northern edge of the Goat Rocks Wilderness with a great trail for most of it leading through wildflower-choked Lily Basin. It is difficult to visit until late July or even August when snow and ice finally melt from the super-steep N-facing slopes off of Johnson Peak's SW ridge in Lily Basin. It's about 6 mi to the intersection with Angry Mountain Trail 90 at a saddle on the SW ridge of Johnson Peak, then another ½ mi and less than 500 ft down steeply to beautiful Heart Lake as an alternate day hike or camping trip. Some people even stop at the little saddle with its great views of Angry Mountain, Middle Fork Johnson Creek valley, and Hawkeye Point, and return by the same route. Northwest Forest Pass required at both THs, and there are no restrooms.

TRAILHEAD: Lily Basin TH or Lily Basin Stock TH. Take I-5 N from Portland to exit 68 (Morton/Yakima), turn right on US-12 E 61 mi (passing Morton and Randle, last rest area at milepost 126), turn right (S) on gravel FR-48 (easy to miss, milepost 129½) for 10½ mi and 10 turns to a small pullout on the left with the signed Lily Basin TH on the right (last 2 mi narrower and slightly rougher with a few potholes, okay for 2WD, AWD preferred).

For Lily Basin Stock TH, continue ¼ mi farther on FR-48, turn right up the gravel driveway less than ½ mi to the end (140 mi, 3 hours from Portland). Lily Basin Stock TH is quieter and begins a few hundred feet higher with a slightly shorter spur Trail 86A to meet the main trail. The only caveat is that you must quickly drop about 100 ft in elevation to meet the main trail, which must be regained on your return at the end of the day.

ROUTE: From Lily Basin (lower) TH at the pullout off FR-48, sign in at the free self-issue Wilderness Permit station and take Lily Basin Trail 86 for ½ mi up to the faint

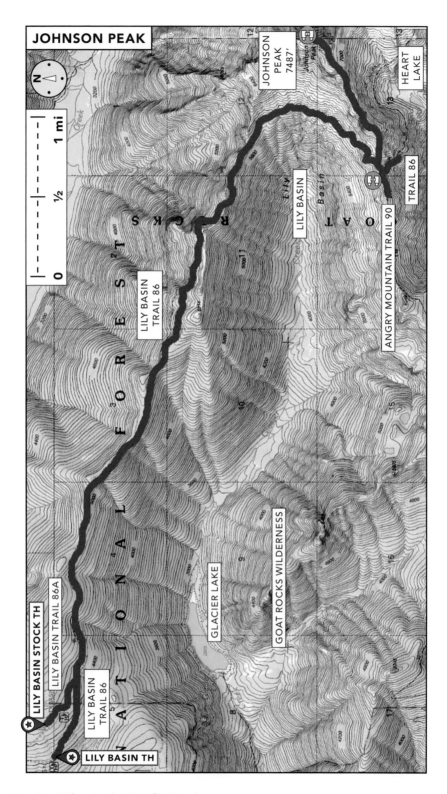

JOHNSON PEAK

JOHNSON PEAK 7487'

HEART LAKE

LILY BASIN

TRAIL 86

ANGRY MOUNTAIN TRAIL 90

LILY BASIN TRAIL 86

LILY BASIN STOCK TH

LILY BASIN TRAIL 86A

LILY BASIN TRAIL 86

LILY BASIN TH

GLACIER LAKE

GOAT ROCKS WILDERNESS

N

1 mi

½

0

FOREST

ROCKS

GOAT

NATIONAL

spur Trail 86A juncture on the left (no sign, sometimes marked with an orange flag). Coming from Lily Basin Stock (upper) TH, hike more than ¼ mi up and down the spur Trail 86A to the juncture with Trail 86.

Continue to traverse E easily through the mossy forest 2000 ft above Glacier Lake on the wider trail with a few larger Douglas fir and cedar another mile to the long NW ridge of Johnson Peak. Then look to the right through the trees for a shot of Angry Mountain across the valley. Follow the center of the sweet ridge SE on the narrow and slightly overgrown path past good-sized cedar with glimpses left of nearby Mount Rainier that only improve as you ascend. The route steepens at 2 mi from Lily Basin TH briefly as you head right (S) under the top of a small ridge bump. At roughly 2½ mi from the THs is one of only a few switchbacks on the entire hike! It's coming down from a tiny ridge bump where the trail has been reworked steeply through fallen trees. Pass through more thick brush and wild berries moving right (S) of another ridge bump to the ridge again. There is a better look at Mount Rainier and Packwood Lake as you hike left (N) well below the ridge for a bit at around 3 mi and an hour from the THs.

In ¼ mi is your first full shot of Mount Rainier while crossing a boulder field across a clearing. Trees become sparser as wildflowers become grander with paintbrush, bear grass, and lupine ¼ mi up the steeper trail at times to the first of many great views of Mount Rainier looming above Packwood Lake below. Be careful along sections of the trail with huge drop-offs even though the route is Class 1 (minus the summit). At around 4 mi from the THs you round a corner to suddenly see Johnson Peak towering above the ridge and the steep green and rocky hillside with the trail visible up to a little saddle on the ridge crest. Move down steeper then up to the ridge with a large rock fin and pinnacle blocking easier travel on the ridge in that direction (NW toward Mount Rainier).

Paintbrush, lupine, and others dazzle before even reaching Lily Basin with Mount Rainier as a fitting backdrop over Packwood Lake.

Cross the saddle to the right (S) side of the ridge again briefly as Trail 86 cuts under Johnson Peak traversing through the very steep and colorful Lily Basin ahead. Descend to another little ridge saddle before the 1½-mi traverse to the SW ridge saddle intersection/viewpoint. Move S across the vibrant wildflower-covered oasis under the W slopes of Johnson Peak without much difficulty (unless snow/ice remain). After ½ mi of the traverse, including a few tiny water crossings and a decent little rocky creek crossing in a steep meadow (between some of the last pines), is a steeper rocky ravine to cross. There are cascades above the narrow ravine with a smaller off-chute to the left from the main trail. Be very cautious down, across, then up; and fortunately it's not as problematic as it appears at first. In ¼ mi is an easier rocky creek bed to pass and the last chance for water if you are hiking to the summit. The wildflower spectacle that blankets these slopes in August during peak season rivals those of any in all of Goat Rocks Wilderness!

Hike down the narrow path a bit to cross a large scree field. The steeper rocky trail turns up to a fake saddle and then the going is easier over dirt to an old sign at the saddle (6150 ft) and intersection with Angry Mountain Trail 90. The great views just got better as you see Hawkeye Point above the beautiful Middle Fork Johnson Creek valley and basin belonging to Heart Lake (out of sight), and the rough ridge to Johnson Peak. Moving SW on Trail 90 takes people below Angry Mountain down the continuation of the ridge to that TH, while staying on Trail 86 moves SE to Heart Lake (with a steep spur path), Hawkeye Point, and Goat Lake in the interior of Goat Rocks Wilderness. See the two huge rocky spires down to the left from the saddle and see toward Angry Mountain with massive valleys on each side. Also see Mount St. Helens, Mount Rainier, and the top of Mount Adams.

For Johnson Peak leave the main trails and scramble a fun mile left (NE) up the steep ridge with only a faint path at times to the rockier summit. There the views extend from the SE ridge to Hawkeye Point, Old Snowy, Ives Peak, Gilbert Peak, and Mount Adams farther S, with Mount Rainier not far to the NW. Several waterfalls and perhaps mountain goats can be seen in the basins below. Goats can even be seen to the summit so be sure to make noise and not compete with them near the top. From the main trail, bushwhack WNW very steeply up the ridge or just right without falling while near the edge. Look for helpful cairns to the summit but don't depend on them. See the bright green Heart Lake in the beautiful open basin under Hawkeye Point quickly from the main trail near the saddle.

Avoid brush along the rocky slender ridge NE as the trees thin and you work just right (S) of the ridgeline near a tiny point (6689 ft) to the ridge again with huge boulders and rocks to descend. The route changes to Class 2 as you must scramble quite steeply down 15 ft with decent holds to more solid ground. Next, climb right of a cruddy ridge section finding your way more easily back to the ridgeline. After that, see boulders on the ridge for the remainder of the route with very few trees ½ mi more to the top.

Continue left of the ridge momentarily, then left (N) of big boulders and short gendarmes blocking the ridgeline. Find the faint path hugging the rock for 100 ft, then climb the loose rock right back to the ridge when it's possible, watching for cairns while checking all of your holds. Cross the ridgeline immediately, moving slightly right of it again, and stay high around a little rocky fake summit to a (usually snowy) small saddle at 7240 ft. Cross the snow without difficulty and then finish the last stretch on an easier approach steeply over the widening rocky ridge to the narrower rocky summit plateau. The exposure is minimal along the SW ridge route and from the top, but a fall or slip over much of it could still be devastating so be extra watchful. Soak in the vistas from this peaceful peak and savor the solitude within this remarkable expanse before descending.

16 HOGBACK MOUNTAIN

ELEVATION: 6793 ft, with 2400 ft vertical gain

DISTANCE: 5¼ mi up, 10¼ mi round-trip clockwise loop down ski area

DURATION: 3–4 hours up, 6–7 hours round-trip loop

DIFFICULTY: Strenuous. Steady, steep only briefly, scrambling, bugs/ticks possible

TRIP REPORT: Often overlooked from the nearby busy Pacific Crest Trail in the summer is this sweet little double-peaked mountain directly above White Pass Ski Area. The E bowl between summits is easily attained via a short climb from the highest chair lift and is skied on powder days. It is also possible to cross-country ski or snowshoe the route in winter, but you will have to contend with downhill skiers and snowboarders while the ski resort is open, making it somewhat unnerving. Better to go before or after they are in operation, which is usually December through April or May. There is plenty of the white stuff for enthusiasts outside of these months and the packed snow can be walked over in June or July with the last of it lingering as wildflowers abound everywhere else on the slopes (be careful with softer snow

Lenticular clouds over Mount Rainier from the White Pass Ski Area.

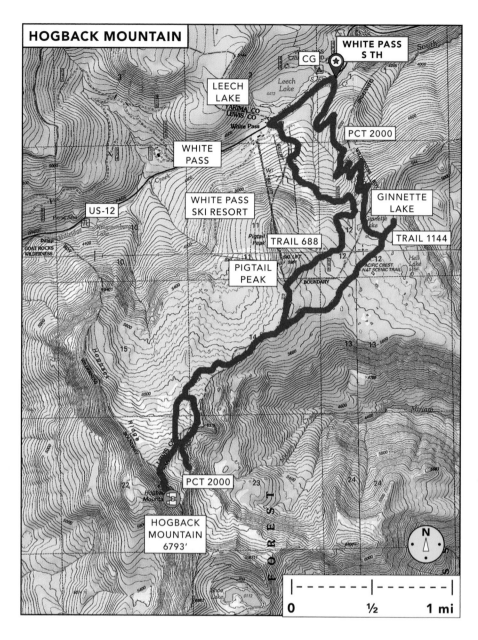

HOGBACK MOUNTAIN

WHITE PASS S TH

CG

LEECH LAKE

PCT 2000

WHITE PASS

WHITE PASS SKI RESORT

GINNETTE LAKE

US-12

TRAIL 688

TRAIL 1144

PIGTAIL PEAK

PCT 2000

HOGBACK MOUNTAIN 6793'

N

|‑ ‑ ‑ ‑ ‑ ‑ ‑|‑ ‑ ‑ ‑ ‑ ‑ ‑|
0   ½   1 mi

around tree wells). Hogback Mountain is the most northern point in Goat Rock Wilderness, which tends to hold snow longer than most regions and is a vast expanse of wonder and amazement tucked away N of Mount Adams (SE of Mount Rainier). Northwest Forest Pass required, and no restroom is present at the small parking circle, but there is a gas station conveniently ½ mi back at the top of White Pass.

TRAILHEAD: PCT on White Pass. Take I-5 S from Seattle to exit 142A (Auburn), merge onto WA-18 E to WA-164 E (Enumclaw) to WA-410 E (Chinook Pass Highway), turn slight right onto WA-123 S, turn left onto US-12 E 13 mi to the White Pass area and the TH on the right (just past the White Pass Campground and Trailheads sign that reads "White Pass S TH" at milepost 151¾). From Portland, take I-5 N to exit 68 (Morton/Yakima), turn right on US-12 E 86 mi passing Morton (hint: speed trap), Randle, and Packwood to White Pass and follow as above (113 mi, 2½ hours from Seattle; 161 mi, 2½–3 hours from Portland).

ROUTE: At the PCT TH on White Pass, fill out a free self-issue Wilderness Permit, then begin the clockwise loop past the sign that barely identifies itself as the Pacific Crest National Scenic Trail 2000. Cross the bridge over S Fork Clear Creek immediately to slowly rise 1½ mi and 4 switchbacks S up through thick forest on a wide trail. Plenty of small pines and brush along the creek before views of Mount Rainier emerge through the trees to the left. Navigate a few blowdowns without much difficulty, as trees aren't too huge, up 5 more switchbacks steadily S to a rock field. On the eleventh switchback (total) pass another rock field and arrive at Ginnette Lake 2 mi and about 1 hour in. The tree-surrounded small lake melts off much slower than Leech Lake at the pass and makes for a nice pit stop.

Stay E of the lake easily on the PCT ¼ mi to a juncture with rougher Trail 1144 taking off left (NE) from a wide saddle toward Twin Peaks a mile away. Head right (SW) on the PCT instead, up a wide, easy ridge section 1 mi to an intersection with a wider ski road moving right (N) toward Pigtail Peak (on the ski area). Make a note that this will be the return route for the loop trail down the more open slopes to finish. Continue ¾ mi, crossing ski runs under a chair lift to stay on the PCT proper to the top of that four-person chair lift.

See Mount Rainier as big as life and finally see the open summit plateau of Hogback Mountain further up the ridge past the top of the next chair lift you'll be aiming for. You could make a beeline toward the top of the lift by crossing a steep meadow; or stay on the PCT hugging closer to the ridgeline on the left with better views of a large, sharp prominent rock just E of a little bump on the ridge, then meet the other path on the more prominent ridge ahead. Either way it's

Curious elk near the TH on White Pass in Washington.

Deep snow still covers most of the route into late June with ice finally melting off Ginnette Lake.

only ¼ mi or so from the top of that four-person chair lift to where you should leave the PCT at about 6200 ft to stay on the high ridge. The other option is to stay on the PCT briefly as it leaves the ridge left (S) and then scramble up a very steep, rocky gully to the right (W) to a small saddle between the double summit area with no trail.

Both options are the steepest part of the hike, the ridge crest being preferential with constant views of the Goat Rocks and others.

From the high ridge, right to left as you see them, are Chimney Rock, Mount St. Helens, Johnson Peak, Hawkeye Point, Old Snowy Mountain, Ives Peak, Mount Adams, and Gilbert Peak! No path necessary to finish the thinning ridge from the fake or first summit (which only appears higher as is usually the case when summits are close to the same elevation) a hundred yards to the highest point crossing a saddle halfway. There is some volcanic pumice-like solid rock, low pines, and a few old gnarls to negotiate without trouble. More fantastic vistas with Twin Peaks, Round Mountain, and Clear and Rimrock Lakes to the NE; Mount Rainier is directly behind the lower summit to the NW. Be careful through late spring with snow cornices building near thin sections of ridge from the protuberant boulder below to the peaks.

Return roughly the same way 1¾ mi down to the ski road intersection near Pigtail Peak. Consider taking the loop, which is only slightly shorter but with more wildflowers. Be careful not to lose Trail 688 due to lingering snow on the wider ridgeline or get pulled too far to the right (S) near the intersection. Turn left (N) on Trail 688 (unsigned) for the loop toward multiple chair lifts on the top of Pigtail Peak but traverse right of the ridge crest on the road around the base of that summit block easily (avoid left fork). Descend the road or steeper ski runs between a few tiny tarn ponds, then stay on the wide gravel road down ski runs for the best route. You come close to the PCT momentarily but stay on the road as it winds WNW down with better views of Mount Rainier, the ski resort, Leech Lake, and Spiral Butte's steep rocky face. Near the bottom of the ski area bushwhack or take trails N to the large parking lot. Follow the driveway briefly left to US-12 or take the path from the NE corner of the lot down to the highway. Walk right (NE) less than ½ mi carefully along US-12 to the TH on the right to finish the loop.

<table>
<tr><td>**17**</td><td>**BEAR CREEK MOUNTAIN**</td></tr>
</table>

ELEVATION: 7337 ft, with 1317 ft vertical gain

DISTANCE: 3½ mi up, 7 mi round-trip

DURATION: 1½–2 hours up, 3–4 hours round-trip

DIFFICULTY: Mix of moderate for the standard route (solid trail, rocky, dusty, steeper last mile, drop-offs near top, wildlife sightings possible including marmot, deer, elk, coyote, black bear, and mountain goats) and very challenging for lollipop loop down N ridge (Class 3, bushwhack, very steep, sharp branches and brush at times, scrambling)

TRIP REPORT: Best side door to the Goat Rocks Wilderness for the easiest summit with the best views without having to hike several miles before it gets good! The only downside is the longer drive from Seattle or Portland. No fee or restroom.

TRAILHEAD: Section 3 Lake TH. Take I-5 S from Seattle to exit 154A for I-405 N (Renton) to exit 4, merge onto WA-169 S to Enumclaw, turn left onto WA-410 E/Roosevelt Ave into WA-123 S, turn left on US-12 E 15 mi to White Pass, then 9 mi more to milepost 158½, turn right on paved Tieton Reservoir Road (FR-1200, signed for Clear Creek Recreation Area) 5 mi easily and quickly winding around Clear Lake. Turn right on gravel Cold Creek Road (FR-1205, signed for Section 3 Lake) more than 2½ mi, turn left on FR-742 for ¼ mi, turn right on FR-1204 (correct signage, follow

Tieton Peak closer in the middle with Gilbert Peak above the Conrad and Meade Glaciers to the left and Ives Peak above McCall Glacier to the right, all from lavender meadows.

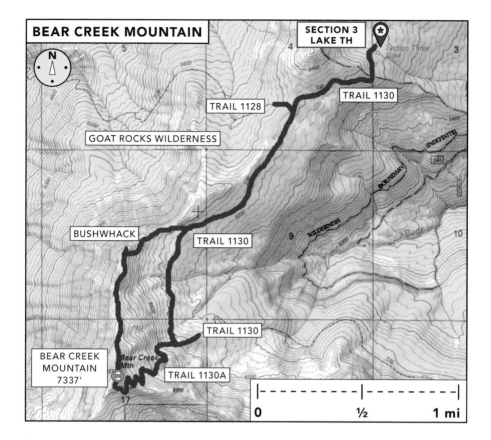

BEAR CREEK MOUNTAIN

N

SECTION 3 LAKE TH

TRAIL 1130

TRAIL 1128

GOAT ROCKS WILDERNESS

BUSHWHACK

TRAIL 1130

BEAR CREEK MOUNTAIN 7337'

TRAIL 1130

TRAIL 1130A

0   ½   1 mi

signs and arrows when in question) 3½ mi, fork right to the end at the circle (roughest road section: narrow, rocky, few pullouts, 2WD okay but high-clearance AWD recommended). From Portland, take I-5 N to exit 68 (Morton/Yakima), turn right on US-12 E 90 mi, turn right on Tieton Road and follow like above (130 mi, 3 hours from Seattle; 180 mi, 3½ hours from Portland).

ROUTE: Walk by the kiosk and old sign for Bear Creek Mountain on Trail 1130 (rutted at times) past Section 3 Lake (more a small tarn pond) immediately, then easily traverse SW and S below the E side of the main ridge. Move through a few smaller pines and then across tiny creeks and open meadows where you can see Bear Creek Mountain ahead. At more than 2½ mi from the TH arrive at a juncture where you stay right (WSW) at the sign posted to an old tree stump on Trail 1130A. The trail will be rockier, dustier, and steeper before and after the intersection as you ascend the wide, rocky gully to the high ridge. Encounter a micro-break in the pitch and then it's steep again with wildflowers mixing in for the remainder.

See Mount Adams and nearby Gilbert Peak from the high ridge. Walk a bit easier up the wide trail with thinning pines to the highest open and narrower ridge section where Mount Rainier pops into view for the final 100 ft along with the entire main ridge of the Goat Rocks Wilderness, including Gilbert Peak, Ives Peak, Old Snowy Mountain, Hawkeye Point, and Johnson Peak! And along the ridge continuing SW from Bear Creek Mountain to the main ridge is the serrated Devil's Horn up to Tieton Peak (pronounced TIE-it-tun peek). Far to the N, Mount Stuart and the Alpine Lakes Wilderness can also be spotted on a clear day from the boulders on top. Return the same way for the simplest descent to the TH.

There is one other option for the descent. Although shorter than the main trail at less than 1½ mi (and about an hour down, which is the only direction recommended), the ridge N then NE back to the meadows from the summit is more trying than it appears—with some drop-offs—but not without its charm and allure to press on as you keep the amazing vistas a while longer. About a hundred yards N from the top, hike left without trouble around black rock, then scramble briefly nearest the ridgeline with a bit of loose rock.

Next, stay on or barely right (E) of the crest to miss some brush (although missing all of it may prove difficult). Continue to bushwhack, with no trail, to meet the ridge at a wide saddle. Following the saddle is a small bump you must climb; be careful to avoid the sheer rock wall to the left. Stay in the center of the ridge for a time, then right again easier. The route becomes narrower and tree-covered in spots to a small saddle before the last little bump (above 6800 ft) with sharp black rock surrounding it.

Down climb around 100 ft steeply to the right (E) from the saddle, through loose rock, leaving the ridge and large pylon; then traverse NE through scree above a boulder-filled meadow back to the wider ridgeline again with some grasses and a few trees. There is one more brief scramble, down workable rock on the ridgeline, before you traverse right of the crest again by old snags and tree roots. It's somewhat rough just as you see the main trail below in the nearby larger meadow to the right. Work down to it slowly to finish the loop and turn left (NE) to the TH on Trail 1130.

Absolutely glorious look past the highest peaks within the Goat Rocks Wilderness to Mount Adams from the boulder-strewn summit of Bear Creek Mountain.

18 | NANNIE RIDGE TO CISPUS PASS

ELEVATION: 6473 ft, with vertical gains of about 2800 ft, and 2000 ft
for Sheep Lake

DISTANCE: 6¾ mi up, 13½ mi round-trip; 4¾ mi to Sheep Lake, 9½ mi
round-trip; add less than 1 mi round-trip for Nannie Peak too

DURATION: 3½–4 hours up, 6–8 hours round-trip; 2 hours or so for
Sheep Lake, 4 hours round-trip

DIFFICULTY: Mix of very challenging to Cispus Pass (quite long, scree,
snowfields, possible wildlife encounters, steady steep) and strenuous
to Sheep Lake or Nannie Peak (switchbacks, ups/downs, narrow)

TRIP REPORT: Travel to Sheep Lake or even Nannie Peak for a more moderate day
in the shadow S of Old Snowy Mountain, Ives Peak, and Goat Rock's highest summit
in Gilbert Peak (8184 ft). Or continue up Nannie Ridge where you will revel within
copious numbers of wildflowers and an increasingly brilliant landscape to Cispus
Pass. Remember Goat Rocks Wilderness holds snow until late in the summer. Check
ahead as always for road and trail conditions (www.fs.usda.gov/recarea/
giffordpinchot/recarea/?recid=31462). Northwest Forest Pass required, and restrooms
are present.

TRAILHEAD: Walupt Lake TH. Take I-5 N from Portland to exit 68 (Morton/
Yakima), turn right on US-12 E 60 mi passing Morton and Randle, turn right (S) at
milepost 128 on washboard gravel FR-21 (2 mi W of Packwood) 15½ mi (signed to
Walupt Lake), turn left on paved FR-2160 for 4½ mi (winding, narrow) up to Walupt
Lake Campground. Park near the second of several vault toilets next to the TH. From
Seattle, take I-5 S to exit 142A (Auburn), merge onto WA-18 E, exit for WA-164 E
(Enumclaw), turn left on WA-164 E 14 mi, turn left on WA-410 E (Chinook Pass
Highway) 40 mi, turn slight right onto WA-123 S 16 mi, turn right on US-12 W 10
mi, turn left (S) on FR-21 and follow like above staying on main wide road (160 mi,
3 hours from Portland; 130 mi, 3½ hours from Seattle).

ROUTE: Fill out a free self-issue Wilderness Permit at the Walupt Lake TH. Begin E
past the signage 150 ft and turn left (N) on Nannie Ridge Trail 98. The wide trail
works up a decent grade with 16 switchbacks and turns through the thick woods as
the route narrows and gains almost 2000 ft the first 2½ mi to the Nannie Peak saddle
S of that tiny summit. The final ½ mi E to the saddle juncture mellows thankfully as

the forest floor opens up and you can see Mount St. Helens and Mount Adams. There are a few tiny creeks to cross all day so finding water is never a problem.

As a much shorter day hike skipping Sheep Lake and Cispus Pass or even an add-on spur, you could turn left (N) on the brief trail at the juncture on the saddle and ridge (unsigned) over the small downed pine onto the clear path ½ mi winding up to the old lookout site on Nannie Peak (6106 ft). There is a great shot of Mount Adams with Mount Rainier sneaking in and Goat Rocks can be seen best from the viewpoint just N of the lookout site.

For the main route, traverse steadily down the wider Trail 98 losing about 200 ft in elevation around the E side of Nannie Peak heading N under a huge sheer rock wall. Pass left of a small pond in a partial clearing with nice reflections and possibly some campers. Hike a couple steeper switchbacks into the woods again and continue traversing to meet the main ridge momentarily. Look SW back to Nannie Peak and Mount Adams. Hike steeply and briefly up the wide ridge section with even more wildflowers working in and the Goat Rocks coming into sight, especially Ives Peak and Gilbert Peak, then walk easier down the meadow and ridge to the bright green Sheep Lake. The astute will notice the top of Old Snowy Mountain left of Ives Peak. It's about 2¼ mi and an hour to the lake from the Nannie Peak saddle and it's 2 mi and 1½ hours more to Cispus Pass. Hang at the lake and return the same way or continue to the goods including mountain goats at times near the pass.

Wildflowers, including intensely red paintbrush, to Cispus Pass in Goat Rocks.

Green is the theme from Sheep Lake, a worthwhile destination for many families.

Directly above Sheep Lake you begin choking on various wildflowers such as lupine and paintbrush ¼ mi N up to the PCT intersection. Fork left (N) on the PCT a mile on an easy traverse up the left (W) side of the ridgeline in and out of the trees with a great look at the enormous gendarme on the ridge ahead from the colorful hillside. From the next saddle on the ridge you reach Klickitat Basin and can see the remainder of the route up the right (E) side of the ridge. The trail becomes dusty and rocky the last mile as the landscape thrills passersby every time.

You will most likely have to traverse lingering snowfields between wildflowers through August (earlier may require traction devices) and will have your best views of Ives Peak left and Gilbert Peak to the right. Between the two summits, the prominent jagged centerpiece holds such named high points as Goat Citadel, Big Horn, and Black Thumb. Big Horn is actually the second highest summit on the ridge being the pinnacle just W of Gilbert Peak and there is a lesser high point between Big Horn and Ives Peak simply called Peak 7478. E of Ives Peak is Tieton Peak, Devil's Horn, and Bear Creek Mountain.

Finish with a couple switchbacks to the usually very windy Cispus Pass and cherish the views of two wonderful basins simultaneously before returning down to Walupt Lake. Or better yet turn left (S) from the tiny pass area steeply up the scree-covered ridge path a hundred yards or so for more solitude and the premier overlook of the day. See another path on the other side of the pass and the continuation of the PCT traveling through Cispus Basin to Snowgrass Flats en route to its second highest point in Washington (7000 ft) N of Old Snowy Mountain.

HIKES 18–20: NANNIE RIDGE TO CISPUS PASS / GOAT LAKE LOOP TO HAWKEYE POINT / OLD SNOWY MOUNTAIN

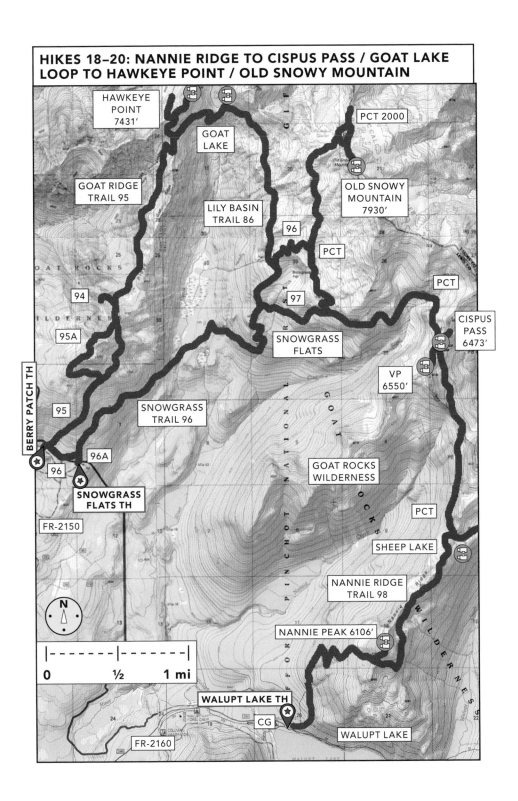

HAWKEYE POINT 7431'

GOAT LAKE

PCT 2000

GOAT RIDGE TRAIL 95

LILY BASIN TRAIL 86

OLD SNOWY MOUNTAIN 7930'

96

PCT

PCT

94

97

CISPUS PASS 6473'

95A

SNOWGRASS FLATS

VP 6550'

BERRY PATCH TH

95

SNOWGRASS TRAIL 96

GOAT ROCKS WILDERNESS

96A

96

SNOWGRASS FLATS TH

PCT

FR-2150

SHEEP LAKE

NANNIE RIDGE TRAIL 98

N

NANNIE PEAK 6106'

0   ½   1 mi

WALUPT LAKE TH

CG

WALUPT LAKE

FR-2160

ELEVATION: 7431 ft; 6650 ft without the summit; with vertical gains of 3281 ft, and 2500 ft for Goat Lake loop alone

DISTANCE: 6¾ mi from Berry Patch TH (5½ mi to the high intersection with Lily Basin Trail, plus ½ mi from Snowgrass Flats TH), 16½ mi clockwise loop including the summit; 14 mi clockwise loop without the summit

DURATION: 3–4 hours directly up Goat Ridge Trail, 8–10 hours round-trip loop; 7–9 hours round-trip loop without the summit

DIFFICULTY: Very challenging. Steady trails, mosquitoes July into August, few steeps, well signed, obvious, fairly long, steeper summit block with snow/ice crossing okay without special gear in late summer, mountain goat encounters possible

TRIP REPORT: Most people camp at various locations throughout Goat Rocks Wilderness including at the THs, but several day hikes surrounding this one prove it's not necessary for those in good shape getting an early start! The Snowgrass Trail to Snowgrass Flats is fairly crowded on summer weekends because of the camping options there and the short season. Northwest Forest Pass required at both THs, and an outhouse is located at Berry Patch TH.

TRAILHEAD: Snowgrass Flats TH or Berry Patch TH. Take I-5 N from Portland to exit 68 (Morton/Yakima), turn right on US-12 E 60 mi passing Morton and Randle, turn right (S) at milepost 128 on washboard gravel FR-21 (2 mi W of Packwood) 13 mi staying on main wide road. Fork left on FR-2150 for 3 mi, ignore the left turn down to Chambers Lake, and then either turn right more than ¼ mi on FR-405 to Snowgrass Flats TH or continue straight more than ¼ mi to Berry Patch TH, both with ample parking. From Seattle, take I-5 S to exit 142A (Auburn), merge onto WA-18 E, exit for WA-164 E (Enumclaw), turn left on WA-164 E 14 mi, turn left on WA-410 E (Chinook Pass Highway) 40 mi, turn slight right onto WA-123 S 16 mi, turn right on US-12 W 10 mi, turn left (S) on FR-21 and follow like above (155 mi, 2½–3 hours from Portland; 125 mi, 3½ hours from Seattle).

ROUTE: For the big clockwise loop from Snowgrass Flats TH, take Snowgrass Spur Trail 96A past a small lake briefly and turn left (W) on Trail 96 for ½ mi to Berry Patch TH (for Hawkeye Point and Goat Lake directly begin from Berry Patch TH). Turn right on Goat Ridge Trail 95 steeply N 1½ mi toward Goat Ridge and Jordan

The spectacular wildflower display in late August under Hawkeye Point en route to Goat Lake.

Basin through the forest. Pass Trail 95A on the left (moves around the cliffy W side of the ridge more than a mile to meet the main trail again) and hike ¾ mi up through meadows E of the ridge to the juncture on the ridgeline.

Continue N on the W side of Goat Ridge almost ½ mi passing Jordan Creek Trail 94 on the left. Traverse up steadily, but never too steep, less than 3 mi more to the high intersection with Lily Basin Trail, passing through the top of the stunningly picturesque Jordan Basin en route to the ridge saddle. See Hawkeye Point ahead as the views are somewhat underrated on this side of the loop. There are open meadows littered with dazzling wildflowers along Jordan Creek (camp spots), waterfalls, ponds, grasses, wildlife, and then the final push easily to the intersection with Lily Basin Trail 86.

See Old Snowy to Gilbert Peak SE across the vast valley belonging to Goat Creek; you'll be descending to the right on Trail 86 for the clockwise loop, but leave Trail 85 to continue on Trail 86 up the ridge ½ mi N to the junction with the summit spur path on the right for Hawkeye Point. Look S to Mount Adams standing impressively behind Goat Ridge with Mount Rainier past the ridge to Johnson Peak. Lily Basin Trail continues NW for several miles, but follow the spur instead ¾ mi NNE along the wide-open treeless ridge to the top as the trail becomes a bit steeper and rockier after cautiously crossing a lingering snowfield in a little saddle. Pick a safe angle past the snow/ice as a very steep wall remains most times of the year. See the

Old Snowy Mountain reflects into a small pond below Snowgrass Flats.

vibrant Goat Lake below, which may be partly frozen until late August or even September, and take in the wonder from the boulder-topped peak before moving on!

From the main intersection at the saddle with the Goat Ridge Trail, walk left (NE) for the loop on Lily Basin Trail a mile to Goat Lake, passing thick, bright wildflowers mid-July into August choking the trail on the downward traverse under Hawkeye Point. The gorgeous lake partially to fully thaws for only a fraction of the year (if that) and thus sees most visitors in late September when the rampant mosquitoes of midsummer are mostly gone. Mountain goats love the rocky and snowy high basin and walls under Hawkeye Point as well as the lake itself for much of the year. Keep your distance from these endearing yet wild animals as you carefully cross the outlet creek coming from the lake and walk down the trail without any difficulty.

Enjoy the views of the cascade coming from Goat Lake behind as you stroll S by more surprises, beautiful creeks, an immense blanket of purple lupine, Western pasqueflower, paintbrush, and others, with Old Snowy looming above to the left. Mount Adams and Mount St. Helens are much farther to the S and SW. In around 2½ mi from Goat Lake is the end of Lily Basin Trail past a stream crossing near part of the Snowgrass Flats camping area, with Snowgrass Trail 96 moving steeply up to the left (E) a mile to the PCT or straight down. Walk down ¾ mi steeper to the lower meadows with Bypass Trail 97 heading left (E) to the PCT or Cispus Pass.

Hike steeply S down turns on Trail 96, then follow a flat traverse right (NW) turning SW past a pond or two with great reflections before you cross Goat Creek over the bridge. Finish the last couple of miles through the thickening forest up around 400 ft in elevation (gradual) and down to the Snowgrass Flats TH as you finish on Trail 96A just past Trail 96 moving right (W) to Berry Patch TH in ½ mi.

<table>
<tr><td>**20**</td><td>## OLD SNOWY MOUNTAIN</td></tr>
</table>

ELEVATION: 7930 ft, with 3680 ft vertical gain

DISTANCE: Almost 8 mi one way, 16 mi round-trip

DURATION: 4 hours up, 7 hours round-trip

DIFFICULTY: Very challenging. Only steep near top, very long, well-marked, brief rocky scramble near summit, lingering snow until late summer, mountain goat encounters possible

---

TRIP REPORT: Rite-of-passage destination for Goat Rocks Wilderness hikers is this magnificent trek within an ancient stratovolcano. The entire wilderness was once a colossal volcano eroded by glaciers over time leaving behind beautiful ridges, peaks, valleys, and lakes that all hold snow until late July or August but then reveal one of the most colorful displays of wildflowers in the Pacific Northwest! Northwest Forest Pass required, and an outhouse is located more than ¼ mi away at Berry Patch TH.

TRAILHEAD: Snowgrass Flats TH. See hike 19 for directions.

ROUTE: Fill out a free self-issue Wilderness Permit at the kiosk and signage for Snowgrass Spur Trail 96A and walk by a small lake to Trail 96 proper. Head right (NE) on Trail 96 almost 2 mi easily up 400 ft, then down just as much with a very mild grade, to cross Goat Creek over the bridge. Continue without much of a pitch for a couple miles as you start N up a little rise in the thinning trees to the juncture with Bypass Trail 97 on the right near the bottom of Snowgrass Flats (a few camp spots at 5600 ft).

As a slightly easier and longer brief loop option, you could traverse Trail 97 a mile E to its end at the PCT, then turn left (N) a mile on the PCT to the junction with the end of Trail 96. Hike more directly left instead, a bit steeper ¾ mi N on the Snowgrass Trail to Snowgrass Flats, which is actually quite hilly between flat areas. Leave what seems like the main trail but is really Lily Basin Trail 86 continuing N to Goat Lake and beyond for the fork right (ENE) on Snowgrass Trail 96, steeper almost a mile winding up the clearing to the PCT.

Turn left on PCT 2000 to traverse 1½ mi N up under Old Snowy Mountain by wildflowers and big cairns into the high alpine environment, then across a lingering snowfield without trouble en route to another intersection. Follow the wood sign right (E) toward Old Snowy on the PCT Alternate Trail up steeper rocky turns ½ mi to the high ridge. Climb right (SSE) more than ¼ mi to the summit over scree and boulders

A hiker revels adjacent to the glaciers under Goat Rock's rugged rim from Old Snowy south to nearby Mount Adams.

on the thinning ridgeline between the Packwood and McCall Glaciers where it becomes steeper, but not too difficult, to the very top finishing over larger rock.

From pretty much the center of Goat Rocks see all of the local mountains, Goat Lake, Packwood Lake, Mount St. Helens, Mount Adams, and Mount Rainier. Words can't quite describe the splendor and sheer awe! Return by the same route (considering the Snowgrass Flats loop) with some glissading possible through lingering snowfields NW of Old Snowy Mountain.

ELEVATION: Around 6520 ft at Hellroaring Canyon Viewpoint; 7895 ft at Iceberg Lake Overlook; with vertical gains of 2220 ft from Bird Creek Meadows TH; 4550 ft from South Climb TH

DISTANCE: 3½ mi to Iceberg Lake Overlook from Bird Creek Meadows TH, 7 mi round-trip; 5½ mi to Hellroaring Canyon Viewpoint from South Climb TH, 7½ mi to the overlook, 15 mi round-trip

DURATION: 2 hours up to the overlook, 3–4 hours round-trip from Bird Creek Meadows TH; 3½–4 hours up to the overlook, 7–8 hours round-trip from South Climb TH

DIFFICULTY: Strenuous. Ups/downs from South Climb TH and very long, many bugs June into August, route-finding to the overlook and rockier, narrower, steeper to the top, wildlife sightings possible including mountain goats, literally half as strenuous from Bird Creek Meadows TH

TRIP REPORT: Bring the family in August through September and traverse a small segment of the Round-the-Mountain Trail through a magnificent sub- and high-alpine environment, with several creeks and wildflower-covered meadows en route to one of the best perspectives on Mount Adams from Hellroaring Canyon Viewpoint. More experienced hikers continue to Iceberg Lake or better yet an overlook above the lake atop a moraine ridge with views comparable to any in the Wallowas, Olympics, North Cascades, or on Mount Rainier! The huge Cougar Creek Complex Fire in 2015 closed the Bird Creek Meadows TH as well as the Mirror, Bluff, and Bird Lakes area for a couple years, but

Luminous Iceberg Lake far beneath Piker's Peak from the SE slopes of Mount Adams.

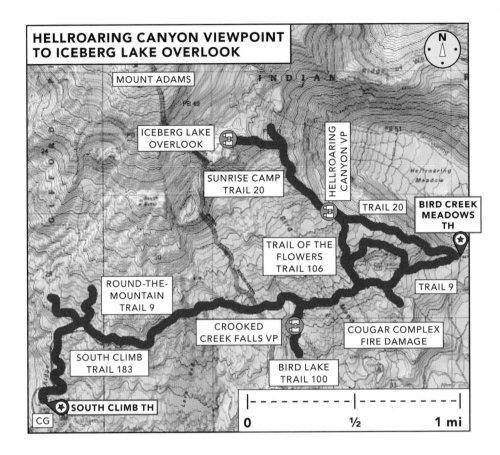

HELLROARING CANYON VIEWPOINT TO ICEBERG LAKE OVERLOOK

MOUNT ADAMS

ICEBERG LAKE OVERLOOK

HELLROARING CANYON VP

SUNRISE CAMP TRAIL 20

TRAIL 20

BIRD CREEK MEADOWS TH

TRAIL OF THE FLOWERS TRAIL 106

ROUND-THE-MOUNTAIN TRAIL 9

TRAIL 9

CROOKED CREEK FALLS VP

COUGAR COMPLEX FIRE DAMAGE

SOUTH CLIMB TRAIL 183

BIRD LAKE TRAIL 100

SOUTH CLIMB TH

CG

0   ½   1 mi

much of the area has reopened and hiking just N and E of the burn area (including the lakes dreadfully) remain immaculate. Cheaters take awful 4WD roads for a longer drive but shorter hike to Bird Creek Meadows TH on a little saddle before Hellroaring Meadow for the Bird Creek Picnic Area, Trail of the Flowers loop, Hellroaring Canyon Viewpoint, or Iceberg Lake. A Cascade Volcano Pass must be purchased for hikes on Mount Adams over 7000 ft all summer and can be found at local Ranger Stations but not all of the THs (www.fs.usda.gov/detail/giffordpinchot/passes-permits/?cid=stelprdb5144542). A small day use fee for Yakima Nation is required and available at all THs except South Climb TH. Northwest Forest Pass is only required at South Climb TH, where the only vault toilets are present.

TRAILHEAD: South Climb TH (almost 5600 ft) or Bird Creek Meadows TH (5676 ft). For South Climb TH, take I-84 E from Portland to exit 64 (Hood River), turn left on OR-35 N (White Salmon), pay the toll to cross Hood River Bridge into Washington, turn left on WA-14 W 1½ mi, turn right on WA-141 N 21 mi to Trout Lake. Fork right on Mount Adams Road (FR-82, sign says "Mt. Adams Rec. Area") 2 mi, fork left on FR-80 for 3¾ mi, fork right on gravel FR-8040 for 5½ mi, fork right on gravel FR-500 for 2½ mi rougher and narrower (2WD okay, AWD preferred) winding to the end with much parking within the trees and some camping (very loud close to TH; 95 mi, 2-plus hours from Portland).

For Bird Creek Meadows TH, follow like above to Trout Lake. Fork right on Mount Adams Road (FR-82, sign says "Mt. Adams Rec. Area"), stay right at two forks (at 1¼ mi and almost 2 mi) 4½ mi turning to dusty gravel to an intersection. Turn right on FR-82 (small brown sign for Bird Creek Meadows 50 ft up the road, narrowing gravel, into Yakima Reservation Tract D, BIA Road 285) less than 6 mi, fork left on unsigned FR-8290 more than 5 mi for the TH to the left on a little saddle with signage and a picnic table (fairly rough road last miles, slow, high-clearance AWD required, GPS device helpful; 100 mi, 2½ hours from Portland).

ROUTE: From Bird Creek Meadows TH, walk left (W) from the road between the signs on the solid Sunrise Camp Trail 20 and stay on it heading NW briefly as you reach a juncture, left (WSW) briefly for Bird Creek Picnic Area on Round-the-Mountain Trail 9. It's almost 1½ mi up on Trail 20 through the thinning forest nearest a developing ridge directly toward Mount Adams to a nondescript open area leveling a bit to Hellroaring Canyon Viewpoint. This will be near another junction left (S) for the remainder of the Trail of the Flowers loop (brief spur to Trail 9 to South Climb TH).

Sizable Hellroaring Falls rips down the rock below the Mazama Glacier from Hellroaring Canyon Viewpoint.

From South Climb TH, begin past the signage and self-issue Wilderness Permit kiosk on the wide South Climb Trail 183, past the campsites at first, then more to the N through the thin pine forest amongst an older burn area. It's about 1¼ mi easily up to a major intersection with the Round-the-Mountain Trail. Turn right (E) on Round-the-Mountain Trail 9 for 2½ mi as it pleasantly rolls with minor ups and downs on a long traverse across the top of Aiken Lava Bed (see Mount Hood), then into a land of color and wonder with many small streams, cascades, and endless wildflowers within the Yakima Nation Reservation.

Large fires in 2015 scorched thousands of acres just S of the main trail including at a few lakes, but trails have reopened to the right (S) including just W of Crooked Creek, and Bird Lake Trail 100 at Crooked Creek with a sweet little option to visit Crooked Creek Falls ¼ mi down the steeper trail to the worthwhile 50-ft high waterfall. Continue E ¾ mi from the waterfall option, and then turn left (N) on Trail of the

Flowers 106 a mile up slightly steeper following signage to the Hellroaring Canyon Viewpoint area left at the ridge juncture on Sunrise Camp Trail.

Hellroaring Canyon Viewpoint (6500–6600 ft) is really a wide swath of ridge you approach from the meadows on Trail 106 coming from the SE to a suddenly mesmerizing perspective. Piker's Peak and Mount Adams tower up to the left (NW) above the Mazama and Klickitat Glaciers. Hellroaring Falls and Hellroaring Canyon (Meadow) are in front of you with Ridge of Wonders on the opposite side down to the cinder cone that is Little Mount Adams (NE)! Return the same way without difficulty after meandering around a bit or press on to even more wild scenery.

To continue on to Iceberg Lake Overlook (less than 2 mi), hike NW up the climber's path (Trail 20), which is narrower but okay, through more wildflowers and the last of the trees to a rocky and icy landscape. Watch for mountain goats as you follow cairns up steeper turns through the moraine to a more solid, thin ridgeline. Climb left (W) up the ridge to a faint juncture, possibly with painted rock. The right fork on Trail 20 leaves the ridge to head almost ½ mi NW on a somewhat rough traverse to Iceberg Lake (glacier travel) then much steeper and farther to Sunrise Camp; all for another day!

Climb the fork left (W) instead roughly ½ mi to a superior overlook atop the moraine ridge S of Iceberg Lake by hiking fairly steeply up the loose rocky trail where it's obvious to the top. From there the panorama is completely mind-blowing. One of the most underrated destinations anywhere in the Cascades! In late August or September the small, milky turquoise Iceberg Lake reveals itself and lives up to its name. The view up the moraine ridge and Mazama Glacier to Piker's Peak and Mount Adams is positively delicious!

22 STAGMAN RIDGE LOOP

ELEVATION: 6075 ft, with about 2000 ft vertical gain

DISTANCE: 12½ mi round-trip loop

DURATION: 6–7 hours round-trip loop

DIFFICULTY: Strenuous. Longer, narrow at times, bugs in early summer, difficult creek crossings until later in summer, not too steep, GPS device helpful

---

TRIP REPORT: This fantastic summer hike takes you up one of several tree-covered little ridges S of Mount Adams, this one just SW and leading up Stagman Ridge, then through colorful pastures including Horseshoe Meadows with great views of the mountain. Enjoy a lollipop loop across multiple creeks and little waterfalls on course to beautiful Lookingglass Lake, and then onto Stagman Ridge again. No fee or restroom.

TRAILHEAD: Stagman Ridge TH. Take I-84 E from Portland to exit 64 (Hood River), turn left on OR-35 N (White Salmon), pay the toll to cross Hood River Bridge into Washington, turn left on WA-14 W 1½ mi, turn right on WA-141 N 21 mi to Trout Lake. Fork right on Mount Adams Road (FR-82, sign says "Mt. Adams Rec. Area") 1¼ mi, fork left on FR-23 for 7½ mi, turn right on gravel FR-8031 for ½ mi staying left briefly past the bridge (White Salmon River) into FR-070 (well signed) 3 mi, turn hard right on FR-120 for ¾ mi up to the end of the turnaround with signage and ample parking (100 mi, around 2 hours from Portland).

ROUTE: Fill out a free self-issue Wilderness Permit and proceed on Stagman Ridge Trail 12 into the woods thick with flora steadily up turns toward the ridge through a burn area at first (providing early views of Mount Adams). After 2 mi of walking NE, the trail becomes steeper the last ¼ mi to an area known as Grassy Hill. Soon leave the main ridge to the left (NNW) dropping 200 ft in ¼ mi. Then slowly climb NE through a long wildflower-covered meadow with tremendous shots of Mount Adams to an intersection at 4 mi from the TH. This is the beginning and end of the loop. It will be less steep to turn left ¾ mi on Trail 12 toward PCT 2000 for a clockwise loop. Turning right on Graveyard Camp Trail 9 would take you to Lookingglass Lake in less than 1½ mi.

Turn right (E) from Trail 12 on the PCT for only ¼ mi or so (see Mount St. Helens through the burn) before it takes off left (N) and you continue straight (E) on Round-the-

Colorful Lookingglass Lake through an old burn to Mount Adams.

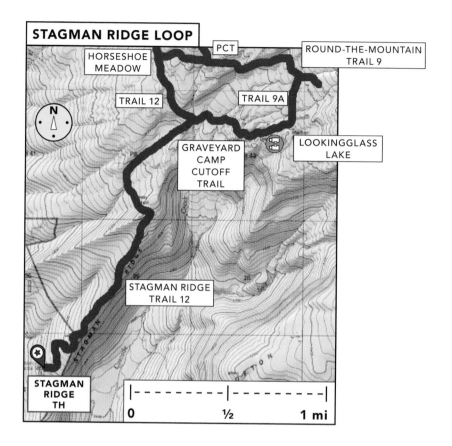

STAGMAN RIDGE LOOP

HORSESHOE MEADOW

PCT

ROUND-THE-MOUNTAIN TRAIL 9

TRAIL 12

TRAIL 9A

N

GRAVEYARD CAMP CUTOFF TRAIL

LOOKINGGLASS LAKE

STAGMAN RIDGE TRAIL 12

STAGMAN RIDGE TH

0   ½   1 mi

Mountain Trail 9 (5 mi from the TH). In another ½ mi and past lovely Horseshoe Meadow is a tough creek crossing during high water that can be pleasantly avoided by walking up next to the water a hundred yards to a narrower crossing well below a cool little hidden cascade. Rock hop across with relative ease finding the trail below.

In ¾ mi (see Mount Hood clearly to the S and Mount Adams above the alpine meadows) stay right (S) on Lookingglass Lake Trail 9A at the sign (1 mi away). The next challenging creek negotiation (before late July/August) is in ½ mi and you may have to scout up and down for a time to find semisafe passage, as fording the swift creek isn't a viable option until late in the season. Continue easier after the crossing to the spur path, left briefly and steeply down to the tree-surrounded shallow lake.

Reach the brilliant, blue-green clear water of Lookingglass Lake at around 7½ mi from the TH on the clockwise loop and enjoy the splendor of new growth and the view of Mount Adams through the burn area. After exploring for that perfect reflection (or not), climb back up a moment, then finish the loop left (NW) on Graveyard Camp Trail across a couple more hiker-friendly creeks (one with a log bridge) up to the Stagman Ridge Trail. Return 4 mi left (SW) to the TH as in the ascent route without any trouble.

<table>
<tr><td>**23**</td><td>**HIGH CAMP / ADAMS GLACIER MEADOWS TO EQUESTRIA LAKE**</td></tr>
</table>

ELEVATION: 6900 ft at High Camp/Adams Glacier Meadows; 7600 ft above Equestria Lake; with vertical gains of 2300 ft, and 3000 ft

DISTANCE: 4 mi to High Camp/Adams Glacier Meadows, more than 8 mi round-trip; 5¼ mi to Equestria Lake, around 10½ mi round-trip

DURATION: 1½–2 hours to High Camp/Adams Glacier Meadows, 3–4 hours round-trip; 2½ hours to Equestria Lake, 5–6 hours round-trip

DIFFICULTY: Mix of strenuous for High Camp (steady steep, fairly easy to follow, lingering snowfields possible, mosquitoes until late September) and very challenging for Equestria Lake with a small loop option (scrambling, route-finding, loose rock, mountain goat encounters possible, much steeper, glissading potential)

TRIP REPORT: This seemingly remote location on Mount Adam's N face actually has great roads to the TH (from the S) and a lot going on if you can only wait until most of the snow melts by August or even September (unless it's a drought year). As per usual, hiking earlier in the season means more wildflowers and lupine but also more flying bugs in your face. Either way, the payoff is an astounding day in the high country breaking out of most of the trees into large, lush, colorful meadows and clear creeks, with expansive views of many big Cascade volcanoes including nearby Goat Rocks! The high alpine glacial Equestria Lake (also known as Glacier Lake on some sites) above High Camp can also be attained. A Cascade Volcano Pass must be purchased for hikes on Mount Adams over 7000 ft all summer and can be found at local Ranger Stations or at the TH ($10–15 per day or $30 per year). No fee or restroom.

TRAILHEAD: Killen Creek TH. Take I-84 E from Portland to exit 64 (Hood River), turn left on OR-35 N (White Salmon), pay the toll to cross Hood River Bridge into Washington, turn left on WA-14 W 1½ mi, turn right on WA-141 N 21 mi to Trout Lake. Fork right on Mount Adams Road (sign says "Mt. Adams Rec. Area") 1¼ mi, fork left on FR-23 for 23 mi (some unpaved), turn right on FR-2329 (mostly rougher gravel) 6 mi including past Takhlakh Lake (worth checking out) to the small parking lot on the right (115 mi, 2½ hours from Portland).

ROUTE: Fill out the free self-issue Wilderness Permit and hike steeply uphill on dusty and wide Killen Creek Trail 113 (shared with equestrians) through the woods a

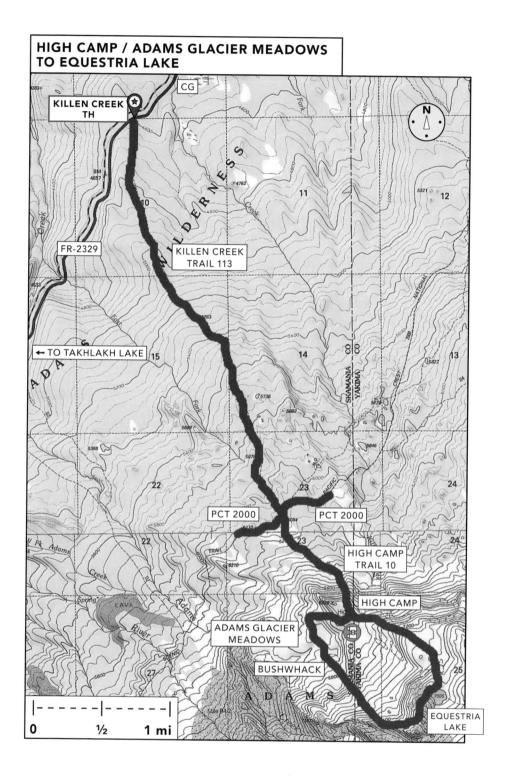

HIGH CAMP / ADAMS GLACIER MEADOWS TO EQUESTRIA LAKE

CG

KILLEN CREEK TH

WILDERNESS

11

12

FR-2329

KILLEN CREEK TRAIL 113

← TO TAKHLAKH LAKE   15

14

13

SKAMANIA CO
YAKIMA CO

22

23

24

PCT 2000   PCT 2000

HIGH CAMP
TRAIL 10

22

23

24

TRAIL

HIGH CAMP

ADAMS GLACIER
MEADOWS

BUSHWHACK

EQUESTRIA
LAKE

A D A M S

0   ½   1 mi

couple miles S before the remainder of the day satiates you with constant eye candy. For the next mile or so the trees are slowly replaced with vibrant sub-alpine meadows littered with lupine and more little stream crossings to the juncture with the PCT.

Cross the PCT to stay SE on narrower High Camp Trail 10 (signed) a mile to Adams Glacier Meadows. The terrain changes to involve more rock and scree over occasional steeper sections and the actual path can be elusive to High Camp if snow remains on a steeper-sloped rocky stretch leading to a rise. Cross the rise (heading directly toward Mount Adams) to High Camp with views back N to Mount Rainier, W to Mount St. Helens, and straight up the mountain past the wildflowers and a long moraine ridge to

Mount Adams and the forest reflected perfectly into Takhlakh Lake near the trailhead close to sunset.

the massive Adams Glacier above. Get your bearings once you reach the High Camp area as meandering is the norm. Return by the same route or climb 700 ft higher to check out a really cool iceberg-covered lake and possible loop option.

For Equestria Lake from High Camp, follow the wide rise on the left (SE), which becomes the rocky moraine ridge you saw from below. It's a mile to the high point just above the glacial lake as you sneak up to it over fairly sharp rock and/or snow (hiking gloves helpful). From here you have a splendid shot of the frosty Equestria Lake and possible reflection of Mount Adams! Adams Glacier, with its stunning icefall, is really in your face now. You can hear it cracking and creaking with ice and boulders falling. Remember your mountain goat etiquette if you see any, and keep a respectful distance from these Bovidae. It is also possible for those experienced with proper gear to continue left of the lake up the ridge another 1000 ft and almost 2 mi to the North Cleaver Overlook (and more difficult summit route option; ice axe and crampons required).

Head back the same way or continue S a few feet on the rocky ridge before it turns quite steep to leave it for the little clockwise loop without discernible trails but is obvious back down to High Camp. For this bushwhack say goodbye to the lake and glacial moraine ridge as you traverse the scree down right (W) then straight (N) carefully. You may have to descend long snowfields, perhaps glissading or sliding on your feet, down to the colorful green meadow again with plenty of water flowing through it. Make your way to the rise and end of the loop above Adams Glacier Meadows, and then finish on trails 10 and 113 more than 4 mi NNW down to the TH.

ELEVATION: 12,276 ft, with around 6700 ft vertical gain

DISTANCE: Less than 6 mi up, almost 12 mi round-trip

DURATION: 7–9 hours up as a day hike, 3 hours down with glissading; around 10–13 hours round-trip

DIFFICULTY: Expert only. Huge vertical, punishing, popular, route-finding, loose rock, very steep, snowfields, crampons/ice axe required most times, no water, no cover from storms, windy, cold on top, high altitude, steep, long glissading/skiing/snowboarding option

---

TRIP REPORT: Suksdorf Ridge holds the least technical route on Mount Adams and under rare conditions it can be summited without any special gear. Most hikers not acclimated to high elevation or able to attain Washington's second highest summit in one day camp partway up at Lunch Counter (9400 ft) or thereabouts. Or perhaps they simply wish to experience the rawness of the mountain at night and in the morning light. Others camp at or near the TH, opting for an alpine start on a single-day adventure to avoid competing with others for a flat camping spot on the side of the mammoth volcano.

Day hikers also avoid carrying a huge backpack not to mention "blue bags" all day (or on your potential glissade)! A Cascade Volcano Pass must be purchased for hikes on Mount Adams over 7000 ft all summer and can be found at local Ranger Stations but not all of the THs. For conditions and pass information: www.fs.usda.gov/recarea/giffordpinchot/recarea/?recid=80023 and www.fs.usda.gov/detail/giffordpinchot/passes-permits/?cid=stelprdb5144542. Northwest Forest Pass required, and a vault toilet is present.

TRAILHEAD: Cold Springs Campground/South Climb TH. Take I-84 E from Portland to exit 64 (Hood River), turn left on OR-35 N (White Salmon), pay the toll to cross Hood River Bridge into Washington, turn left on WA-14 W 1½ mi, turn right on WA-141 N 21 mi to Trout Lake. Fork right on Mount Adams Road (sign says "Mt. Adams Rec. Area") 2 mi, fork left on FR-80 for 3¾ mi, fork right on gravel FR-8040 for 5½ mi, fork right on FR-500 for 2½ mi rougher and narrower (2WD okay, AWD preferred) winding to the end with much parking and some camping (very loud close to TH; 95 mi, 2 hours from Portland).

ROUTE: Begin beyond the signage and self-issue Wilderness Permit kiosk on the wide South Climb Trail 183, past the campsites at first, then more to the N through the thin pine forest amongst an older burn area about 1¼ mi easily up to a major intersection with Round-the-Mountain Trail 9. Cross to stay N on Trail 183, straight up briefly, then to the left a bit at 6600 ft through meadows with fir and hemlock, working up gradually to cross Morrison Creek (dry if still frozen above) 2½ mi from the TH.

Hike almost a mile steeper out of the drainage following cairns with posts, perhaps already on a snow-packed trail at times, through a bench under Crescent Glacier. Head up a steep rise that ascends the rock and boulders just left (W) of the glacier to the snowfields above. Mount Hood and Mount Jefferson can be seen to the S on a clear day. Trudge up the snowfields or the rocks to the left (W) steadily toward the Lunch Counter plateau. Mount St. Helens to the W is popping into view. And you can see the more defined Suksdorf Ridge on the other side of Lunch Counter (at almost 4 mi up)

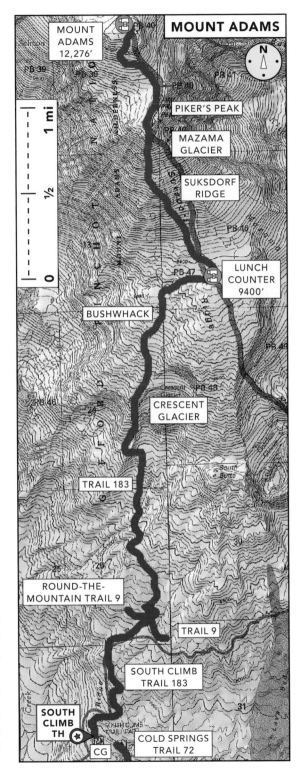

MOUNT ADAMS

MOUNT ADAMS 12,276'

PIKER'S PEAK

MAZAMA GLACIER

SUKSDORF RIDGE

LUNCH COUNTER 9400'

BUSHWHACK

CRESCENT GLACIER

TRAIL 183

ROUND-THE-MOUNTAIN TRAIL 9

TRAIL 9

SOUTH CLIMB TRAIL 183

SOUTH CLIMB TH

CG

COLD SPRINGS TRAIL 72

Far above Hellroaring Canyon is Iceberg Lake, a whopping 400 ft below as you near Piker's Peak!

with the endless snowfield on the SSE slopes that you will need to ascend to an area S of Piker's Peak (11,657 ft).

From Lunch Counter use crampons and head a mile NNW straight up the middle of the super-steep snowfield; or, as a less snowy option, climb either side of the slope up the rocky shoulders with faint paths to follow (left or near side more direct). The rocks may be looser than the snow, however it's much easier to take a relatively safe break or picture without resting against the steep snowy slope wearing crampons, but it's your choice. The mountain's severe elevation gain makes you do a double take when gazing down past the snow. See tiny Iceberg Lake to the SE.

Near Piker's Peak, the snow and rocky routes join to traverse W of and below that summit as you finally see your goal N past the saddle. You'll have a momentary rest on the traverse as you try to catch your breath, and then the route becomes very steep again. Hike left briefly at the summit block past the more cliffy area on the ridgeline and turn right (ENE) up the steep slope. Icy sun cups might make this part more difficult at certain times of the day in the fall without traction devices. In fact, early birds coming from Lunch Counter may find more ice than they bargained for or questionably dangerous glissading chutes until later in the day or season.

Immerse yourself in the moment from this remarkable vantage point. See from Mount Baker up N with the Olympics and Glacier Peak past Goat Rocks and Mount Rainier. Also see all the way S to Three Sisters with Broken Top and everything in between! Return the same way. There are several steep and exciting glissading options for the descent saving you thousands of feet and much time and energy, but more importantly it's a whole lot of fun when done properly (remember to remove your crampons). Correct use of your ice axe as an anchor and rudder is essential for most options near the summit and S of Piker's Peak. Mind your bearings on the descent as it's easy to get off course heading too far left (E) above Lunch Counter and then sadly down the Mazama Glacier. Tack right (SW) instead, when in question, toward the snowfield above Crescent Glacier and the steep rise on Trail 183, and then continue easier to South Climb TH.

MOUNT HOOD

SALMON-HUCKLEBERRY WILDERNESS

25 Wildcat Mountain 91

26 Salmon Butte 94

27 Hunchback Mountain 97

28 Devil's Peak Lookout 99

29 Tom Dick and
Harry Mountain 101

30 Trillium Lake Snowshoe
Loop 104

31 Palmateer Point 106

32 Lookout Mountain 108

33 Tamanawas Falls 110

34 Tilly Jane Snowshoe Loop.........112

35 Cooper Spur 115

36 Lamberson Butte to Newton
Creek Canyon Loop.................. 118

37 Little Zigzag Canyon Loop 121

38 Paradise Park to
Mississippi Head Loop 125

39 Illumination Saddle................... 128

40 Ramona Falls Loop 131

41 Yocum Ridge............................. 134

42 Lost Lake Butte......................... 137

43 Buck Peak.................................. 139

44 McNeil Point 142

45 Vista Ridge to
Cairn Basin Loop...................... 146

46 Barrett Spur Summit 148

<table>
<tr><td>**25**</td><td>**WILDCAT MOUNTAIN**</td></tr>
</table>

ELEVATION: 4480 ft, with vertical gains of 1030 ft plus 200 ft for the spur trail on McIntyre Ridge

DISTANCE: 2½ mi up directly, 5 mi round-trip; almost 7 mi round-trip with the spur

DURATION: 1 hour to summit, 3–5 hours round-trip with or without the spur

DIFFICULTY: Moderate. Narrow at times, no signage, easy grades, not long

---

TRIP REPORT: On the W edge of the Salmon-Huckleberry Wilderness is Wildcat Mountain. One of its redeeming qualities is that it's Washington County's greatest prominent point (CoGPP) for those hikers who like to summit all of the state's most prominent peaks by county; a slightly odd peak bagger indeed, but why not? Prominence here is defined as the vertical distance between the summit and the lowest topographic contour line around the mountain with no higher peak. In other words, it is understood to be the elevation of a summit relative to the highest point one descends to before immediately ascending to a higher summit. The historical lookout site holds an okay view of Mount Hood above blooming rhododendrons in late June. The bonus kicks in on a very brief bushwhack past the mostly forested summit to a small opening with a great look at five big Cascade volcanoes. The spur trail on McIntyre Ridge takes folks to a superb in-your-face look of Mount Hood from a small wildflower-draped meadow. No fee or restroom.

TRAILHEAD: Douglas TH. Take US-26 E from Portland 2 mi E of Sandy, turn right on Firwood Road ¾ mi, turn right to stay on Firwood Road 2½ mi, turn hard left on SE Wildcat Mountain Drive (FR-36 into FR-3626) 9 mi (paved, slightly rough, last ½ mi very narrow), turn right on narrow FR-105 for ¾ mi turning to gravel near a rough turnaround with the TH lying at the end (within earshot of a local shooting range, but improves tenfold soon). Please protect your valuables.

ROUTE: Begin up to the old fire lookout (removed years ago) on the solid wide trail (no signs, next to 2-ft tall large wood post) ¼ mi S through the woods to an old rock quarry near an open section on the ridge NW of Wildcat Mountain. There are views to your tree-covered goal and S to Old Baldy across Eagle Creek valley. Continue left (E) following the rocky path through the quarry past the rock wall to a faint juncture. Walk left past a steel post on Douglas Trail 781 with a quick shot of Mount St. Helens to the left before moving back into the trees.

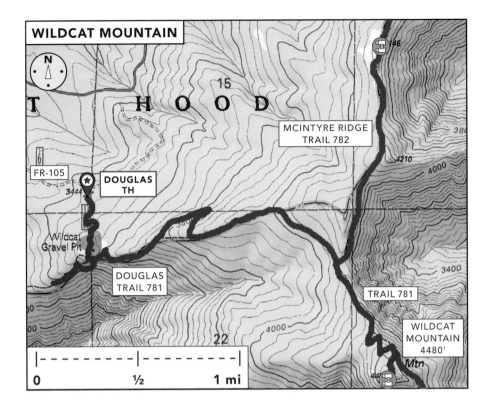

At ½ mi into the hike are 4 quick turns past thin pines and plenty of rhododendrons. Do not dismay if they are not in bloom (June into July) as they very well may be once you are higher in elevation. About a mile from the TH is a switchback leading up the wide and easy ridge. Soon, a brief traverse off the ridge takes you SE to a juncture before a Salmon-Huckleberry Wilderness kiosk near a small saddle (1¾ mi in). McIntyre Ridge Trail 782 heads left (N, no sign) at a faint three-way juncture on an easy traverse with little elevation change for a side trip now or saved for later. There is a great viewpoint and a bench in an open wildflower-covered meadow on the ridge almost a mile away with the best look to Mount Hood all day. See below for the description for this better picnic setting than on Wildcat Mountain.

Continue straight for the direct route to the Wildcat Mountain summit on narrowing Trail 781 upwards with Mount Adams and Mount Hood seen through the trees. More than ¼ mi from the three-way juncture the path widens to the first of 3 switchbacks with an easy grade to follow. There may be a few downed trees across the trail that are simple to hop over or bypass.

Find Wildcat Mountain Trail 781F (no sign) on the right at the apex just before the trail begins to descend at more than 2¼ mi from the TH, and move S without any trouble up the slightly overgrown route to the mostly reclaimed top. The summit is on a small, flat, rocky circle (with an old fire pit) surrounded by trees, bear grass, and

Mount Hood is the perfect backdrop with wildflowers blooming in the meadows from McIntyre Ridge.

rhododendron. Blooming rhododendron with Mount Hood as a backdrop is a wonderful sight. If the numerous flies don't scare you off the mountain, then a bushwhack "path" not even 50 ft more (farthest S on the narrow summit block) has a superior payoff. Continue exactly where you think you would, carefully fighting through rhododendron and brush just right of the ridgeline (getting a good glimpse of Mount Jefferson), then work immediately back to the narrow summit plateau where the rhododendrons give way to a brief open swath to stand. You are rewarded with a decent vista through a few trees of the nearby tree-covered ridge belonging to Huckleberry Mountain (E of Boulder Creek canyon) to the much larger Mount Hood. There are also great views of Mount St. Helens, Mount Rainier, and Mount Adams all in one eyeshot on a clear day!

Return to the TH or tack on the McIntyre Ridge viewpoint to get some more exercise. Trail 782 on McIntyre Ridge undulates gently nearly a mile N without much for outward views except close to the start. The path narrows as you reach the open meadow with the bottom of an old dead tree still standing near the middle. Numerous wildflowers dot the meadow just below another little high point on the ridge with the exact same view (of Mount Hood) thanks to trees blocking the vista to the S. Return to the Douglas Trail moving right down to the TH when you've had enough.

26   SALMON BUTTE

ELEVATION: 4877 ft, with 3250 ft vertical gain

DISTANCE: 5¾ mi up, 11½ mi round-trip

DURATION: 2½–3 hours up, 5–6 hours round-trip

DIFFICULTY: Strenuous. Very long, continual steep but not unbearable, minimal signage but obvious, crowded in summer near the bottom, wildlife sightings possible may include mule deer, coyote, mountain lion, and black bear

TRIP REPORT: Within Mount Hood National Forest and Salmon-Huckleberry Wilderness is this summit with great vertical and exercise, only an hour from Portland. The old lookout burned and was removed many years ago and even though some of the top is overgrown, views are more far-reaching than many expect! Try the hike from June to perhaps mid-July for the wildflower and rhododendron show in full bloom. Northwest Forest Pass required, and outhouses are located at nearby Salmon River W TH just N of the river and Green River Campground (open May through September).

TRAILHEAD: Salmon Butte TH. Take US-26 E from Portland 16 mi E of Sandy, turn right (S) in Zigzag past Hoodland Fire District Station on E Salmon River Road (FR-2618) 5 mi, cross the bridge over the Salmon River into gravel less than ½ mi more to the end (50 mi, 1 hour from Portland).

ROUTE: Begin S beyond the boulders on the continuation of old FR-2618 more than 1¼ mi, first across the bridge over S Fork Salmon River, then winding up across small creeks past wildflowers with some fairly big Douglas fir as the narrowing Salmon River Trail 791 dives into the forest to the right. Follow the slightly overgrown Trail 791 through the thick woods with a steady steep grade. Most of the undergrowth nearly disappears except for

Beginning of the route through the lively forest to Salmon Butte.

ferns through the moss-covered forest before you cross a partially cut tree at 2 mi from the TH. The path widens as you soon round the bottom of a NW shoulder off the N ridge of Salmon Butte and stay W of the ridge a while. More than ¼ mi farther (2¾ mi up) is an opening to a good view of a large rock monolith known as Green Knob far to the S (just W of Salmon Butte which is out of sight) and of Salmon Mountain across the valley NW.

Continue to traverse the fairly steep slope SSE steadily and somewhat easier around another NW shoulder below the main ridge to the first of 5 switchbacks as the route becomes steeper (more than 3½ mi up). After the fifth switchback (more than 4½ mi up) you soon turn up the actual ridge a bit easier (at 4240 ft) with a full shot of Mount Hood over the tall rhododendrons.

Walk the overgrown trail on the ridge through the old pines and turn up through rhododendrons to the first of 4 more undisputable switchbacks. Hike SW ¼ mi steeper up the narrow path and head right at the top of the switchbacks onto the wider trail (5½ mi up) with bear grass, paintbrush, and others. Wind more than ¼ mi to the rocky top as the path steepens with 1 easier switchback to the summit.

Past the wildflowers near the summit you see the entire local wilderness including tiny Salmon Lake SW (to complete the list of everything nearby named "Salmon"). And outwardly you may be able to gaze at most of the big volcanoes in two states from Mount Rainier down to Three Sisters on a clear day! Of course Mount Hood is the centerpiece towering over nearby Devil's Peak and you hardly notice trees blocking the nominal views to the W.

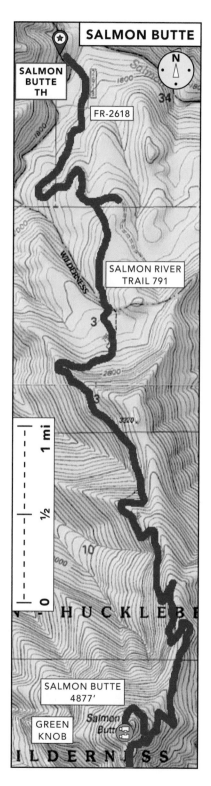

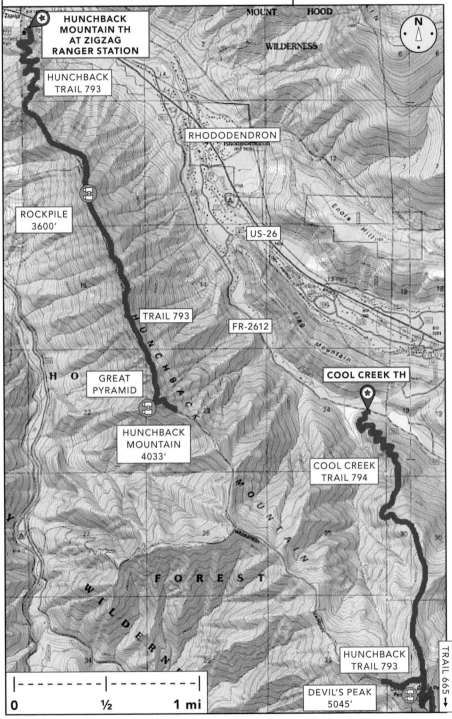

HIKES 27–28: HUNCHBACK MOUNTAIN / DEVIL'S PEAK LOOKOUT

MOUNT HOOD

WILDERNESS

N

HUNCHBACK MOUNTAIN TH AT ZIGZAG RANGER STATION

HUNCHBACK TRAIL 793

RHODODENDRON

ROCKPILE 3600'

US-26

TRAIL 793

FR-2612

H O O

GREAT PYRAMID

COOL CREEK TH

HUNCHBACK MOUNTAIN 4033'

COOL CREEK TRAIL 794

F O R E S T

W I L D E R N

HUNCHBACK TRAIL 793

TRAIL 665

DEVIL'S PEAK 5045'

0   ½   1 mi

27	HUNCHBACK MOUNTAIN

ELEVATION: 3600 ft on Rockpile; 4033 ft on the summit; with vertical gains of around 2175 ft for Rockpile, and 3000 ft for the summit including ups/downs

DISTANCE: 2½ mi to Rockpile, 5 mi round-trip; 4½ mi to the summit, 9 mi round-trip

DURATION: 1½–2 hours up to Rockpile, 3 hours round-trip; 3 hours to the summit, 5 hours round-trip

DIFFICULTY: Strenuous. Friendly grade then steeper, narrow at times, obvious, wildlife sightings possible but not probable including mountain lion and black bear

---

TRIP REPORT: This tiny volcano opposite Mount Hood is a high point along a lengthy and mostly tree-covered ridge with just enough viewpoints to make the trek worth it. Plus there's the easy TH access and abundant exercise to be had. Devil's Peak (5045 ft) is the highest summit on the same ridge and is described in the next hike. Some folks stop at the Rockpile viewpoint to cut the hike nearly in half. Hunchback Mountain can be hiked year-round although snowshoes may be desired at times in winter near the high ridge. No fee required, and restrooms are located at the Ranger Station.

TRAILHEAD: Zigzag Ranger Station. Take US-26 E from Portland 16¾ mi E of Sandy to Zigzag Ranger Station on the right with a parking lot on the left. The signed TH lies to the right in the lot (45 mi, less than 1 hour from Portland).

ROUTE: Walk past multiple signs, the first for Hunchback Trail 793 and Devil's Peak (which can be attained more directly from the next hike's northern route above Cool Creek). Head S a mile on Trail 793 through the thick forest teeming with flora up 8 easy switchbacks as the highway traffic noise dissipates. Then the trail becomes much steeper for the next mile S with 9 switchbacks, several s-turns, and a couple more switchbacks near the high ridge past more rhododendron, bear grass, Douglas fir, and western hemlock.

After catching a breather, briefly move to the right where you arrive at the top of a cliff band with a great look out past the funky, mossy rock formations to the Salmon River valley and more of the Salmon-Huckleberry Wilderness. Continue over the ridge or just E of it on the thin trail undulating around ¼ mi (with tacky pine needles to aid with traction) to the sign and spur path for Rockpile on the right. Scramble the rocks

The boulder-covered steep finish to Rockpile in autumn.

and boulders very steeply (slippery when wet) a hundred yards to the top. There you will be rewarded with a fine shot of Mount Hood past closer Zigzag Mountain across the valley. Return to the TH or press on for the longer hike and similar views.

Hike SE up and down 2 mi more on Trail 793 (sometimes steeply) near the narrowing ridge to the summit with more side paths leading to fleeting views (thanks to overgrowth) and cool rock outcrops. Walk past the sleepy top (identified only as a tall, mossy boulder) carefully out a few hundred feet to the right (SW) scrambling to better views of most of the high ridge and more from the cliffy rock promontory known as the Great Pyramid (signed). Return back to the TH by the same route.

28 DEVIL'S PEAK LOOKOUT

ELEVATION: 5045 ft, with 3200 ft vertical gain

DISTANCE: 4 mi up, 8¼ mi round-trip

DURATION: 2 hours up, 3–4 hours round-trip

DIFFICULTY: Strenuous. Very steep sustained, signed, well-defined trail, not crowded, wildlife encounters may include black bear or a rare mountain lion

TRIP REPORT: The highest peak in the Salmon-Huckleberry Wilderness is still home to an old fire lookout not in use but open to the public as a small sanctuary, as long as people are respectful (no reservations). The Cool Creek Trail described here is the Goldilocks of the three possible routes, the others being too long or too short for most day hikers, plus the drive to the TH is super simple. Expect snow and more difficult travel with some elevation in winter until June (snowshoes may be necessary). No fee or restroom.

TRAILHEAD: Cool Creek TH. Take US-26 E from Portland 18 mi E of Sandy (1½ mi past Zigzag Ranger Station), turn right (SSE) on Still Creek Road (FR-2612) more than ¼ mi, stay right on FR-2612 for 2½ mi paved, then more than ½ mi gravel (crossing over the Cool Creek bridge) to the tiny, signed TH on the right. Park off the left side of the road or wherever there is room (50 mi, 1 hour from Portland).

ROUTE: Take Cool Creek Trail 794 across a small creek then SE for 3½ mi through the lively thick forest that only opens briefly to expose Mount Hood (once at a mile up and a few more sightings from short spurs at 2 mi up), past the blooming rhododendrons, huckleberries, western hemlock, big red cedar, and huge Douglas and Noble fir. The hike starts pretty darn steep, up multiple switchbacks, but mellows the

Rhododendrons fill the forest with color in late June as Mount Hood can't hide on a blue day.

Devil's Peak Lookout rises just enough above increasing trees to provide excellent views of the Cascades.

final mile or so to an intersection with Kinzel Lake Trail 665 on the left. You will climb the more open ridge section with a shot to Mount Adams as the route will become rockier and more colorful with wildflowers to the juncture. Then fork to the right onto Hunchback Trail 793.

Traverse SW 350 ft W of and below the ridgeline, then turn left (ESE) on the spur path almost ¼ mi easily to the lookout and summit area. Growing trees are slowly obscuring the outlook but there are still views of Mount Adams, Mount Hood, and even Mount Jefferson with part of the Sisters Range on a clear day. And look to the nearby E slope from the high point for the basalt monolith called the Devil's Tooth. Check out the old lookout and return down steeply to the TH after a picnic.

29 | TOM DICK AND HARRY MOUNTAIN

ELEVATION: 4970 feet (Tom Peak); 5066 feet (Dick Peak); 5027 ft (Harry Mountain), with vertical gains of (700 ft for Mirror Lake alone) 1570 ft for the W-most summit (Tom Peak), 1666 ft for the highest summit (Dick Peak), 1700 ft or so for the counterclockwise loop down ski runs

DISTANCE: 2¼ mi to Mirror Lake, 4½ mi round-trip; 4¼ mi to Tom Peak, 8½ mi round-trip; 4½ mi to Dick Peak, 9 mi round-trip; around 8 mi round-trip counterclockwise loop around Tom Dick and Harry Mountain

DURATION: Less than 1 hour to the lake, 2 hours round-trip; 2 hours to Tom Peak, 4 hours round-trip; 2-plus hours to Dick Peak, 3½–4 hours round-trip; 4–5 hours round-trip loop

DIFFICULTY: Mix of easiest to Mirror Lake (wide, solid trail, gradual, very popular), moderate to the W-most or highest summits (rocky, narrowing, scree), and strenuous loop (longer, trail-finding, wide, steep ski area/roads)

TRIP REPORT: This charming mountain with a strange name and three separate little summits shares half its terrain with Mount Hood Skibowl and lies directly across the highway from Mount Hood and the town of Government Camp. The other half of the terrain is highlighted by Mirror Lake, which lives up to its name, and a mellow hike to the lowest of the three summits along an open ridgeline. Part or all of the latter also makes for a great snowshoe in winter. Both the trail to Mirror Lake and the TH were relocated and finished late in 2018. The new TH is much safer and larger (fifty spots) a few feet off of US-26 at the W end of Mount Hood Skibowl. The old TH will become inaccessible and the old trail will be revegetated. Northwest Forest Pass is required at the primary TH (Sno-Park Pass required in winter and also at Mount Hood Skibowl), and restrooms are present and also at the ski area open mid-June through Labor Day and in winter.

TRAILHEAD: Mirror Lake TH or Mount Hood Skibowl. Take US-26 E from Portland to milepost 52 just W of Mount Hood Skibowl's sizable parking lot. The town of Government Camp with more facilities is another mile up the road (55 mi, more than 1 hour from Portland).

ROUTE: Begin W of the parking lot and the larger parking lot at Mount Hood Skibowl on Mirror Lake Trail 664 more than 1½ mi WSW to a juncture with the old trail. You will rise up around a half-dozen switchbacks SW through the woods to cross the bridge over Camp Creek, then continue SW then WNW easy up steadily through the beautiful forest with some good-sized trees and rhododendron (blooming in late June) to the juncture. Stay left (S) on Trail 664 at the old trail juncture more than ½ mi up steady switchbacks to Mirror Lake.

Popular shot of Mount Hood into Mirror Lake that most Portlanders own.

Explore the lake on either side, the left (E) continuing over a bridge at first, but the right (W) side is more popular with more options for swimming or sightseeing. The Tom Dick and Harry Mountain Trail takes off from the right as well, toward the end of the lake at a signed juncture. From there, take the quick spur left first only a hundred yards over wooden planks around the end of the lake to the viewpoint for the reflection of Mount Hood into the lake on a clear day. Return the same way or visit one of the summits above to claim you actually hiked!

Continue a mile (WSW) on Trail 664 to the high ridge with a pleasantly graded contour, crossing another scree field after the first ¼ mi. The rock-embedded trail is easy to follow to a gigantic 6-ft tall rock cairn where the trail turns left (ESE) up the wide ridge face. Follow the rocky path without any difficulty ½ mi while falling off the ridge center to the right (S) a bit before you have to make up for it and hike steeper ¼ mi back to a more pronounced ridgeline near the fake summit. The trail turns to scree on the rockier section of ridge where, as a rule of thumb, you can walk straight over, following cairns. Or take the more distinct trail just to the right (S) of the ridgetop less than ¼ mi to the W-most summit (whether it be Tom Peak or Harry Mountain; there are arguments for both depending on what map you have). There's no argument however that Dick Peak is in the middle and the highest of the triad.

Have a picnic and return the same way to Mirror Lake and the TH as most do or if it's near winter and the ski area is open or running ski-related operations. If snowshoeing back, you may be tempted to run down the steeps to the right (N) from the popular summit (Tom Peak), but you should wait until you are well out of any potentially avalanche zones and much closer to the lake (for a 200-yard-long section where it is safe) since the W side of the mountain is not maintained or watched by ski patrol.

For the high point and loop, continue SE down the ridge crest from the W-most summit (Tom Peak) as Trail 664 pitters into a user/animal trail. Follow it interestingly or take the brief bailout trail just right around a steeper section of larger rock, back to easier walking on the ridge. You see Mirror Lake and others N over to Mount Hood; to the S are the rolling forested mountains of the Salmon-Huckleberry Wilderness with Mount Jefferson far behind. The final bit through the trees is steeper to Dick Peak almost ½ mi from the W-most summit. Notice the solar-powered seismograph station with a small antenna and a couple rock fire pits on a flatter area that is the top.

From Dick Peak to the last summit ½ mi away, follow the thin user/animal trail and pass the ski area boundary on the counterclockwise tour ESE over the wider easier ridgetop; there are more trees closer to the crest and snow lingering until early summer, but it's not a nuisance. Walk past a satellite tower with attached green structure then past a small A-frame building up a thin path to the left of the main trail/road to the nearby top of the final bump, another small flat spot, this unassuming peak just above the highest chairlift at Mount Hood Skibowl.

For the descent on the loop, take the wide gravel road, down the signed "Easiest" route right of the ridge, ¼ mi steeply to an alright viewpoint off to the left of the ski area. Stay on the wide ski area road N for better shots of Oregon's tallest mountain a bit easier. Then go down 2 big switchbacks to a large blue sign that shows the "Base Area." Move to the left on the thin path just before the third actual switchback. Come down to the clearing above the warming hut and just below the highest chairlift. Follow the gravel road down left a few hundred yards as it curves to the signed Gnar Gnar Trail in the middle of the open ski runs. Follow the Gnar Gnar bike trail toward the lodge as it winds quite a bit, or bushwhack the faint trail straight down less than a mile passing the summer Alpine Slide on your right (and tons of wildflowers including lupine and Indian paintbrush), to the bottom. Ascend briefly to the huge parking lot for Mount Hood Skibowl and walk left (W) to the nearby TH.

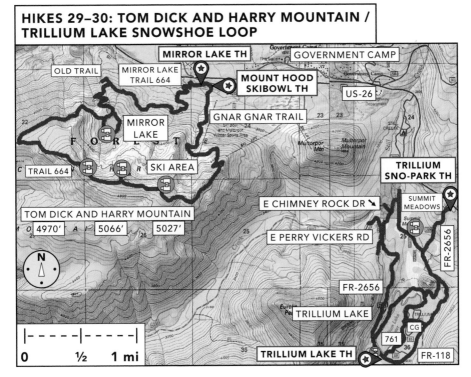

HIKES 29–30: TOM DICK AND HARRY MOUNTAIN / TRILLIUM LAKE SNOWSHOE LOOP

30 | TRILLIUM LAKE SNOWSHOE LOOP

ELEVATION: 3800 ft at the TH (3600 ft at Trillium Lake), with almost 400 ft vertical gain total for the loop as the route begins downhill

DISTANCE: 2 mi to the primary viewpoint at the lake, 4 mi or so round-trip; 4¾ mi round-trip loop

DURATION: 1 hour to the lake, 2–3 hours round-trip directly or with the loop

DIFFICULTY: Moderate. Ups/downs, steeper only briefly, popular, easier in summer from the lake without snow on a shorter loop

---

TRIP REPORT: Teeming with campers and lake enthusiasts in summer, Trillium Lake is a different story in winter and worthy of a hike listing or more specifically a snowshoe or cross-country ski route. It's a bit more work with snow when the 2-mi-long road closes in winter extending the day. P.S.: It's still worth it! Sno-Park Pass required November through April, and there are restrooms at the campground, but only open in summer.

TRAILHEAD: Trillium Sno-Park TH or Trillium Lake TH. Take US-26 E from Portland past Government Camp, turn right for Trillium Lake (signed) on gravel FR-2656 near milepost 55½ and park immediately in the large lot left of the gated road. When the gate is open in spring those with AWD can make it 2 mi more to the day use area at Trillium Lake TH as snow lingers until late June or so (57 mi, 1¼ hours from Portland).

ROUTE: From Trillium Sno-Park TH begin past the big green gate, snowshoeing SSW down the wide road (FR-2656) that is constantly groomed but receives much snow throughout the winter. Be respectful of cross-country vs. snowshoe tracks when possible. In a little more than ½ mi of the steepest stretch of the day is the first signed juncture and end of the longest clockwise loop option on the right (E Perry Vickers Road). One sign correctly states the dammed end of Trillium Lake is 2¼ mi away and Summit Meadows is ½ mi away, but ignore those for now and continue straight (SE). The pitch will be less steep, then flat, then steady up a stretch between the pines, hemlock, and cedar without much outward for views.

After 1 mi from the winter TH, walk SW down the road less than ½ mi to a four-way intersection with the campground on the right. Stay straight again as you level to the day use area turn on the right, 1¾ mi from the TH. Stay straight again past a small sign directing traffic for the loop to the right, and walk ¼ mi down FR-118 to the primary viewpoint. At 2 mi from the TH is the end of the road (with parking) at the dammed end (S) of the lake. This is your first great look at Mount Hood over the lake, and whether thawed or frozen, it makes no difference: the brilliance is exceptional!

In summer, some people forgo the only slightly longer snowshoe loop to Summit Meadows for a more local 2 mi loop (with several boardwalks) around the lake by taking the lakeside trail to the right (N) from the dam area past the sign denoting Trillium Lake Trail 761 and also that

The winter wonderland around Trillium Lake makes for a nice family day without working too hard.

bikers should reduce their speed in the campground. Enjoy views of the ski areas under Mount Hood's impressive S face (from the E side of the lake) on the walk over to the campground trails or thereabouts, and then head for the main trail (FR-2656). From there, turn left in winter less than 1½ mi undulating up the wide road to the Trillium Sno-Park TH.

For the arguably easier clockwise Summit Meadows loop from the S end of the lake, continue left around the lake past another little sign for Trillium Lake Trail 761. Stay on the wider road from the W side of the lake, rolling up and down some but effortlessly, to the N 1¼ mi from Trillium Lake to a four-way signed juncture ("Still Creek Campground, Hwy 26, Rhododendron"). Stay hard right on E Chimney Rock Drive down for the TH. In ¼ mi are shots of Mount Hood through the trees as you pass left of a small pond leveling out.

At 3¾ mi from the TH on the Summit Meadows clockwise loop reach another signed juncture (for Trillium Lake ski loop and others). Turn right (SSE) on E Perry Vickers Road ½ mi to the end of the loop as you cross scenic Summit Meadows with more outstanding views of the big Cascade volcano over the level trail. End back through the forest down a tad to the three-way juncture with FR-2656. Turn left on FR-2656 more than ½ mi up steeper to the winter TH.

ELEVATION: 4410 ft, with at least 1300 ft vertical gain including ups/downs

DISTANCE: 5 mi to the point, 9¾ mi round-trip clockwise loop with Twin Lakes

DURATION: 1½ hours to the point, 3–4 hours round-trip loop

DIFFICULTY: Moderate. Long loop, many ups/downs, not too steep

---

TRIP REPORT: Great family outing with most of the elevation gain achieved from multiple ups and downs over the hills S of Barlow Pass near Barlow Butte, Bird Butte, Frog Lake Buttes, and Twin Lakes. Snowshoe and cross-country ski around Twin Lakes in winter. Northwest Forest Pass required all summer (Sno-Park Pass in winter), and a restroom is present.

TRAILHEAD: Frog Lake Sno-Park at Wapinitia Pass. Take US-26 E from Portland past Government Camp less than 4½ mi S of the intersection with OR-35 near milepost 62, turn left for Frog Lake Sno-Park and left again immediately into the large lot (62 mi, less than 1½ hours from Portland).

ROUTE: Begin from the NW corner of the parking lot (left of the restroom) on the spur 50 ft to PCT 2000. Turn right on the PCT, (ignoring the next trail right for Frog Lake) through the firs and western hemlock with rhododendron and bear grass, up gradually about 500 ft, then down a bit to a little saddle and juncture 1½ mi from the TH. Right (E) is Twin Lakes Trail 495, which is the return path from Upper and Lower Twin Lakes on the clockwise

Palmateer Point poking above the trees from Twin Lakes.

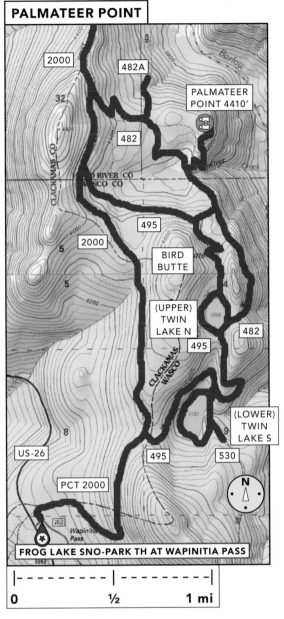

PALMATEER POINT

2000

482A

PALMATEER POINT 4410'

482

RIVER CO
WASCO CO

495

BIRD BUTTE

2000

(UPPER) TWIN LAKE N

482

495

CLACKAMAS WASCO

(LOWER) TWIN LAKE S

US-26

495

530

PCT 2000

N

FROG LAKE SNO-PARK TH AT WAPINITIA PASS

Wapinitia Pass

|---------|---------|
0   ½   1 mi

loop. Continue N on the wide PCT undulating almost 1½ mi to the next juncture, the top end of Twin Lakes Trail on the right. Stay left on the PCT traversing through the pines up easily ¾ mi to the highest part of the trail back to the ridgeline, then turn hard right on Palmateer View Trail 482 SE almost a mile down (staying on the main trail) and E, directly up toward Palmateer Point.

Turn left at the spur trail signed for Palmateer Point up ¼ mi N to the nearby top of the wide-open summit with wildflowers and an immediate full shot of Mount Hood (past Barlow Butte). Back down from the point stay straight (S) ¾ mi on Trail 482 for the Twin Lakes loop down across Palmateer Creek (dries up in late summer), and then up (passing a trail on the right, W) to another great look of Mount Hood, Palmateer Meadows, and Barlow Creek. Walk down through the woods gradually ¾ mi to the E side of Upper Twin Lake turning left around it briefly with a nice truncated look at Mount Hood across the water N.

Continue S from Upper Twin Lake at the junction, now on Trail 495, for ¾ mi down switchbacks to the N end of the slightly larger Lower Twin Lake; stay to the right at any crossroads ¾ mi more around it (or try the mile-long forested trail around the sparkling lake), and then walk up to the end of the loop on the saddle at the PCT. Turn left on the PCT (S then W) for 1½ mi up and down to the TH.

32 LOOKOUT MOUNTAIN

ELEVATION: 6525 ft, with 1925 ft vertical gain

DISTANCE: 3½ mi up, 7-plus mi round-trip

DURATION: 1½–2 hours up, 3–4 hours round-trip

DIFFICULTY: Moderate. Wide, not very steep, family-friendly

TRIP REPORT: A favorite route option of at least three known THs. From the top on a clear day you can see from the Columbia River to Mount Rainier and also past Three Sisters Wilderness down S. No fee required, and a restroom is present at nearby Fifteenmile Forest Camp.

TRAILHEAD: Fret Creek TH. Take I-84 E from Portland to exit 64 (Hood River), turn right from the off-ramp more than ¼ mi to a stop sign, continue straight on OR-35 S 25 mi, turn left on FR-44 (milepost 71, Lookout Mountain/Camp Baldwin/Dufur) more than 5 mi winding up, turn hard right to stay on FR-44 (Dufur Valley Road, closed in winter) 3 mi, turn right more than ½ mi S toward Cold Springs Road. Continue straight on FR-4420 (Cold Springs Road) 3¾ mi to the small, signed TH on the right. There are a couple pullout parking spots on the left, ¼ mi past Fifteenmile Forest Camp (100 mi, 2 hours from Portland, all paved).

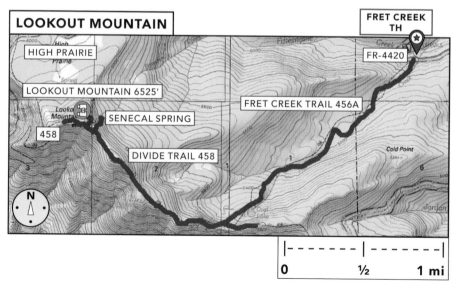

Mount Adams, due north in Washington, standing larger than life from Lookout Mountain.

ROUTE: Begin on Fret Creek Trail 456A, past the signage, SW more than 2 mi to the high ridge; pass Opal Lake just before the ridge. The wide trail through the vibrant forest is steeper the first ½ mi then mellows to cross Fret Creek a few times over footbridges. The route becomes steeper again to the brief spur path left to Opal Lake, which is quite small, surrounded by trees, and has a view up the rock formations to Palisade Point on the high ridge.

Continue ¼ mi on Trail 456A from the Opal Lake juncture steeper to the end near the high ridge. Turn right on Divide Trail 458; head WNW just N of the ridge crest for less than ½ mi to improving vistas (see Mount Jefferson S) as the flora (including huckleberries in late summer) thins and you travel up, down, then up the center for the remaining 1 mi to the peak. Pass by a helispot and then a short spur on the right (N) down ¼ mi to Senecal Spring (source of Fifteenmile Creek: hint if you're thirsty) as the trail becomes rockier to finish. The old lookout foundation is barely there on the open top with other trails converging and outstanding views W a half-dozen miles to Mount Hood, the Badger Creek Wilderness to the S, and High Prairie just N of Lookout Mountain.

ELEVATION: Under 3500 ft at the falls; 3580 ft on a potential loop; with vertical gains of about 720 ft from Polallie TH on a loop; 530 ft from E Fork–Tamanawas Falls TH directly

DISTANCE: 4½–5½ mi round-trip for the loops, the longer being from E Fork–Tamanawas Falls TH; 3½ mi round-trip directly from E Fork–Tamanawas Falls TH without a loop

DURATION: 2–4 hours round-trip

DIFFICULTY: Moderate. Narrow at times, family-friendly, rocky briefly, loop option, trail-finding in winter, slippery rocks near falls

TRIP REPORT: Simple walk to an impressive waterfall NW of Mount Hood tucked away N of Bluegrass Ridge on Cold Spring Creek. Great year-round and very popular on summer weekends. A more difficult loop in winter can be avoided without Elk Meadows Trail although skis, snowshoes, or traction devices may be used there or elsewhere. Northwest Forest Pass required at both THs, and there are no restrooms except at nearby Sherwood Campground (open in summer) just S of the primary TH.

TRAILHEAD: Polallie TH and E Fork–Tamanawas Falls (primary) TH. Take I-84 E from Portland to exit 64 (Hood River), turn right from the off-ramp more than ¼ mi to a stop sign, continue straight on OR-35 S 21½ mi to Polallie TH (small sign, quieter TH, milepost 73½) at a little pullout on the left past Cooper Spur Road. Continue less than 1½ mi to the larger gravel pullout for Tamanawas Falls TH (another small sign) on the right (85 mi, less than 1½ hours from Portland).

ROUTE: From the primary TH (near milepost 72) walk a few feet W through the trees to cross E Fork Hood River over the solid footbridge. Turn right (N) at a vague junction onto E Fork Trail 650 (no sign) that undulates gently ½ mi up through the big evergreens to views of the basalt cliff band across the highway. Walk 150 ft to the next signed juncture (beginning/end of the loop). From there, Polallie TH is right 1 mi away on Trail 650 following the river quite effortlessly to the N.

Continue straight (left, W) instead on Tamanawas Falls Trail 650A 100 ft and cross Cold Spring Creek over another bridge. Turn left and follow the lively creek (with steelhead possibly running in summer or winter) upstream through the forest a mile to a faint fork as the trail becomes a bit rockier with tree roots, but it's not too bad. Patches of snow may remain until late spring. Tamanawas Falls Tie Trail 650B (loop option, unsigned) is on the right fork continuing up a steeper switchback heading NE just right (E) of the boulder field.

Hike left instead, staying on Trail 650A, around ¼ mi to the falls by tackling the boulder field up 2 very solid switchbacks, then working up to a little shoulder. After the shoulder, Trail 650A begins the brief descent through the woods SW to the open amphitheater belonging to Tamanawas Falls. The roaring waterfall (110 ft high, 40 ft wide) comes into view from downstream as you break out of most of the trees with several vantage points at different times of day and year. The path peters out near the rocky creek bed and several dreamy picnic spots, before the steep mossy rock under the cliff wall. The constant spray may make photography more difficult, but it sure feels nice on a hot day! On the lowest flow under the driest conditions, a few reckless souls seek the small cave behind the falls and must cross very slippery rocks to do so risking injury.

Tamanawas Falls never disappoints throughout the seasons.

Return back along Trail 650A past the boulder field to the juncture for the clockwise loop and skip it to return by the same route for the simplest option. Turn left on narrow Trail 650B for the interesting loop, sharply and steeply (at first) up the switchbacks and through the trees easy enough, ½ mi NE from the boulder field to the high ridge. Once you reach the wide ridge line, turn right (NE still) on Elk Meadows Trail 645 (signs) and begin to descend pleasingly through the thicker old forest 1¼ mi to Polallie TH.

There is a fleeting look at Mount Adams through the trees above and below the first switchback as you navigate the narrow and slightly overgrown trail scattered with a few fallen trees. Rhododendrons line the forest floor here, and then after the second switchback you see Mount Hood standing largely behind you through the thick trees. Finish pleasantly around the last corner to the nearby intersection and signed spur trail fairly steeply left (NE) 100 ft down to Polallie TH.

From Polallie TH, cross the highway carefully and climb the trail steeply 100 ft SW up to the juncture with E Fork Trail. Turn left on Trail 650 to hike to Tamanawas Falls (only somewhat easier than on Elk Meadows Trail) or to take the loop in a clockwise fashion. Begin steeply up 100 ft, then roll down and up with less pitch but continually (views across highway to cliffs) as you parallel the E Fork Hood River on its W side almost a mile S. You'll cross a little creek without a problem, then carefully pass a 15-ft partially eroded section of trail along the way before the path becomes a bit rougher crossing Cold Spring Creek over the solid bridge. A few feet later you reach the intersection with Tamanawas Falls Trail. For the falls take that trail right (W) and follow like above or return left (S) on Trail 650 up, then down, ½ mi to Tamanawas Falls TH.

ELEVATION: 5718 ft at the Tilly Jane Guard Station and Tilly Jane A-Frame, with around 1900 ft vertical gain

DISTANCE: 6 mi loop with Polallie Ridge

DURATION: 3 hours round-trip loop

DIFFICULTY: Strenuous. Steady steep, mileage deceivingly brief, short steep slope crossing difficult at times, GPS device helpful in winter

---

TRIP REPORT: Best to wait till after New Year's through the spring for the snow to pile up so you may enjoy some great snowshoeing and cross-country skiing on Mount Hood's NE flank below Cooper Spur near the historical Cloud Cap Inn. The Tilly Jane A-Frame (rented with reservations only: www.recreation.gov/camping/tilly-jane-aframe/r/campgroundDetails.do?contractCode=NRSO&parkId=72353) is always a good goal in winter with the nearby campgrounds open during the short summer season. Of course this can be hiked quite pleasantly in summer too. Northwest Forest Pass required in summer and Sno-Park Pass required November through April (purchase locally or from Hood River Ranger Station 14 mi S on OR-35 from Hood River), and there is no restroom.

TRAILHEAD: Tilly Jane TH. Take I-84 E from Portland to exit 64 (Hood River), turn right from the off-ramp more than ¼ mi to a stop sign, continue straight on OR-35 S 21½ mi (milepost 74), turn right on Cooper Spur Road (FR-3510) 2¼ mi, turn sharp left on Cloud Cap Road (FR-3512) less than 1½ mi to the closed gate with the parking lot on the right and the TH on the left, just past Cooper Spur Ski (and Winter Sports) Area.

ROUTE: Start WSW across the road past the kiosk on Tilly Jane Ski Trail 643 more than ½ mi through the forest to a juncture and the end of the loop. The ¼-mi-long connector trail left (SE) to the other ski area ridgeline (Polallie Ridge Trail 643A) heads in the same basic direction up toward the Tilly Jane A-Frame. Stay right at the signage instead on Trail 643 up, on and off the smaller ridge, 2 mi more through an old burn affording fantastic views straight ahead to Mount Hood. The final ½ mi requires traversing a very steep slope (25 degrees or so) and it may be arduous in winter or slightly problematic if it's icy and no solid trail is visible through the snow. Some people opt to climb left up across the top of Doe Creek to nearby Polallie Ridge and follow Trail 643A along the ridge instead.

Just before the top, from the main approach, is the faint junction with the loop

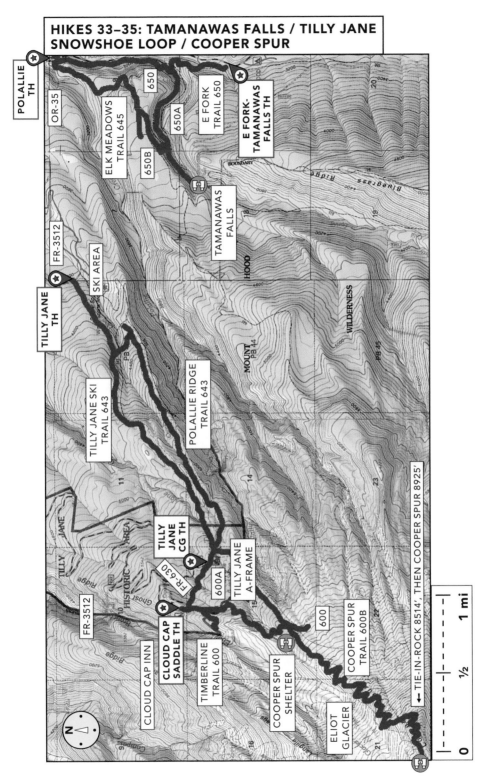

HIKES 33–35: TAMANAWAS FALLS / TILLY JANE
SNOWSHOE LOOP / COOPER SPUR

POLALLIE TH

OR-35

650

650A

ELK MEADOWS TRAIL 645

650B

E FORK TRAIL 650

E FORK-TAMANAWAS FALLS TH

BOUNDARY

TAMANAWAS FALLS

HOOD

Bluegrass Ridge

WILDERNESS

FR-3512

SKI AREA

TILLY JANE TH

PB

TILLY JANE SKI TRAIL 643

POLALLIE RIDGE TRAIL 643

MOUNT

PB 44

PB 45

TILLY JANE
Ridge

HISTORIC AREA

Ghost Ridge

TILLY JANE CG TH

FR-630

TILLY JANE A-FRAME

600A

15

TIE-IN-ROCK 8514', THEN COOPER SPUR 8925'

CLOUD CAP INN

FR-3512

CLOUD CAP SADDLE TH

TIMBERLINE TRAIL 600

600

COOPER SPUR SHELTER

COOPER SPUR TRAIL 600B

ELIOT GLACIER

Compass Ridge

N

0   ½   1 mi

TILLY JANE SNOWSHOE LOOP 113

taking a hard left on Trail 643A down to the TH, but continue up a moment to the Tilly Jane A-Frame emergency lodging, which is visible through the woods and perhaps half buried in snow. Cross-country skiers or hikers may wish to continue another mile or so left (SW) from the A-frame to Cooper Spur Shelter on Cooper Spur Trail 600B before returning the same way to the A-frame area. Or from the Cooper Spur Shelter, take Timberline Trail 600 (NW of Trail 600B) down to Cloud Cap Inn. Cross-country skiers may wish to ski down nearby Cloud Cap Road (FR-3512) from the Inn 9 mi to the same TH for a much longer adventure.

Near the campground next to the A-frame is the Tilly Jane Guard Station (also rentable: www.recreation.gov/camping/tilly-jane-guard-station/r/campgroundDetails. do?contractCode=NRSO&parkId=72357). From this area, you can choose one of two paths to the historic Cloud Cap Inn ½ mi away. One is FR-630 from the campground moving down NW (turning into FR-3512) then up encircling the Inn. The other is Timberline Trail 600A heading up W then NNW from the A-frame. Cloud Cap Inn is only open late June until Labor Day and run by the oldest search and rescue group in the U.S. (Hood River Crag Rats). Investigate further or begin to snowshoe down for the remainder of the loop. See hike 35 for more detail in this general area.

Head from Tilly Jane A-Frame ENE down the solid ridgeline (which is only faint to begin) on Polallie Ridge Trail 643A for 2 mi of the best walking all day! Around 4280 ft near the bottom of the ski area is the easy-to-miss return ¼ mi left down easily on the connector trail NW across Doe Creek to Cloud Cap Ski Trail 643. Turn right (NE) almost ¾ mi to the TH.

The partially open-air Tilly Jane A-Frame packed in snow for most of the year.

<table>
<tr><td>**35**</td><td>**COOPER SPUR**</td></tr>
</table>

ELEVATION: 8925 ft at the top of Cooper Spur; 8514 ft at Tie-In Rock; with vertical gains of 3200 ft for the very top from Tilly Jane Campground, 2800 ft to Tie-In Rock, 2665 ft directly from Cloud Cap Saddle to Tie-In Rock (3355 ft for the loop from Cloud Cap Saddle)

DISTANCE: Almost 4½ mi up from Tilly Jane Campground, 8 mi round-trip loop; 3¾ mi directly from Cloud Cap Saddle, 7½ mi round-trip

DURATION: 2–3 hours up, 4–5 hours round-trip for Tie-In Rock directly or with a loop; 6-7 hours round-trip for Cooper Spur directly or with a loop

DIFFICULTY: Strenuous. Mostly friendly grade, rocky, pumice, high altitude, mostly signed, not many trees

---

TRIP REPORT: This extremely difficult alternate climbing route to the summit of Mount Hood ends for most normal people at the top of the Cooper Spur moraine ridgeline where the Eliot Glacier meets the Newton Clark Glacier. The vantage point from nearly 9000 ft is attained from the highest established trail on Mount Hood. The incredible day hike beginning from one of two neighboring high THs takes visitors through alpine terrain and affords fantastic close-ups of the glaciers, Mount Hood, and several other Cascade Mountains without having to trudge up steeply for thousands of feet all day before you get to the views!

Snow lingers until July or so making trail-finding more difficult but alternates or the proper trails are usually packed out and obvious. Opt for a nice bluebird day when it's scalding hot in the Willamette Valley to cool off with the nice breeze at higher altitudes for hours. Check ahead to be sure the rougher gravel Cloud Cap Road is open (www.fs. usda.gov/recarea/mthood/recarea/?recid =53164). Northwest Forest Pass required at Cloud Cap Saddle and Tilly Jane Campground, and outhouses are present at both locales.

TRAILHEAD: Tilly Jane Campground or Cloud Cap Saddle. Take I-84 E from Portland to exit 64 (Hood River), turn right from the off-ramp more than ¼ mi

Tilly Jane Guard Station adjacent to the peaceful campground.

to a stop sign, continue straight on OR-35 S 21½ mi (milepost 74), turn right on Cooper Spur Road (FR-3510) 2¼ mi, turn sharp left on Cloud Cap Road (FR-3512) less than 1½ mi to a gate past Cooper Spur Ski Area and just after parking for the Tilly Jane snowshoe route. The road becomes gravel for a slow 3 mi to Inspiration Point located on the first of 10 more switchbacks (less than 5 mi more, a bit rougher with several drainage ditches, narrow, okay for 2WD, AWD preferred) to an intersection. Turn right less than ½ mi to Cloud Cap Saddle on the right (less than ¼ mi before the Cloud Cap Inn at the top—worth checking out), or for a much quieter TH turn left at the intersection less than ½ mi easily to Tilly Jane Campground. Tilly Jane Campground TH is less busy on summer weekends, roughly the same distance directly, and only 150 ft lower than Cloud Cap Saddle (refer to the previous map; 95 mi, 2 hours from Portland).

ROUTE: From Tilly Jane Campground parking, head right (SW) where it's only vague for a moment instead of walking straight toward the buildings (Guard Station). Then fork right almost immediately on Timberline Trail 600A, 100 ft to another juncture. For the counterclockwise loop, stay right (WNW) on Trail 600A ½ mi on an easy traverse up to the Cloud Cap Campground. Turn sharp left (S) on Timberline Trail 600. Walk S through the primitive campground from Cloud Cap Saddle TH and stay left of the River Crossing Safety sign and Mount Hood Wilderness kiosk at the four-way intersection on Trail 600 (not sharp left on Trail 600A to Tilly Jane) past a free self-issue Wilderness Permit station a few more feet to a signed fork.

Climbing steeper right on Trail 600 heads W toward Elk Cove and Barrett Spur. Take the left fork instead, toward Gnarl Ridge on Trail 600 as you continue S around 1 mi past the last of any tall trees (ignoring the upcoming Climber's Trail right). Hike somewhat steeper up the thin Tilly Jane canyon (turning to rock and sand), noting large rock cairns with wooden posts marking the route through the changing landscape as you leave the rocky gully left (SE). See Mount Hood ahead plus Cooper Spur left of the big volcano. Back into the thinning short pines with wildflowers nearby August into September, you can see out to Mount Adams, Mount Rainier, and Mount St. Helens up to a rocky four-way junction.

Leave Timberline Trail 600 and turn right (SW) on Cooper Spur Trail 600B (opposite the return for the loop left on Trail 600A). Walk 100 ft to the Cooper Spur Shelter, a small, intact old rock shelter on the open boulder-filled slope just off the main path to the right. Check it out along with the Cascades including Mount Hood as a backdrop, while the Columbia River Plateau lies to the E.

Continue up steeper s-turns leaving the last of the scrub brush to the first of 22 fairly gentle switchbacks through scree and pumice with ever improving vistas of the icefalls on nearby Eliot Glacier (second largest in Oregon) 1¾ mi from the four-way junction. Alternate routes exist up the rocks where lingering snow across a rather steep slope may block easier travel on the uppermost switchbacks, but no worries. Also

Intensifying vista from Cooper Spur Shelter to Mount Rainier and Mount Adams.

there are routes directly up the steeper and more difficult ridge crest, which are actually more suited for downhill travel and quite fun while saving time and mileage.

It's steeper to finish ½ mi to the Tie-In Rock where most people stop (with an option to continue less than ½ mi to the very top). Climb the steepest part of the day for nearly 30 make-your-own, tight switchbacks up the loose sand and rocks to the high ridge where you are greeted with a few open-air rock wind shelters (for summit climbers). See Mount Jefferson and walk along the high ridge easier briefly to the sizable boulder within the little saddle left of the trail known as the Tie-In Rock; this is where most people picnic and turn around. It is possible (if snow doesn't persist late into summer) to hike up another 400 ft fairly steeply to another older wind shelter at the top of Cooper Spur between the glaciers under the Chimneys on Mount Hood (watch for constant rock falling). Absolutely exquisite!

Return down safely and pretty quickly to the four-way junction under Cooper Spur Shelter and head straight on Trail 600A (NE) for the counterclockwise loop past Tilly Jane Guard Station and A-frame, instead of returning left on Trail 600 down Tilly Jane canyon. It's about a mile down the steeper ridge without switchbacks, but quite pleasant, as the rocky trail turns to dirt, then sand, finishing in the trees N of Polallie Creek canyon. Be cautious while checking out views into the decent-sized canyon with no further shots back to Mount Hood.

Arrive at another Wilderness Permit station and keep left at any faint forks to a more pronounced three-way juncture near a larger kiosk, some old buildings, and the Tilly Jane A-Frame to the right. Check out the A-frame if you wish, or just turn left on Trail 600A down past an open-air amphitheater and across a small but lovely creek over a footbridge, and then ascend a few feet to the Guard Station and Tilly Jane Campground. Walk straight briefly to the TH or left (WNW) at the fork on Trail 600A around ½ mi to Cloud Cap Saddle.

ELEVATION: 6633 ft; 5660 ft at the high point on the loop; with vertical gains of about 2400 ft for the butte with the loop, and 1420 ft for the loop without the butte

DISTANCE: About 5 mi directly to Lamberson Butte, almost 11 mi round-trip with the loop; 7¼ mi for the loop without the butte

DURATION: 2–3 hours to the butte, 5–6 hours round-trip for the butte with the loop; 3 hours round-trip for the loop without the butte

DIFFICULTY: Strenuous. Long, only steep near butte, difficult creek crossings with high water possible: trekking poles might help, bugs in high summer

TRIP REPORT: The quieter E side of Mount Hood is just as stunning as anywhere else on the mountain and sees fewer visitors except for a few weekends in July. The best time to see the entire region however is mid- to late August without snow being an issue (fewer bugs) and with wildflowers still thriving. The Elk Meadows area may be a fine destination for families and is described below, but what follows only becomes more spectacular for hikers who like to hike! Northwest Forest Pass required, and a portable outhouse is present late May through September.

TRAILHEAD: Elk Meadows TH. Take US-26 E from Portland 30 mi past Sandy, exit right for OR-35 N (Hood River) 7½ mi to a small brown sign and then a road left for Elk Meadows TH (near milepost 65). Follow it ¼ mi NW to the pullout on the right with the proper trail farthest to the left (N; 65 mi, less than 1½ hours from Portland).

ROUTE: From the signed TH near Hood River Meadows Nordic Center walk NNE on Sahalie Falls Trail 667C easily passing a juncture with Umbrella Falls Trail 667 to the left, and then arriving to the juncture of Elk Meadows Trail 645 near the self-issue Wilderness Permit station at more than ½ mi from the TH. Fill out the permit and continue NE across the bridge over Clark Creek on Trail 645 traversing ½ mi to Newton Creek Trail 646 on the left heading NW (signed). That is the return trail for the slightly longer loop. Stay straight on Elk Meadows Trail instead ¼ mi to cross Newton Creek carefully one of two times (the top portion of the creek on the potential loop can be more difficult). The continuation of the trail into the woods (marked by cairns) is directly across the creek, but walk left on the rocky path along the water up to 100 ft while searching where to cross. Mount Hood is visible NW up Newton

Creek Canyon. Use the logs (plus one huge one) or rock hop where it is safe to the solid trail, then move a few feet right before heading left into the trees.

Hike right immediately at the first of 9 well-graded switchbacks N a mile up through the forest on Trail 645 to a four-way intersection. After the eighth switchback you see Mount Hood and Mount Jefferson through the trees. Right (SE) from the intersection a mile is Elk Mountain on Bluegrass Ridge Trail 647. Straight (NE) only ¼ mi down on Trail 645 is Elk Meadows Perimeter Trail 645A around beautiful wildflower-laced Elk Meadows (smaller loop worth exploring another day or without the butte). N of the open meadow is Gnarl Ridge Cutoff Trail 652A that heads NW to meet the main route to Lamberson Butte or the Newton Creek Canyon loop on Trail 600.

For this hike and the main route up Gnarl Ridge, turn left (NW) on narrower Gnarl Ridge Trail 652 at the

LAMBERSON BUTTE TO NEWTON CREEK CANYON LOOP

four-way intersection. Hike ¾ mi through the forest without any trouble to the juncture with Trail 652A on the right. Stay left on Trail 652 through the pines ¼ mi to the crossroads with the counterclockwise loop. If you are omitting the butte, go left (W) at the fork on Trail 600 down into Newton Creek Canyon.

Scrambling the final feet to Lamberson Butte without any trouble in late September.

For Lamberson Butte, move right (NNW) at the fork onto Timberline Trail 600 1½ mi only a bit steeper up the opening terrain encircling the butte from the E. There are a couple sweeping turns through the thinning trees past the stone foundation of an old structure 50 ft to Gnarl Ridge, NW of Lamberson Butte. The view suddenly becomes remarkable with a close-up of the Newton Clark Glacier to Mount Hood! Trail 600 continues N several miles to Cooper Spur and beyond; but instead you'll have an obvious, fun scramble up off the main trail less than ½ left (S).

Climb much steeper up the rocky bushwhack path toward the summit of Lamberson Butte past the old snags just left (N) of the ridge crest to a small bump on the high ridge with improved vistas. See the top of the butte about 150 ft farther S. Continue carefully, with serious drop-offs down the cliff band to the right (S), as you stay left (NE) of the ridgeline somewhat easier past more snags and short pines to the rocky top. The amazing full-length view of Newton Creek Canyon up to the Newton Clark Glacier and Mount Hood makes that last stretch to Lamberson Butte completely worth the effort! Of course you could see Mount Adams from far below and on top, but while on the summit (and on Gnarl Ridge from Trail 600) you can also see Mount Jefferson and the Sisters Range on a clear day. And the constant breeze should keep the flies at bay. Hear the creek raging below and bushwhack down N very steeply and briefly from the top to the main trail, or return NW along the high ridge cautiously less than ½ mi to Trail 600 and continue down the more established route.

Return (SE) 1½ mi down Timberline Trail to the junction with Trail 652 on Gnarl Ridge; continue right (W) on Trail 600 toward Newton Creek for the immensely interesting loop option. Traverse easily almost ¾ mi down the narrow, slightly overgrown trail through the forest, then move up a hundred yards before pulling out of the trees. Follow the pumice path with cairns right (NW) briefly through boulders on the rocky canyon floor at the creek with a full shot of Mount Hood's E face. You may have to move a few feet right at the water to rock hop where it is safe, and then locate the elusive path heading left up the steeper slope on the W side. There are cairns and a tall post near the trees you reenter.

Immediately cross a small creek over two thin logs as the trail moves right to climb a couple hundred feet in elevation W fairly steeply up turns to the next juncture. Leave Trail 600 at the juncture for the left turn on Newton Creek Trail 646 (old sign). Hike SE pleasantly down less than 2 mi to the end of the loop over the moraine ridgeline with expansive views much of the way. There are 2 switchbacks just right (W) of the ridge as you leave it for a bit with the route steepening for a short time. Then be mindful past all the snags near the edge of the ridge (far above the creek) as erosion is ongoing in a big way. Bushwhack somewhat away from the edge and trail if necessary. There are great shots of Gnarl Ridge up to Lamberson Butte and part of Mount Hood. The route mellows and narrows through more pines off the moraine to finish over tiny creeks, and is truly a delightful and peaceful loop option not to be missed. Turn right at the end of Trail 646 for 1 mi to the TH. You will cross more water, then Clark Creek, halfway to your vehicle.

37 | LITTLE ZIGZAG CANYON LOOP

ELEVATION: 7000 ft, with 1500 ft vertical gain total

DISTANCE: 6 mi round-trip clockwise loop

DURATION: 3–4 hours round-trip loop

DIFFICULTY: Strenuous. Steeper after Zigzag Canyon Overlook, scree, route-finding, snow-filled gullies to ascend, traction devices helpful but not required in summer

TRIP REPORT: The following few hikes require some high alpine experience and route-finding skills with year-round snow coverage possible. But because you are mostly above tree line, the ski area and chairlifts can always be seen or found leading to the TH. This hike includes the family-friendly option to turn around at Zigzag Canyon Overlook (4½ mi round-trip), while other hikers either continue down toward Paradise Park or climb up the ridge, looping above Little Zigzag Canyon to the ski area near Silcox Hut (private lodge rental). No pass required in summer, and restrooms are located inside the lower building at Timberline Lodge 50 ft to the right.

TRAILHEAD: Timberline Lodge. Take US-26 E from Portland 28½ mi E of Sandy just past Government Camp after milepost 54, fork left on Timberline Road (brown sign for "Timberline Lodge 6 mi" but closer to 5 mi) winding up as it turns into a one-way to the largest parking lot (60 mi, 1½ hours from Portland).

ROUTE: Begin from the huge parking lot and proceed between lodge buildings onto the paved trail that moves right of the upper building, or simply walk steeply from the parking lot up the path leading to railroad tie steps past the welcome sign to meet the paved trail. Walk a hundred yards farther N to the first intersection at Timberline Trail 600 (sharing a stretch with PCT 2000).

Head left (W) easily on Trail 600/2000 for ½ mi under the ski area. Pass Mountaineer Trail 798 on the left that moves back to the lodge and TH (right moves up toward Silcox Hut), and proceed another ½ mi near tree line (fill out free self-issue Wilderness Permit). The rocky trail undulates then descends to cross Little Zigzag Canyon. Continue W downwards passing Hidden Lake Trail 779 on the left after ¼ mi or so. You walk 1 mile (from Little Zigzag Canyon) through the thinning pines and more lupine-covered meadows with much of Mount Hood behind, and Mount Jefferson with Three Sisters to the S.

Suddenly you come up a tad to the stunning Zigzag Canyon Overlook (5500 ft) before a steep descent takes the trail down another mile crossing Zigzag River in the enormous canyon. From the overlook you can see a whole lot more of Mount Hood, and also Mississippi Head at the top of the canyon above the cliff band to the left. Return to the TH by the same route after investigating from the viewpoint when you are ready.

Wildflowers, including these asters, abound near Timberline Lodge up to Mount Hood.

For the clockwise loop around Little

Zigzag Canyon, you will leave Trail 600/2000 for the obvious bushwhack path right (NE) up the open ridge E of Zigzag Canyon for about 1¼ mi and then traverse E ½ mi, to the bottom of the Palmer Lift area. You will see lakes and Tom Dick and Harry Mountain SSW and Illumination Rock straight ahead under Mount Hood. For this loop hike up the steep widening ridge (path disappears) and adjacent large snowfields with only minor difficulty. Then carefully begin the traverse (at around 7000 ft with no trail or markers) to the right (E), past rocky outcrops, and across the top of Little Zigzag Canyon to the Silcox Hut near the top of the Magic Mile chairlift.

Return to Timberline Lodge and the TH to the S by taking the ski area service road under the Magic Mile chairlift down several well-graded switchbacks or a bit shorter directly down the paths under the Silcox Hut (avoiding active ski runs) E of the chairlift. These trails meet near a maintenance area where you continue briefly to the paved path leading to the TH. See Illumination Saddle (hike 39) and the final paragraph for the longer but interesting Mountaineer Trail as a third option down from the bottom of the Palmer Lift.

The path from Zigzag Canyon looking up to Mississippi Head under Oregon's highest volcano.

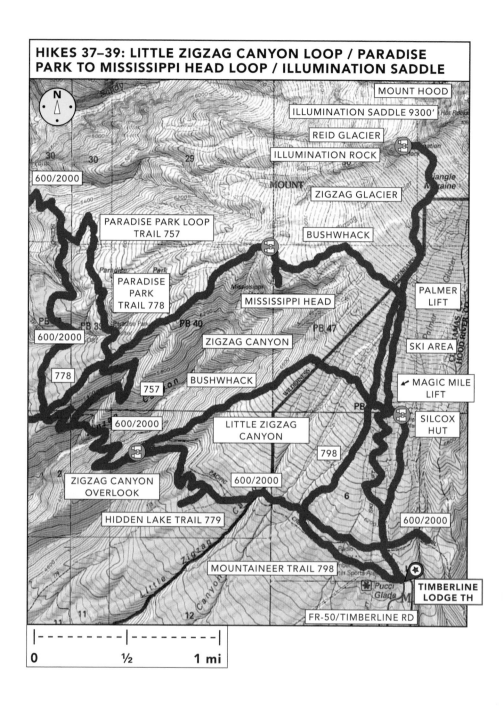

HIKES 37–39: LITTLE ZIGZAG CANYON LOOP / PARADISE
PARK TO MISSISSIPPI HEAD LOOP / ILLUMINATION SADDLE

N

MOUNT HOOD

ILLUMINATION SADDLE 9300'

REID GLACIER

ILLUMINATION ROCK

600/2000

ZIGZAG GLACIER

PARADISE PARK LOOP
TRAIL 757

BUSHWHACK

PARADISE
PARK
TRAIL 778

PALMER
LIFT

MISSISSIPPI HEAD

PB 40   PB 47

SKI AREA

600/2000

778

ZIGZAG CANYON

757

BUSHWHACK

MAGIC MILE
LIFT

600/2000

LITTLE ZIGZAG
CANYON

SILCOX
HUT

798

ZIGZAG CANYON
OVERLOOK

600/2000

6

HIDDEN LAKE TRAIL 779

600/2000

MOUNTAINEER TRAIL 798

TIMBERLINE
LODGE TH

11   12

FR-50/TIMBERLINE RD

0   ½   1 mi

ELEVATION: 8040 ft, with around 3400 ft vertical gain total; 2000 ft vertical gain Paradise Park loop only

DISTANCE: 11 mi max round-trip clockwise loop; 12 mi Paradise Park loop instead

DURATION: 5–7 hours round-trip for each loop

DIFFICULTY: Mix of very challenging (steeper, route-finding, rocky, long, ups/downs, snow travel probable, traction devices helpful above Mississippi Head) and strenuous for Paradise Park loop (long, never steep, good signage, ups/downs)

TRIP REPORT: This hike is like the previous one with its many options but on an even grander scale! It's longer, steeper, contains an option to descend the tip of Mississippi Head to view or visit an old B-26 bomber plane crash site (only part of a propeller remains), and climbs part of a glacier before descending the ski area to the TH. You also happen to pass by the Paradise Park wildflower show (alternate loop option without Mississippi Head), which in high summer is one of the very best in all of the Oregon Cascades! No pass required in summer, and restrooms are located inside the lower building at Timberline Lodge, 50 ft to the right.

TRAILHEAD: Timberline Lodge. See hike 37 for directions.

ROUTE: See the beginning of hike 37 for the description 2¼ mi to the Zigzag Canyon Overlook (for both hikes). Continue on Timberline Trail 600/ PCT 2000 down 3 gradual switchbacks 1 mi through the forest to the Zigzag River crossing (lowest point on this hike at 4900 ft), which is usually more like a small stream and no problem to hop over. Notice the nice little cascade up the canyon some and move up the trail ½ mi to the first of several signed junctures around

Paintbrush, aster, and others light up Paradise Park in late August.

Endless lupine-covered meadows delight all who pass through en route to Mississippi Head on Mount Hood.

Paradise Park. Take the fork right (NE) on Paradise Park Loop Trail 757 for 1¼ mi without any difficulty, crossing another stream easily en route to the next intersection as the wildflower display becomes immaculate from July well into August, even lasting until Labor Day some years.

Take a right (NE) on Paradise Park Trail 778 (for Mississippi Head) at 5 mi from the TH, continuing easily through large meadows blanketed with endless bright purple lupine, aster, paintbrush, Western pasqueflower, arrowleaf groundsel, fireweed, and others. A much shorter loop option is to turn left on Trail 778 from the intersection and head 1 mi SW down to Trail 600/2000, then left back down into Zigzag Canyon.

For the longer, laid-back loop around Paradise Park with multiple easy water crossings and interesting sights sans any more elevation gain, stay on Trail 757 a mile N through the park, and then walk down W to the Timberline Trail juncture. Note that Timberline Trail 600 and PCT 2000 run concurrently near Timberline Lodge to Bald Mountain above Ramona Falls. Turning right at this juncture moves very steeply NW on Trail 600/2000 with difficult river crossings (6½ mi to Ramona Fall TH). Turn left instead and continue S on Trail 600/2000 ambling quite pleasantly for almost 1½ mi through the beauty to the Trail 778 junction. Continue ¼ mi more on Trail 600/2000 down quick turns to Trail 757 at the end of the Paradise Park loop, then back into Zigzag Canyon en route to the TH.

From the intersection of Paradise Park Loop Trail 757 and Paradise Park Trail 778 towards Mississippi Head, with or without the loop, take the wildflower-choked path (continuation of Trail 778 unofficially) for about 20 amazing minutes NE to where the route finally becomes a bit steeper near the top of the vegetation into a world of rock, tiny pebbles, sand, ash, and snow—all the things you'd expect from hiking a major Cascade volcano. Notice the waterfall in upper Zigzag Canyon, and Mount Jefferson over several local lakes to the S as you continue past the rock cairn to the more obvious moraine ridgeline under Mount Hood and Mississippi Head. Many people settle for these views and bail on the rest at around 7000 ft (1 mi from Trail 757) to return down the same way on solid trails to Paradise Park.

To continue, follow the path best as possible; you must scramble at least ¼ mi up much steeper, including possibly across snow near the top of the narrow gully, just W of the cliffs under Mississippi Head. Take your time as you end up directly above Mississippi Head and can see the trail down the wider and rocky slope a couple hundred feet to the viewpoint atop the cliff band. See Mount Rainier to the N plus much more; continue the loop to the ski area. A few experienced hikers carefully scramble with no definable trail down a couple hundred more feet in elevation to the tip of Mississippi Head to view, or even visit, the propeller of the old plane on a small ledge directly above the huge cliff at the head of Zigzag Canyon. Climb back up and proceed for the clockwise loop.

Hike NE (slightly right) up the loose rock then snow at the bottom of Zigzag Glacier from the Mississippi Head area for another ½ mi fairly steeply. Traction devices will help to completely and safely clear the very top of Zigzag Canyon at more than 8000 ft. See the ski area and the top of the Palmer Lift as you traverse E directly toward the lift (perhaps through rock and scree). Mountaineer Trail 798 is reached around 8000 ft, close to the lift, where you begin to descend S almost immediately a fun 1½ mi or so to Timberline Trail. Feel free to glissade down snow-filled gullies W of Palmer Lift that double as ski runs in winter. Continue down these gullies W of Magic Mile chairlift, or the adjacent rocky Mountaineer Trail, to the right (W) along the ski area boundary markers, without difficulty to Trail 600/PCT. Turn left on Trail 600 ½ mi easier to the final juncture near the TH. Or cross Trail 600 to stay on Trail 798 traversing roughly the same distance to Timberline Lodge.

ELEVATION: 9300 ft, with 3400 ft vertical gain

DISTANCE: 3½ mi up, 7 mi round-trip with or without a loop; 3 mi round-trip alternate Mountaineer Trail loop (see Trip Report) without Illumination Saddle

DURATION: 3–3½ hours up, 5–6 hours round-trip with breaks; 1½-2 hours round-trip alternate loop

DIFFICULTY: Strenuous. Route-finding, rocky, narrow, multiple paths, possible rocks falling from above Illumination Saddle, crossing snowfields, glissading, traction devices helpful but not necessary most times in summer, crevasses not likely but not unheard of late fall on Zigzag Glacier

TRIP REPORT: Illumination Rock, a prominent sub-summit of Mount Hood, is known as one of the most difficult summits to climb in all the Pacific Northwest. Illumination Saddle lies just E of the prominent massif between the Reid and Zigzag Glaciers on Mount Hood's SW side and is very attainable most times of the year, the late summer being best for most. For cross-country or other winter activities without using the ski area you will be directed left (W) of Timberline Lodge and Ski Area up the Mountaineer Trail utilizing part of the loop described below. A much easier 3 mi loop is also possible using the clues below with Mountaineer Trail 798 and leaving/finding it at about 6900 ft near the bottom of the Palmer Lift.

Unearthly scenery day hiking Mount Hood toward Illumination Saddle.

For an even easier day, pay $18 round-trip to ride the Magic Mile chairlift (from June to Labor Day) up and down after investigating the area. You can also walk down a myriad of trail options back to the lodge. Sno-Park Pass required in winter. No pass required in summer, and restrooms are located inside the lower building at Timberline Lodge 50 ft to the right.

TRAILHEAD: Timberline Lodge. See hike 37 for directions.

ROUTE: Begin from the huge parking lot and proceed between lodge buildings onto the paved trail that moves right of the upper building, or simply walk steeply from the lot up the path leading to railroad tie steps past the welcome sign to meet the paved trail. Walk a hundred yards farther N to the first intersection at Timberline Trail 600 (sharing a stretch with PCT 2000). This is the end of the little counterclockwise loop with Mountaineer Trail 798 (½ mi W on Trail 600/2000).

Continue straight up the paved path instead (in summer) briefly to the end to catch the main gravel trail left of the maintenance area. One option up the mountain is a steeper and slightly briefer path that follows the long ditch and gully (avoid active ski runs) to the right to meet the service road higher or at Silcox Hut. If you take the main dusty, gravel trail, it becomes a wide ski service road under the Magic Mile chairlift at only ½ mi from the TH. See Mount Jefferson and Three Sisters S, and Mount Hood Skibowl (Tom Dick and Harry Mountain) off the SW flank of Mount Hood. Wind up steadily under the lift a half-dozen more turns and walk between chairlift structures at 1½ mi from the TH. The Silcox Warming Hut (closed to general public) is down to the right. Avoid any active ski runs (E of the chairlifts in summer) as the area is known to stay open through Labor Day most years.

Follow the cairns on the steep hillside straight ahead N for another mile with a thin trail over the boulder-strewn slope just W of the Palmer Lift. Arrive at a large cairn with an orange-tipped pole near the top of the chairlift you've been paralleling. You will rise between long snow and rock-filled gullies and finish up to the cairn near the Palmer Glacier.

Begin an upward traverse NW a mile toward Illumination Saddle and the pinnacle (visible the entire hike), tackling the bulk of the steepness early on through semiloose rock and pumice. Traverse somewhat easier to the saddle after crossing several snowfields carefully on Zigzag Glacier including a possibly steeper one where you should pay attention the last few feet to the saddle. Traction devices are helpful even in late summer, while snowshoes, skis, crampons, and ice axe are not required unless it's spring, winter, or icy. Always be aware of the avalanche danger in winter as well as skiers and snowboarders descending from above.

In summer, from the saddle, you can literally hear the basalt crumbling and falling down from the sheer sides of Illumination Rock and from Mount Hood even with no one else climbing in the region. The 360-degree view is one of the overall best

Closing in on Illumination Rock with the saddle just right.

from the slopes of the volcano. See Mount St. Helens N over the top of Yocum Ridge above the beautiful Reid Glacier and Leuthold Couloir. The wild aspect of Mount Hood from this angle has you looking straight up NE toward the summit and all that lies in between like the Hot Rocks, the Hogsback (below the Bergschrund), Crater Rock, the Devil's Kitchen (with active fumaroles occasionally bringing the smell of sulfur or rotten eggs down to the ski areas), the Pearly Gates, and the colorful Steel Cliff to round out the panorama.

On the return, you may be able to ski or glissade part of the way. Just don't begin too soon down Zigzag Glacier or you'll end up near the colossal cliffs at Mississippi Head above Zigzag Canyon. Closer to the Palmer Lift, make your way down Mountaineer Trail 798 or long snowy gullies. Stay right (W) of the lower chairlifts, including the one under Palmer Lift (Magic Mile) while keeping it in sight along the ski area boundary signs (safely away from any skiers, snow cats, and snowmobiles). Then stay on the solid but rocky Mountaineer Trail down little rises on the open slope for the remainder of the enjoyable loop variation SSW to the Trail 600/2000 intersection. Turn left (E) on Timberline Trail 600 and traverse by meadows with wildflowers including lupine, aster, and paintbrush ½ mi to the end of the loop above Timberline Lodge. Turn right to finish down the paved trail to your vehicle.

40 | RAMONA FALLS LOOP

ELEVATION: 3500 ft, with about 1100 ft vertical gain

DISTANCE: 7½ mi round-trip loop

DURATION: 3 hours round-trip

DIFFICULTY: Mix of moderate in late summer or fall easily across the Sandy River over choice of logs (fairly easy to follow, partial bushwhack near river, gentle grade) and very challenging during high water with logs covered or wet at the Sandy River (dangerous river crossing in spring, not recommended for larger dogs any time)

TRIP REPORT: Without a bridge in place over the rushing Sandy River, this once family-friendly bustling hike is far less busy, but most people who aren't too young or old still seem to go for it under the best conditions with low water (usually late August/September). The lighting on these mystical, sparkling falls in a dense emerald forest changes intensely throughout the day and year. The lollipop loop adds a wonderful dynamic to this hike without adding much mileage. Northwest Forest Pass required, and portable outhouses are present.

TRAILHEAD: Ramona Falls TH. Take US-26 E from Portland 16¼ mi E of Sandy, turn left (NE) across from the Zigzag Inn and Zigzag Ranger Station on E Lolo Pass Road (FR-18) 4 mi, fork right on Muddy Fork Road (FR-1825) ¾ mi crossing the bridge over the Sandy River, and continue 1¾ mi (becomes winding one-lane). Fork

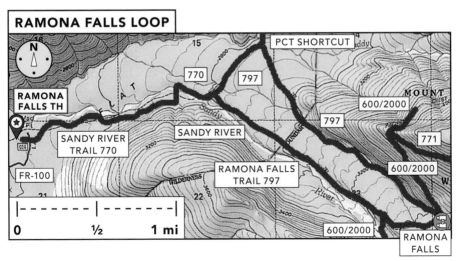

left on FR-100 (a bit rougher, also signed for Ramona Falls, all paved) almost ½ mi to the end at a sizable parking lot (50 mi, more than 1 hour from Portland).

ROUTE: Begin E on Sandy River Trail 770 almost ¼ mi to a kiosk and free self-issue Wilderness Permit at a stop sign. Continue about 1 mi easily up to the river crossing following the wide pumice trail along the high sandy bank through the woods with shots to Mount Hood from the rocky, wide riverbed with steep embankments. You will have to negotiate one of several large, fallen trees directly upriver (right) a few feet or up to a hundred feet farther with higher flows (or rock hop under very low flow) to cross carefully over the cold, rushing stream. Anyone with good balance should be able to get across the dry logs later in the summer.

Walk up through a well-used notch in the bank to climb out of the riverbed. If you had to cross farther upriver, turn left briefly onto the solid trail once you climb the bank to find the main trail (770) again, and then turn right on it. Work your way NNE carefully ¼ mi, or go straight across the confusing open boulder-laden area into the woods remembering your route. Head up to a nearby juncture with the beginning/end of the lollipop loop after getting a really good look at Mount Hood up the valley.

For the direct route (counterclockwise loop), walk straight (SE) on Ramona Falls Trail 797 along the river through the thin trees with ample sun 1½ mi up to the junction with Timberline Trail 600/PCT 2000 (newer signage). Those trails run

Shimmering Ramona Falls is a brief pilgrimage locals make multiple times per year!

concurrently with part of the Ramona Falls loop before moving N up the mountain or moving right here at the fork down SE over the Sandy River, then fairly steep several miles up to Paradise Park and beyond. Resume left instead up dusty Trail 797 about ½ mi without difficulty past rhododendrons to the falls within the thicker forest and enjoy the splendor even though there's a good chance you won't be alone. Check out different angles of the dazzling, splayed-out, year-round cascade (120 ft high) before departing.

For the more interesting segment of the loop, walk across the footbridge below the falls to an immediate intersection (right is Trail 600) and walk left (NW) at the fork nearest Ramona Creek on Trail 797 for a more scenic return losing the equestrians for the next segment. The path down is only slightly narrower but quite enjoyable as you pass a huge cliff wall at the bottom of Yocum Ridge, several tiny cascades on the creek, and a few footbridges throughout the beautiful green forest almost 2 mi from Ramona Falls to the next juncture in the flats. The trail only becomes a bit sandier and rockier to the juncture.

Turn left (SW, opposite the PCT Shortcut) on Trail 797 for ½ mi to the end of the loop, passing the equestrian spur then a solid bridge over Ramona Creek in the woods to the intersection near the Sandy River. Turn right at the end of the loop to the parking lot by continuing more than 1½ mi to the TH using utmost caution crossing the river again.

Thick logs help day hikers cross the mighty Sandy River under ideal conditions.

41   YOCUM RIDGE

ELEVATION: 6285 ft, with 3850 ft vertical gain

DISTANCE: 9 mi up, 18 mi round-trip

DURATION: 4 hours up, 6–7 hours round-trip

DIFFICULTY: Very challenging. Dangerous Sandy River passage under high water if logs cannot be crossed safely, partial bushwhack near river, gentle grade, very long, only snow-free at higher elevations August into September

---

TRIP REPORT: One of the most beautiful, and certainly the longest, day hikes on Mount Hood (excluding Timberline Trail) is also remarkably one of the most peaceful once you are past Ramona Falls near the bottom! Northwest Forest Pass required, and portable outhouses are present.

TRAILHEAD: Ramona Falls TH. See hike 40 for directions.

ROUTE: See the first part of hike 40 for the description directly to Ramona Falls (3½ mi in). Continue right at the fork after the bridge below the memorizing waterfall onto Timberline Trail 600 another ½ mi or so NW up through the woods to the next juncture. Turn right (ESE) up the ridge at the sign onto Yocum Ridge Trail 771 almost 5 mi more to the end of the official trail. The walk is tranquil, mostly through huge Douglas fir, and gains elevation slowly and methodically up 6 switchbacks total with minimal views outward. Pass a picturesque little pond (5180 ft) halfway up after a few

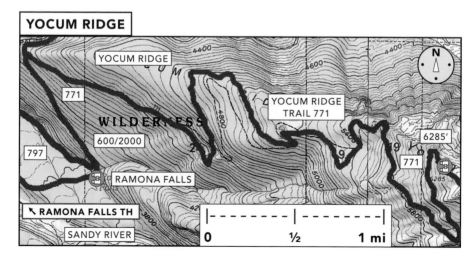

YOCUM RIDGE

Ascending above the clouds on Yocum Ridge for a clear shot to three big Cascade volcanoes in Washington.

turns. Your patience will be rewarded (and then some) in the final mile of the hike.

You slowly break out of the old forest into a high alpine meadow with the W face of Mount Hood looming rather imposingly in front of you (Illumination Rock is just to the right). Soon see the beautiful multi-tiered waterfall carving through the rock at the top of the Sandy River Canyon below the Reid Glacier. You'll have wildflowers to work through late in the summer and snow into October and beyond.

Head NW at the last switchback on Trail 771 ½ mi to the main ridge again where the route becomes a bit steeper and narrower for ¼ mi to another meadow. This meadow is just before a small pine-covered saddle on Yocum Ridge where the official trail ends and a faded climber's path appears occasionally. Most people turn around here, but some folks press on steeper from the saddle to the higher ridgeline; remember every step forward is another to return on. Beware of tumbling rocks near the cliffs a mile or so from the end of the established trail.

From Yocum Ridge, the views on a clear day of Mount St. Helens, Mount Rainier, and Mount Adams to the N are quite glorious. To the S past Zigzag Canyon is Olallie Butte and Mount Jefferson with Three Sisters Range barely visible behind to the left. Return all the way to Ramona Falls and consider taking the slightly longer, but more picturesque, trail along Ramona Creek. Either way, after following the river or creek walk, you must cross the Sandy River cautiously again en route to the TH.

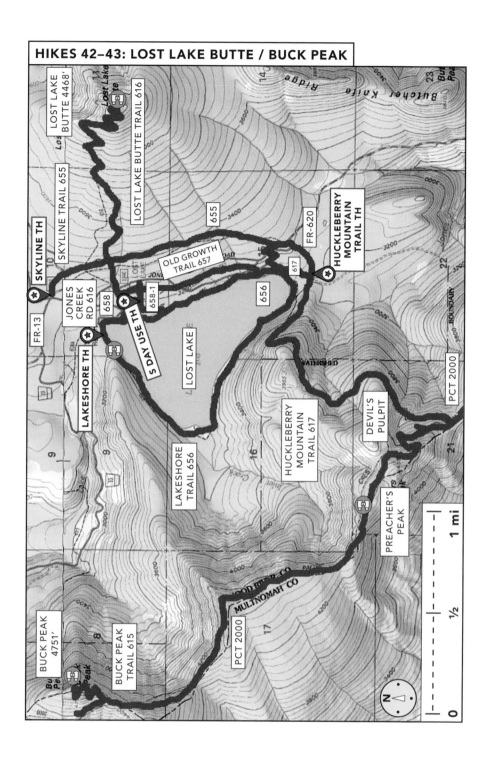

HIKES 42–43: LOST LAKE BUTTE / BUCK PEAK

LOST LAKE BUTTE 4468'

LOST LAKE BUTTE TRAIL 616

SKYLINE TRAIL 655

SKYLINE TH

655

FR-620

HUCKLEBERRY MOUNTAIN TRAIL TH

OLD GROWTH TRAIL 657

656

617

JONES CREEK RD 616

658

658-1

S DAY USE TH

LAKESHORE TH

LOST LAKE

FR-13

DEVIL'S PULPIT

PCT 2000

LAKESHORE TRAIL 656

HUCKLEBERRY MOUNTAIN TRAIL 617

PREACHER'S PEAK

BUCK PEAK 4751'

BUCK PEAK TRAIL 615

MULTNOMAH CO

PCT 2000

N

1 mi

½

0

42   LOST LAKE BUTTE

ELEVATION: 4468 ft on the butte; 3143 ft at Lost Lake; with vertical gains of 1270 ft, and only about 50 ft for a lake loop without the butte

DISTANCE: 2¼ mi up, 4½ mi round-trip; almost 3½ mi round-trip loop around lake

DURATION: 1 hour up, 1½ hours round-trip; 4 hours round-trip with lake loop too

DIFFICULTY: Mix of moderate for the butte (steep, brief, narrow, overgrown) and easiest for the lake loop (not much elevation change, boardwalks, very popular, signed, family-friendly)

TRIP REPORT: Aptly named, as Lost Lake gets easily lost equidistant between the Columbia River Gorge and Mount Hood. It does, however, feel more like a Mount Hood hike, so here we are. Open May through October; check conditions online (www.fs.usda.gov/recarea/mthood/recarea/?recid=53228, lostlakeresort.org/) as multiple lava tubes have been known to completely drain the lake before it refills itself! Spend quality family time at the lake with an easy loop around it through big old cedar, hemlock, fir, and rhododendron, or tack on the equestrian trail to the butte for much more exercise. Lost Lake Resort and Campground is privately owned and an $8 day use fee can be paid at the entrance station on the way in (if open) or at the Lost Lake General Store. Restrooms are located throughout the resort and nearby campgrounds, but not the S day use TH. Use Skyline TH to forgo the fee if Lost Lake Butte is your only goal (no fee or restroom).

TRAILHEAD: Skyline TH, S day use TH, or Lakeshore (N day use) TH. Take I-84 E to exit 62 (Hood River), turn right on US-30 for 1¼ mi through town, and turn right at the signal onto OR-281 S (13th Street into Tucker Road) almost 5 mi. Cross Hood River by Odell, then turn right (SW) on OR-281 S (past Tucker County Park on Dee Highway) 6 mi to Dee, turn right over the railroad tracks (past an old mill, then over the bridge), and turn left at the signage for Wahtum and Lost Lakes. Stay on Lost Lake Road (FR-13) 13 mi to Lost Lake, following signs. Be alert on the narrow, twisting, paved road and watch for oncoming traffic and natural obstacles. For Lost Lake Butte, stop short of the road to the resort on the brief, gated spur road (gravel) on the left with a small sign for Skyline Trail 655. Park on the sides where there is room without blocking anything. For the main parking near the resort, pass the entrance station following the road and signs (ignoring the left turn onto Jones Creek Road toward

A rock cairn is engulfed with wildflowers as Mount Hood dominates the horizon.

camping or Huckleberry Mountain Trail TH) down briefly to an intersection. Lost Lake Butte Trail 616 is immediately to the left with day use parking after (FR-1340) on the right and also less than ¼ mi farther at the S day use TH turnaround. Turn right at the intersection past the small store (info center, more parking) and lodge around the N side of the lake over the bridge, and to the parking circle at Lakeshore (N day use) TH (85 mi, more than 1½ hours from Portland).

ROUTE: To begin from Lakeshore TH for Lost Lake Butte or for the clockwise lake loop, see the map and take any established trail down from the parking area heading left, or take Lakeshore Trail 656 to the nearby fork and proceed hard left past the picnic/viewing areas, big cedars, and hemlock back around the N side of the lake. You can see why this is one of the most photographed perspectives of Mount Hood! Cross the outlet creek (Lake Branch) over the footbridge and pass by Lost Lake General Store.

Remain nearest the lake for the loop alone, but for the butte find the first trail left (616, at the amphitheater) and then head straight (E) on Trail 616 (no sign) at junctures (including past Rhododendron Trail 658-1 and Old Growth Trail 657) through the campground somewhat confusingly. You can also follow the road from the store or S day use TH to the signed trail (Lakeshore Express Trail 658) at the road intersection in between. Or find Lost Lake Butte Trail 616 (also signed) across from Jones Creek Road (just S of B- and C-Loop campgrounds). Follow Trail 616 less than

¼ mi more to the intersection with Skyline Trail 655 and continue to the summit on Trail 616.

From the Skyline TH outside the resort, follow Skyline Trail 655 almost ½ mi S easily through the woods to the intersection with Lost Lake Butte Trail 616. You pass an old clear-cut, cross an old gravel road, and resume through the beautiful old growth forest to the signed juncture.

Take the summit trail (616) left (E) less than 2 mi steeply to the top (9 switchbacks after an upcoming turn) with little fanfare. There aren't many outward views until the summit meadow where you suddenly break out into the open with wildflowers (along with flying bugs late June into August) and great shots of Mount Adams and Mount Hood. Return to Lost Lake or the Skyline TH by the same route.

For the clockwise loop around the lake once you are down from Lost Lake Butte past the Skyline Trail juncture, take Old Growth Trail 657 left (S) a few feet to Lakeshore Express Trail where you can walk to the right briefly down to the lake. Take the Lakeshore Trail 656 left (S) and walk less than a mile along the lake, through the big trees, over several picturesque boardwalks, and past fishing piers to the junction with Huckleberry Mountain Trail 617 on the left (to the PCT and Buck Peak). Continue right on the charming Lakeshore Trail W of the lake 2 mi to Lakeshore TH crossing multiple boardwalks, Inlet Creek, and cedar bogs en route. The view of Mount Hood across the lake is partly obscured at times but remains stupendous. Enjoy one of several swimming spots to put a cap on your day before a barbeque or your happy hour plans!

43 | BUCK PEAK

ELEVATION: 4751 ft, with 1600 ft vertical gain

DISTANCE: 5½ mi up, 11 mi round-trip

DURATION: 2½ hours up, 4½–5 hours round-trip

DIFFICULTY: Strenuous. Longer, steady easy grade, narrow, overgrown, signed, snow lingers into July

TRIP REPORT: A favorite route of the few possible to the highest point in Multnomah County, which is funny because very few of the county's 800,000 residents would know this fact or its location just NW of Mount Hood! Lost Lake Resort and Campground is privately owned and an $8 day use fee can be paid at the entrance station on the way in (if open) or at the Lost Lake General Store. There is no fee at

Huckleberry Mountain Trail TH closest to Buck Peak. Restrooms are located throughout the resort and nearby campgrounds, but not the Skyline TH, S day use TH, or Huckleberry Mountain Trail TH. And FYI: This Huckleberry Mountain Trail does not go to Huckleberry Mountain.

TRAILHEAD: Huckleberry Mountain Trail TH or S day use TH. For both THs, check the Trip Report and see hike 42 for directions past the resort's entrance station for S day use TH. For Huckleberry Mountain Trail TH from the entrance station, turn left on Jones Creek Road keeping S for 1 mi as the pavement narrows and you pass between the horse camp and group camping area. Continue ¼ mi narrowing, turn right before the road blockage on gravel FR-620 (unsigned) ¼ mi to the TH on the right and park in the few small pullouts on either side without blocking the road (easy, mostly paved, ½ hour from Hood River; 85 mi, 2 hours from Portland).

ROUTE: From the S day use TH, continue S from the end of the parking loop on the trail briefly and turn right down to Lakeshore Trail 656. Turn left (S) a mile along the beautiful lake over boardwalks through the woods to the signed junction for Huckleberry Mountain Trail 617 on the left. For Buck Peak, take Trail 617 less than ¼ mi up past a small tarn on the right to the primary TH (and spur path 30 ft left to FR-620). Continue right (left from the primary TH) at the signage ("Lakeshore Trail ¼ mi and Attention Hikers…") up 30 ft more to another sign correctly indicating PCT 2000 is 1¾ mi away.

Work gradually up the narrow trail through dense fir, hemlock, and cedar to the PCT. Follow a traverse after 2 quick switchbacks along a fairly steep slope without

Snapshot of Mount Hood past nearby Sentinel Peak from Lost Lake.

Beautiful from Buck Peak over Bull Run Lake to Oregon's tallest mountain.

much flora. Well after the third switchback, and more than ½ mi from the primary TH, is a decent look out of the tight trees to Lost Lake, Lost Lake Butte, and Mount Hood. Next is a wooden sign on a tree that is the 1 mi marker. The forest becomes a bit lusher with a few rhododendrons as you can see Mount Hood between the big old trees on an easier traverse SW across little creeks to the end of the trail.

Turn right (NW, sign for Huckleberry Mountain Trail 617/Lost Lake "2 mi" and Buck Peak Trail 615) onto the PCT up almost ¼ mi to a small sign on a tree left for Salvation Spring camping area 100 ft down the spur path to the right. Stay left ¾ mi on the PCT up 4 switchbacks to a saddle between Preacher's Peak and the rockier Devil's Pulpit. Soon after the tree-covered saddle you will have a great look at Mount Adams far behind Lost Lake. Continue down easier about ½ mi to a rock outcrop on the left; some people scramble briefly to find rare views SW into the Bull Run Watershed and Bull Run Lake. Hike NW without difficulty or much elevation change almost 2 mi more (below and E of the ridgeline at times) to the turnoff for Buck Peak Trail 615. Halfway to the turnoff is a good shot of Buck Peak with Mount St. Helens in the background. Then you see the top of Mount Hood and Mount Adams behind Mount Defiance, all of which improve from the summit.

Leave the PCT far above and just E of Blue Lake bearing right for the overgrown signed path ("Buck Peak") winding up N slightly steeper ½ mi to Buck Peak (huckleberries in late August). See all of the above plus Mount Jefferson and Mount Rainier on a clear day from the tiny top; have a nice picnic within the wildflowers near the old lookout foundation before returning without difficulty to the TH or Lost Lake.

44 McNEIL POINT

ELEVATION: 6930 ft at McNeil Point Summit; 6100 ft at McNeil Point shelter; with vertical gains of about 3000 ft, and 2100 ft

DISTANCE: 5 mi up the standard route, 10 mi round-trip; 12 mi round-trip including the summit and Bald Mountain scenic loop spur (subtract almost 3 mi round-trip from all routes using super-steep shortcut under McNeil Point both ways)

DURATION: 2½–3 hours to McNeil Point, 4–5 hours round-trip; another ½ hour one way up to the summit boulder

DIFFICULTY: Mix of strenuous (long, decent grade, possible steep snow fields) and very challenging for the summit and/or the shortcut (very steep to extremely steep, slick, dusty, exposure on summit boulder)

TRIP REPORT: One of the finest summer gems and not much of a secret is this fantastic hike with waterfall sightings, babbling brooks to cross easily, wildflowers, inspiring views, beautiful ridges, and a very doable grade for most day hikers on the NW slopes of Mount Hood. The hardest part will be waiting until late July or August when the snow finally melts enough in the high country and you won't have to cross dangerously steep or icy snow fields near the point. Listed below are the briefest routes from the TH and the best options to and above McNeil Point. Northwest Forest Pass required, and a portable outhouse is present during summer months.

TRAILHEAD: Top Spur TH. Take US-26 E from Portland 16¼ mi E of Sandy, turn left (NE) across from the Zigzag Inn and Zigzag Ranger Station on E Lolo Pass Road 4 mi (FR-18), fork right on Muddy Fork Road (FR-1825) ¾ mi, stay straight (as opposed to crossing the bridge) 2 mi on FR-1828 (Top Spur Trail 785 sign), fork right 3½ mi on the main road (all previously paved), fork right 1½ mi on FR-118 over rough gravel and a few potholes to the signed TH on the right with parking on the left (55 mi, less than 1½ hours from Portland).

Looking north to Mount St. Helens, Mount Rainier, and Mount Adams near McNeil Point Summit on a bluebird day.

HIKES 44–46: MCNEIL POINT / VISTA RIDGE TO CAIRN BASIN LOOP / BARRETT SPUR SUMMIT

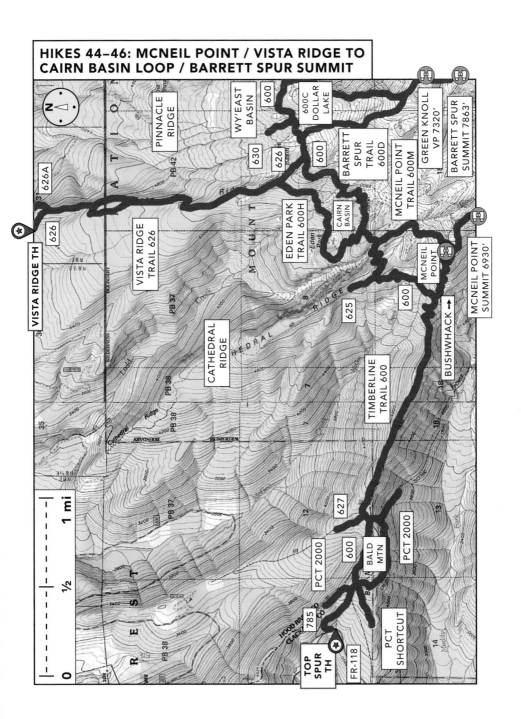

N

PINNACLE RIDGE

WY'EAST BASIN

600

600C DOLLAR LAKE

GREEN KNOLL VP 7320'

BARRETT SPUR SUMMIT 7863'

630

626

600

PB 42

BARRETT SPUR TRAIL 600D

MCNEIL POINT TRAIL 600M

626A

626

EDEN PARK TRAIL 600H

CAIRN BASIN

VISTA RIDGE TRAIL 626

VISTA RIDGE TH

MCNEIL POINT

MCNEIL POINT SUMMIT 6930'

PB 37

625

600

CATHEDRAL RIDGE

BUSHWHACK

PB 38

PB 38

TIMBERLINE TRAIL 600

PB 37

627

PCT 2000

PCT 2000

1 mi

½

0

PCT 2000

600

BALD MTN

785

TOP SPUR TH

FR-118

PCT SHORTCUT

MCNEIL POINT   143

ROUTE: Begin across the road N on Top Spur Trail 785, then quickly SE for ½ mi to the end. Turn right (SE) on PCT 2000 for 100 ft to a major intersection, information board, and mandatory free self-issue Wilderness Permit station. Continue left (SE) on Timberline Trail 600 for ½ mi through the woods more directly to a faint juncture with the Bald Mountain loop near a saddle, or you could walk right (SW then SE) to stay on the PCT for 1 mi with incredible views traversing down and up a bit around Bald Mountain. If you stay on the PCT, look for a spur path (and cairn) left at a small saddle E of Bald Mountain, and then walk N briefly off the PCT and more easily through the forest to meet the Timberline Trail again.

Turn right (NE) on Trail 600 and pass McGee Creek Trail 627 on the left (N). Hike more SE as the solid Trail 600 meets the wider section of Bald Mountain ridge through the lovely forest over a comfortably steady grade. At 2½ mi from the TH (if you took the scenic PCT Bald Mountain loop spur), the ridge narrows as the views become even grander. You've got waterfalls in the Muddy Fork River Canyon up to the Sandy Glacier under Mount Hood, and McNeil Point (shelter barely discernible) straight ahead with the ridge to the summit boulder in the background.

Descend a bit on Trail 600, then climb steeper up a few turns to begin a northerly traverse from the bottom of an open narrow meadow (5400 ft). This skunk cabbage-covered (in summer) meadow on the right at 3 mi from the TH holds the ½-mi-long bushwhack trail and shortcut scramble directly to the McNeil Point shelter. The detailed description is for the descent only. It is not recommended for most, and although not exposed, it is extremely steep, loose, rocky, and fairly tracked out ESE up what quickly becomes the thin ridge section S of the cliff band below McNeil Point. For the scramble from the McNeil Point shelter, you would head W straight down the most prominent thin path through bushes seemingly off the cliff at first. You would stay left (S) of the cliff descending just left or on the narrow, broken ridgeline itself following the most worn path rather abruptly down the boulders and obstacle course with loose scree and pumice until near the bottom.

From Timberline Trail in the open narrow meadow (5400 ft) on the more attractive main route, it's 2 mi farther to McNeil Point's old rock shelter. Easily negotiate around five little streams on the traverse N and then cross a large scree field. Proceed up 2 switchbacks and cross two more tiny creeks before leveling off at the first of two tarn ponds in a sizable clearing. The main trail heads into the woods steeper between the ponds, but take a moment to check out the reflection from the second pond into McNeil Point and Mount Hood. Another option is the bushwhack path in the clearing which peters out up at a juncture with Mazama Trail 625 (moving NW down Cathedral Ridge) and curves right (SE) up a rise to meet the Timberline Trail 600 again. On Trail 600, cross another clearing and revegetating area, then hike steeper up 3 switchbacks to the small McNeil Point sign on the right in another clearing. Leave Timberline Trail and the route to Cairn Basin, Eden Park, Wy'East Basin, Barrett Spur, and Elk Cove.

Hike McNeil Point Trail 600M steeply SE up the clearing (or snowfield

Droves of Western pasqueflower tickle the senses near McNeil Point shelter in mid-August.

depending), catching a few tight switchbacks in the thin trees near the top. Soon meet and climb the N ridge of McNeil Point Summit for ¼ mi more to the S, mostly in the open with a few boulders and then pines. Soak in the vistas of Mount St. Helens, Lost Lake, Mount Rainier, Mount Adams, and of course Mount Hood.

Begin to traverse right (SW) on Trail 600M more than ½ mi over to the shelter on the bluff by crossing wildflower-covered meadows, boulder fields, and snowfields (carefully), finally descending a few feet over to the doorless, old, stone shelter where there are many fine picnic spots scattered about. Return the same way; or use the super-steep shortcut described above; or continue to McNeil Point Summit, nestled between several glaciers, nearly 900 ft more up the open ridge to the best views of the day.

For the summit, and more of a workout, it's ¾ mi farther SE up the steep path. Move up the meadow, then slowly and very steeply gain the rounded ridge crest past the stunted wind-blown trees (krummholz). Finish up slick pumice to the boulder at the top. There are two routes side by side from the S for confident, experienced hikers that work 25 ft up the giant boulder (Ho Rock) seen from far below. It's airy but quite exciting on top. From the base of the boulder, walk around to the right finding a makeshift camp and flat spot on the side. Notice the continuation of the narrow, jagged ridge up to another challenging rocky bump (Co Rock) ¼ mi away, if you haven't had enough yet. See the long Glisan Glacier to the left (E) and the sizable Sandy Glacier to the S with Yocum Ridge W and S of that.

45 VISTA RIDGE TO CAIRN BASIN LOOP

ELEVATION: 5950 ft, with 1450 ft vertical gain plus almost 400 ft more for the loop into Eden Park

DISTANCE: 8 mi round-trip loop

DURATION: 3–5 hours round-trip

DIFFICULTY: Strenuous. Steeper only briefly, creek crossings easier later in summer, signed, narrow, ups/downs, popular but not crowded

---

TRIP REPORT: When the snow finally melts off the N ridges and slopes of Mount Hood, the relatively easier hikes to rolling lush meadows reveal themselves in full grandeur with a spectacle of wildflowers from late July through September! The Cairn Basin loop (described here) down into Eden Park then back up to finish down Vista Ridge is the shortest route of many to visit the area. It is also possible to use this TH to reach other destinations like McNeil Point, Barrett Spur, Elk Cove, and Dollar Lake. No fee or restroom.

TRAILHEAD: Vista Ridge TH. Take US-26 E from Portland 16¼ mi E of Sandy, turn left (NE) across from the Zigzag Inn and Zigzag Ranger Station on E Lolo Pass Road (FR-18) 10½ mi to the pass, turn right onto the second gravel road (FR-1810, toward Lost Lake) 5½ mi into paved 5 mi more, turn sharp right 5½ mi on FR-16 (into gravel), turn sharp right on FR-1650 for 3½ mi to the end (staying left at forks) with parking wherever there is room on the sides. It may be difficult to turn around if congested with vehicles (90 mi, 2 hours easy drive from Portland).

ROUTE: Begin SE up the overgrown section of road briefly to the better trail (Vista Ridge Trail 626) through the woods with medium-sized Douglas fir and western hemlock. Hike less than ½ mi to a saddle. Take Trail 626 right (S) up the ridge more than 2 mi to the next major intersection (for Eden Park) in the high country. Once on the ridge, fill out a free self-issue Wilderness Permit. Then follow Trail 626 right (opposite Old Vista Ridge Trail 626A actually heading left) quite easily for the entire length of the ridge through mostly burnt forest from the Dollar Lake Fire (autumn 2011). The ground cover has been making a great comeback with avalanche lilies, bear grass, and others coming through. About ¼ mi S of the juncture with the registration station is a faint fork with Trail 626 splitting into two trails. Take the easier angle which heads left, straight over the ridge crest, through the burn, and down to a saddle before moving right to meet the other path, then continuing left (S) again. The rest to the Eden Park intersection is fairly straightforward. Newer views through the burn along the way include the Clear Branch valley to Laurance Lake, and Owl Point to the top of Mount Adams.

You break out into the first of many wildflower-covered meadows near the three-way intersection with Eden Park and can see out to Mount Hood, Mount Adams, Mount Rainier, and Mount St. Helens. Stay left (SE) on Vista Ridge Trail toward Wy'East Basin ignoring the turn right down into Eden Park (end of the clockwise loop). Walk easily into Wy'East Basin less than ½ mi to another three-way juncture. The Cairn Basin loop continues right on Timberline Trail 600 at the sign; but as long as you're here, head left (E) deeper into Wy'East Basin on Trail 600 only a hundred yards or so through the meadows and sparse trees to the faint juncture for Barrett Spur on the right (S). The wildflowers are striking near the little creeks right after the snow melts in August or so.

Walk W back from the bottom of Barrett Spur Trail 600D to the three-way juncture and continue left (W) on Timberline Trail almost ¼ mi to outstanding views down Vista Ridge to some big volcanoes in Washington, and Barrett Spur up to Mount Hood. Traverse less than a mile to Cairn Basin and the stone shelter near the next intersection (to McNeil Point on Trail 600 or your next goal on Eden Park Trail 600H). For the basin and shelter you will pass through more meadows below steep rocky drainages and then move down turns to cross Ladd Creek wherever it is safe to do so. If it is too rough, then it may also be rough at the lower crossing of the same creek in Eden Park. Again, late summer into August and September it's usually not a problem. Climb the other side of the creek on Trail 600 to enter the thin forest in Cairn Basin with campsites scattered around to the old open stone shelter just off the trail, most likely surrounded by many wildflowers, including paintbrush, avalanche lilies, lupine, and trillium. Follow the obvious path with rocks lining the trail to the nearby intersection near a tiny colorful babbling brook.

For McNeil Point, stay left on Trail 600 for ½ mi (crossing yet another arm of Ladd Creek), and then take the McNeil Point Trail left (signed) with more difficulty up

almost a mile to the point (11 mi round-trip). For the loop on Eden Park Trail 600H, follow the signage right (N) down tight switchbacks ½ mi through a few trees to the scenic meadow. From there, Mount Hood is in front of you standing proudly above the park. Work down to cross Ladd Creek carefully finding Trail 600H on the other side up a tad. Hike less than a mile NE to the Vista Ridge juncture up steeper turns through more wildflower-covered meadows with views of the Cascades prevailing (as well as the local mountains to the Columbia River including Lost Lake Butte next to Lost Lake). Once you are finally at the top and end of the loop, it's all downhill to the left (N) on the Vista Ridge Trail 2½ mi to the TH.

Glowing paintbrush encroach the trail in Eden Park.

ELEVATION: 7320 ft at Barrett Spur Viewpoint (Green Knoll); 7863 ft on Barrett Spur Summit; with vertical gains of 2820 ft, and 3365 ft

DISTANCE: Less than 4½ mi up directly to the viewpoint, 9 mi round-trip; Less than 5 mi up to the true summit, 9¾ mi round-trip loop with Dollar Lake near Elk Cove

DURATION: 3–4 hours up, 6–8 hours round-trip loop

DIFFICULTY: Mix of strenuous for Barrett Spur Viewpoint (long, steady steep, narrow at times, trail-finding, rocky, above tree line) and very challenging for Barrett Spur Summit (loose scree and rock, more difficult with lingering snow, steep summit block, narrow but solid, slightly exposed near big boulders on top)

TRIP REPORT: Portlanders can easily see the huge rocky moraine ridge and summit N of Mount Hood on a clear day. And from the viewpoint or Barrett Spur Summit you can see into Washington's Cascades as well as the outrageous local panorama, including being directly between the (gigantic) Coe and Ladd Glaciers! The Vista Ridge TH provides the briefest route and loop option for this hike. No fee or restroom.

TRAILHEAD: Vista Ridge TH. See hike 45 for directions.

ROUTE: See hike 45 for the description to Wy'East Basin, taking a left (E) at the second three-way juncture from the top of Vista Ridge Trail 626 onto Timberline Trail 600 a hundred yards or so through the pretty meadows and sparse trees. Arrive at the faint juncture for Barrett Spur on the right (S) at one of two arms on Clear Branch Creek crossing the Timberline Trail within a few feet of each other (less than 3 mi from the TH).

Leave Trail 600 for Barrett Spur Trail 600D up ¼ mi S through the meadows (staying on Trail 600D at a nearby faint juncture); the route steepens only somewhat and will be more difficult to follow with snow coverage. Keep heading toward the moraine shoulder on the right (between Wy'East and Cairn Basins) that curves SE to meet the main (N) ridge (and return route for the loop) near Barrett Spur. You will follow the E side of the shoulder up a mile with trees shrinking to old gnarled snags along the wild setting as you see your goal for the remainder.

After hiking up snowfields and past more stunted whitebark pines, reach the main ridge (between Elk Cove and Wy'East Basin at about 7000 ft) near a cairn which

Barrett Spur under Mount Hood from the last vegetation.

marks the brief scenic return lollipop loop option down Dollar Lake Trail 600C near Elk Cove. Stay right (S) on Trail 600D instead another ¼ mi and 400 ft up to Barrett Spur Viewpoint (a wide, rocky, flatter saddle out of the wind zone) at the base of the stunning Ladd Glacier, with the Coe Glacier just below the summit of Mount Hood. Survey the area and return by the same route down the N ridge (or the slightly longer lollipop loop past Dollar Lake on Trail 600C; see below) to finish N down Vista Ridge.

For Barrett Spur Summit from Barrett Spur Viewpoint, hike up the steep narrow ridge left (SE) of the saddle a long ¼ mi to a little fake summit. From the high ridge you see the boulder-topped summit 100 ft or so away. Work easier past bigger rocks and loose scree, and scramble the last bit briefly without difficulty. Be careful not to fall down onto either glacier or into the Coe Glacier's many crevasses. Above you under Mount Hood is Pulpit Rock with Cooper Spur to the left (SE) and Yocum Ridge to the right (SW), as well as every other view you've had all day, only better; much, much better!

Return down Trail 600D carefully to the viewpoint saddle and then head down the main ridge to the juncture for the counterclockwise lollipop loop past Dollar Lake. You will enjoy the splendor from the open, wide ridge down a friendly grade N less than a mile to the cairned juncture for Trail 600C; then you will move a bit to the right (E) of the ridge following Trail 600C easily another ½ mi to Trail 600. The pines become larger again as you see the 6300-acre burn area from Elk Cove to Stranahan Ridge and much to the immediate N too. You cross a wash to the right (E) side of tiny Dollar Lake, which is the name of the famous fire that destroyed thousands of acres of forest in 2011 but ironically and thankfully left the lake area somehow completely unscathed!

Continue N on Trail 600C less than ¼ mi from Dollar Lake (slightly misplaced on USGS maps) to the Timberline Trail 600. Turn left (W), traversing Wy'East Basin ¾ mi across little streams surrounded by wildflowers (past Pinnacle Ridge Trail on the right and Barrett Spur Trail on the left) to the three-way juncture with Cairn Basin. Turn right down Vista Ridge Trail 2¾ mi N to the TH.

MOUNT JEFFERSON

OPAL CREEK

BULL OF THE WOODS WILDERNESS

47 Silver Falls State Park 151

48 Butte Creek Falls to
Abiqua Falls 155

49 Table Rock................................. 158

50 Rooster Rock to
Pechuck Lookout 160

51 Little North Santiam Loop to
Three Pools 163

52 Henline Mountain and
Henline Falls............................. 167

53 Opal Creek................................. 170

54 Whetstone Mountain 173

55 Dome Rock 177

56 Big Slide Mountain to
Bull of the Woods Loop............ 180

57 Lower Soda Creek Falls............ 183

58 Iron Mountain Lookout to
Cone Peak Loop 185

59 Maxwell Butte............................ 189

60 Three Fingered Jack Loop 190

61 Porcupine Rock to
Cirque Lake Loop...................... 194

62 Upper Downing Creek Falls 197

63 Grizzly Peak 199

64 Triangulation Peak 201

65 Bear Point 202

66 Pacific Crest Trail to
Park Ridge Summit 204

67 Jefferson Park to
Park Ridge Summit 207

47   SILVER FALLS STATE PARK

ELEVATION: 1565 ft at Upper North Falls, with more than 1000 ft vertical gain total including ups/downs

DISTANCE: 9 mi round-trip loop including all waterfalls and spur trails

DURATION: At least 4 hours round-trip for the long loop

DIFFICULTY: Moderate. Some steeper areas, stairs, ups/downs, well signed, popular, can be shortened

---

TRIP REPORT: The Trail of Ten Falls Loop is an Oregon classic to be enjoyed by waterfall enthusiasts of all ages at any time of year with spring weekends being the busiest. The longer loop can be shortened to at least four smaller ones, a South Falls loop, an upper and lower loop (that are less than 3 mi each) and a middle loop (5 mi) beginning at Winter Falls TH or South Falls TH. A special $5 day use fee is required at all three THs, and there are restrooms at North Falls TH and South Falls TH (flush toilets).

TRAILHEAD: Silver Falls State Park. Take I-5 S from Portland to exit 253 in Salem, turn left for OR-22 E (Detroit Lake/Bend) briefly to exit 9 for OR-214 N around 16 mi to Silver Falls State Park South Falls Day Use Area. Continue on OR-214 N 1 mi to the Winter Falls TH (small pullout on left), and 1 mi more to North Falls TH on the left (72 mi, less than 1½ hours from Portland). Alternately shorter and less time-consuming from Portland proper, take I-205 S to exit 10 (Molalla) for OR-213 S 30 mi to Silverton, turn left on OR-214 S winding 13½ mi to North Falls TH (57 mi, 1¼ hours from Portland).

ROUTE: Begin from the one of many parking areas (A or F) at the busy South Falls TH (complete with info center, old lodge, café, restaurant, gift shop, nature

The intriguing Winter Falls worth the brief effort.

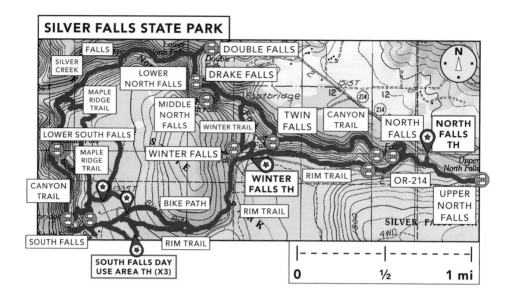

SILVER FALLS STATE PARK

FALLS
SILVER CREEK
LOWER NORTH FALLS
DOUBLE FALLS
DRAKE FALLS
MAPLE RIDGE TRAIL
MIDDLE NORTH FALLS
WINTER TRAIL
TWIN FALLS
CANYON TRAIL
NORTH FALLS
NORTH FALLS TH
LOWER SOUTH FALLS
MAPLE RIDGE TRAIL
WINTER FALLS
CANYON TRAIL
WINTER FALLS TH
RIM TRAIL
OR-214
UPPER NORTH FALLS
BIKE PATH
RIM TRAIL
SILVER FA
SOUTH FALLS
RIM TRAIL
SOUTH FALLS DAY USE AREA TH (X3)
N
0   ½   1 mi

store), the tiny Winter Falls TH (no pay station but fee required) in the middle, or the quiet North Falls TH (with fee station). For this hike, we begin from North Falls TH and complete the longest loop heading clockwise to bang out the more boring section of trail that parallels the highway first, albeit through some big old growth Douglas fir and Western hemlock.

Follow the signage from the parking lot across the footbridge and turn right at the juncture under the same bridge and highway bridge on the spur to Upper North Falls for a (¾ mi round-trip) side trip. Follow North Fork Silver Creek on its S side along the lush overgrown trail with some pretty big trees. Walk up less than 100 ft in elevation to this midsized little gem that plunges 65 ft off a basalt cliff into a nice pool. See the falls from the path before you arrive at a few stone steps down to the creek for the best perspective. Return down the spur past North Falls TH to the fork for the Rim Trail. Continue left of the fence for the clockwise loop instead of heading right down Canyon Trail to North Falls.

See a small cascade on the main creek as you take Rim Trail W up a bit then down gradually more than ¼ mi to a faraway view of North Falls high in the valley surrounded by evergreens. Hear the falls first from the beautiful forest lined with ferns and more. For an even better shot, climb the steep and rough spur path left 30 ft up to a fence at a pullout on the nearby highway. Continue on the wide trail slightly down ¾ mi to the signed Winter Falls TH. With a decent flow (unless it's summer when they nearly dry up), it's worth it to take another side trip right (N) down Winter Trail ¼ mi and a long switchback to Winter Falls directly above the second switchback (134 ft, partly as cascade). There's a nice bench and a narrow spur below the switchback you can take 10 ft for a better picture of the lovely or disappointing waterfall depending on the season.

From the Winter Falls TH at about 1 hour and less than 2½ mi with spurs into the longest loop, take the Rim Trail left (W) 1¼ mi, which undulates gently to the large South Falls Day Use Area. You walk next to the highway and a bike path, ignoring the first junctures left, then taking Rim Trail left when the bike path crosses and heads more to the right in a somewhat confusing area. No worries though, as the trails meet once you cross a side road and arrive at parking area A. Follow the stone trail briefly to a stone circle with many signed trails emanating (3½ mi from North Falls TH including spurs). Walk left to the lodge area for the unexciting look behind the lodge to catch a glimpse of Frenchie Falls (48 ft), which dries up in summer.

From the stone circle, follow signage straight past the nearby nature store (with restroom) en route to the top of South Falls from the fenced-in area. Walk far left along a rock wall for a poor view from the very top of the falls or walk right for South Falls Viewpoint (ignoring Maple Ridge Trail). Both ways lead people to the gravel (then roughly paved) path along a wooden fence down an easy switchback that takes you through a cavern behind the park's most prestigious waterfall (177 ft). Continue around past South Falls and down left on Canyon Trail beyond a picturesque footbridge (taking folks back to the day use area for the shortest loop) at ½ mi from the top of the trail.

The main route on Canyon Trail is fairly level for ½ mi and then you see the top of the wider Lower South Falls (93 ft high) down through the trees from some wooden fencing. It's another ½ mi to gaze outward from the water as you follow the railing

The popular South Falls, like many in the State Park, allows visitors to walk behind the flowing water for multiple great angles.

down 48 steps to a switchback, 20 steps to a second switchback, 19 steps to a third switchback, 37 steps to a fourth switchback, 41 steps to a fifth switchback, and then 19 more steps to additional wooden fencing and a rocky path that goes behind the wide and attractive waterfall. There are many great angles as the water cascades near the bottom and actually looks best from under the falls. Walk ¼ mi, down a tad and up steeper, to the next juncture (5½ mi from North Falls TH with spurs).

Stay left on Canyon Trail along Silver Creek instead of turning right on the steeper Maple Ridge Trail (lower loop to the day use area) for 1½ mi to the juncture with the Winter Trail and more options; there are several notable waterfalls in between. Along the way to the Winter Trail juncture, the wide path moves down then is level as it's very jungle-like in the canyon. You see a 25-ft seasonal waterfall on the left falling into Silver Creek, then hike up a bit easier and down a switchback to cross the bridge back to the N side of the creek. Move E up slightly and see Lower North Falls (30 ft) to the right. This is a wide and short true cascade right off the trail. Immediately after is the sign and spur left (NE) less than a hundred yards to Double Falls (141 ft with 43 ft above) in another splendid alcove on a decent side creek that rarely dries up. For a better picture take the steep spur left for 15 ft before the end of the trail.

From the main trail see miniscule Drake Falls (27 ft) from the viewing platform and walk up some to the fork for Middle North Falls (106 ft). Take this spur path down right behind yet another waterfall and continue briefly to the end for the best view from the mossy amphitheater. Return and turn right back on Canyon Trail quickly to the Winter Trail juncture (7 mi from North Falls TH with spurs). Turn right (S) over the bridge ¾ mi fairly steeply to shorten the loop on Winter Trail to the Winter Falls TH and Rim Trail, otherwise stay on North Fork Silver Creek ¼ mi to Twin Falls (30 ft). You move up, then down, to poor views of the mediocre falls, the safety fence being partially to blame.

Stay on the creek (Canyon Trail) almost another mile E to the grand finale in North Falls (136 ft). The trail there is level but overgrown at times in summer with salmonberries and others as you pass a bonus 5-ft cascade across the entire creek. Then you head up steadily and can finally see North Falls plunging off the lip before you walk behind the striking waterfall with its humongous underhanging cavern. From here, it's less than ½ mi to the TH. There are many good angles as you climb 80 stone steps, then follow the narrowing trail next to a green fence adjacent a rocky cliff band, to one more great shot of North Falls within the emerald amphitheater. Arrive briefly at the end of the loop and take the trail over the footbridge briefly to North Falls TH or walk right a mile to the Winter Falls TH on the Rim Trail.

ELEVATION: 1820 ft at Upper Butte Creek Falls; 1720 ft at Butte Creek Falls; 1150 ft at Abiqua Falls; with vertical gains of about 200 ft for both falls on Butte Creek, and about 850 ft for Abiqua Falls where most people park before the road becomes too rough for 2WD passenger cars (only 300 ft from the official TH)

DISTANCE: 1 mi round-trip loop for Butte Creek Falls; 4 mi round-trip for Abiqua Falls where most people park (1 mi round-trip from the official TH)

DURATION: 1 hour round-trip with breaks for either falls from the official THs; 2–3 hours round-trip for Abiqua Falls with the longer route; 3–5 hours round-trip combining both hikes

DIFFICULTY: Mix of moderate for Butte Creek Falls (brief, solid trails, drop-offs, steeper overlook for Butte Creek Falls may be omitted) and strenuous for Abiqua Falls (very steep bushwhack paths, tough if muddy, ropes in place, fairly brief, negotiating riverbank)

TRIP REPORT: Avid hikers will combine both areas within only a few miles of each other as the crow flies, however Abiqua Falls is not family-friendly in the least and injuries on the trail are not uncommon. In fact, the drive down to Abiqua Falls TH has deteriorated over the years and is only really suitable for high-clearance or AWD vehicles. To get more of an actual hike in, most people park in tiny pullouts 1½ mi from the TH and walk the steep rocky road. Because the nearby Silver Falls area receives all the attention, the local waterfalls here have escaped most people's radar but should not be overlooked, even with rougher roads. Please be considerate, and for everything you bring down to the falls remember to pack it out. Abiqua Falls is on private property granting public access as long as people are respectful. For these jaunts we warm up with the lovely Butte Creek Falls area first, then move onto the grand prize in Abiqua Falls, which is very similar to waterfalls in the Columbia River Gorge in grandeur. There are no fees, and an outhouse is present at Butte Creek Falls TH (B.Y.O.T.P.).

TRAILHEAD: Butte Creek Falls TH or Abiqua Falls TH. For Butte Creek Falls TH, take I-205 S from Portland to exit 10 (Molalla) for OR-213 S 22½ mi, turn left at a yellow caution signal in Marquam onto S Nowlens Bridge Road 2½ mi, turn left after the bridge onto winding Crooked Finger Road 9 mi into gravel 2 mi more S, turn left on FR-400 (small sign for Butte Creek Falls-Rhody Lake) 1¾ mi down the narrow,

Abiqua Falls thunders into a bright green pool.

slightly rougher, steep washboard gravel road, passing through an old clear-cut, then back into the woods steeply to a signed small pullout on the left (50 mi, less than 1½ hours from Portland).

For Abiqua Falls TH, return up to Crooked Finger Road and turn right about ½ mi, turn left on gravel FR-300 (small signs for Abiqua Falls) down very steeply with loose rock 2½ mi to a locked gate at the official TH with parking on the sides. Those with 2WD should park after several forks 1 mi down FR-300 (directly after or at a right-hand fork that leads to a huge open area) with only a few small pullouts available. From the pullouts there is at least ½ mi of undesirable road (steep, monstrous potholes, rough gravel, narrow, 40-minute drive from Butte Creek Falls TH).

ROUTE: For the short counterclockwise loop, head straight down N from the pullout (right of the kiosk) on Butte Creek Falls Trail to visit Upper Butte Creek Falls first. Immediately notice the lush mossy forest with ferns and much more between giant Douglas fir, Western hemlock, and Vine maple. Move NW down friendly turns to a three-way juncture after first hearing, and then seeing, the upper falls through mossy trees around a corner before the spur trail. At ¼ mi from the TH turn hard right (SE) from the three-way juncture onto the spur trail down 2 steeper switchbacks briefly to Upper Butte Creek Falls (26 ft high, 40 ft wide); its broad curtain falls off the lip within the mossy grotto into a lovely pool suitable for swimming on a hot day! There is even a huge cavern to get a different perspective looking out from underneath the falls.

Back on Butte Creek Falls Trail from the three-way juncture at less than ½ mi in, continue right less than ¼ mi NW to the main falls. Walk past the return path on the left (little lollipop loop) back to the TH and stay right down 2 switchbacks to the slightly rougher trail. See the top of the Butte Creek Falls on the right below a 10-ft cascade and avoid a very steep and dangerous bushwhack path down to poor views of both. Cross a solid footbridge and walk down to a narrow rise with an opening and decent views of Butte Creek Falls (78 ft), a narrow ribbon that widens a bit with a decent flow and cascades somewhat into a pretty pool.

Be very careful if you continue down steep rocks 30 ft or so to a wide-open

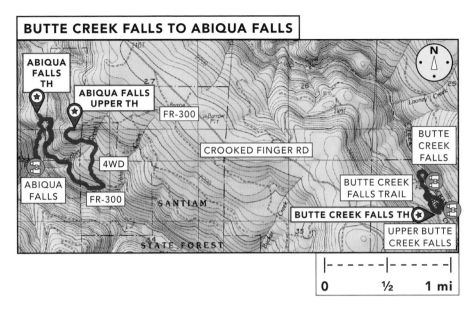

BUTTE CREEK FALLS TO ABIQUA FALLS

ABIQUA FALLS TH

ABIQUA FALLS UPPER TH

FR-300

CROOKED FINGER RD

BUTTE CREEK FALLS

4WD

ABIQUA FALLS

FR-300

SANTIAM

BUTTE CREEK FALLS TRAIL

BUTTE CREEK FALLS TH

STATE FOREST

UPPER BUTTE CREEK FALLS

0   ½   1 mi

perch without a fence, far above the creek. The thin, picturesque canyon formed by the falls holds another cascade below the main drop, as the water cuts through bigger rock in the creek for yet another small waterfall difficult to see from the overlook (be cautious gazing over the edge). A narrow spur that continues to the right from the overlook quickly drops super-steeply down uneven, possibly wet rock ledges all the way to the creek and is not at all recommended. Return back up to the loop trail on the right and move up a switchback with stone steps through the beautiful forest very easily leveling out SE to the TH.

For Abiqua Falls only a few miles W of Butte Creek Falls, follow the rocky road from the upper parking pullouts for about 1½ mi to Abiqua Falls Trail on the left denoted by a large white sign (Abbey Foundation of OR) down on a mossy tree. Step aside for vehicles navigating the difficult road section, as you will encounter brief uphill stints too. From the official TH near the rusty old gate, walk back along the road 50 ft and turn right onto the trail. Descend the wide path S that narrows through the lush forest with abundant undergrowth. The route quickly becomes so steep that several ropes are in place as an option to aid enthusiasts briefly down to the creek ¼ mi from the road.

Hike left (S) along Abiqua Creek as a couple paths move in the same direction a few feet from each other, one on the creek and one that leaves it at times of high water to move with a bit more difficulty past trees, boulders, and mossy rocks. Either way, hop and steer by obstacles briefly until you round the corner and reach the vast, colorful, columnar basalt amphitheater. Abiqua Falls (92 ft high, 20 ft wide) is quite a spectacle as the water roars into a large green pool. Explore both sides of the pool with the best pictures coming from the far left side of the falls, although constant spray is slightly problematic. Spend some quality time before returning steeply to your vehicle.

49 | TABLE ROCK

ELEVATION: 4881 ft, with 1500 ft vertical gain

DISTANCE: 4½ mi up, 9 mi round-trip

DURATION: 1½ hours up, 3–4 hours round-trip

DIFFICULTY: Moderate. Steady, not steep, boulder field, more difficult with snow, drop-offs near top

---

TRIP REPORT: The 6000-acre Table Rock Wilderness gets overlooked, except by locals, as most Portlanders drive farther toward Mount Jefferson if heading in that direction. This closer drive takes people to surprisingly rugged mountains known as the Old Cascades; basalt cliffs and pinnacles above the Molalla River corridor afford distinguished views of several big Cascade Mountains in three states on a clear day! Except for the clear-cutting, the region remains fairly pristine with plenty of wildlife, taking hikers through Douglas fir, hemlock, wildflowers, thick flora, and a recovering forest section from an old fire. No fee required, and a portable outhouse is present April through October.

TRAILHEAD: Table Rock TH. Take I-205 S from Portland to exit 10 (Molalla) onto OR-213 S 12½ mi, turn left on S Union Mills Road 3¾ mi, turn right on OR-211 S ¾ mi, turn left on S Wright Road 1½ mi, turn right on S Feyrer Park Road ½ mi, stay straight on S Dickey Prairie Road 5¼ mi. Turn right over the Molalla River across Glen Avon bridge and stay left on narrowing S Molalla Forest Road 12½ mi (watching for logging trucks, two outhouses en route), fork slight left on gravel Upper Molalla Road 7 mi to the end (with two more signed forks to watch for: a sharp right at 2½ mi and a left fork 1 mi farther with a junction at Quarry Road) with parking on the sides (55 mi, less than 2 hours from Portland).

ROUTE: Begin past the signage over the berm on Table Rock Trail immediately passing a nasty, old, open-air outhouse on the right. The scenery improves from there as

Final feet to Table Rock with snow lingering in early May.

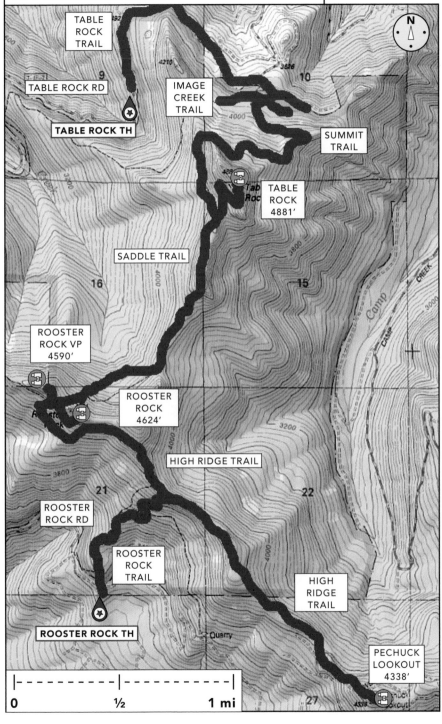

TABLE ROCK TRAIL

N

TABLE ROCK RD

9

IMAGE CREEK TRAIL

10

TABLE ROCK TH

SUMMIT TRAIL

TABLE ROCK 4881'

SADDLE TRAIL

16

15

ROOSTER ROCK VP 4590'

ROOSTER ROCK 4624'

HIGH RIDGE TRAIL

21

22

ROOSTER ROCK RD

ROOSTER ROCK TRAIL

ROOSTER ROCK TH

Quarry

HIGH RIDGE TRAIL

PECHUCK LOOKOUT 4338'

0   ½   1 mi

27

you easily walk (N then SE) up the old road with tiny creek crossings around 1½ mi to the Summit Trail on the right. The path will undulate through the tall forest a bit under huge cliffy pinnacles leading up to Table Rock. Turn right (S) on the obvious narrower Summit Trail from the road at a little creek 100 ft to a sign where rhododendrons bloom in late June and early July. Snow may still be lingering. Stay on the main trail instead of turning left or right onto Image Creek Trail at the turns.

It's 1¾ mi to the next intersection at a small saddle S of Table Rock. You will follow the rhododendron- and wildflower-choked Summit Trail SE without trouble along a sharp slope adjacent to a little creek. Then you will hike right (SSW) up a petite shoulder under a rocky spire, traverse right (W) underneath a cliff, and soon turn left (SSE) around Table Rock's NW ridge through more firs, pines, and hemlocks. You cross a scree field to the small saddle intersection with Saddle Trail, S of Table Rock. That trail moves right (S) to a little viewpoint, then up and down the connecting ridge toward the rock outcrop known as Rooster Rock. That route descends several hundred feet, however, from the ridgeline before climbing fairly steeply just as much to the other ridge between Rooster Rock (hike 50) and Rooster Rock Viewpoint.

Stay left (N) instead on the much easier Summit Trail ½ mi up a switchback, and then another switchback as the trees thin onto the high ridge with views opening widely. Follow the trail left less than ¼ mi along the open ridge N attentively to the very top; you might be able see over the clear-cuts to all of the major Cascade volcanoes from Mount Rainier to Mount Shasta (on a very clear day)! Return by the same route.

50 ROOSTER ROCK TO PECHUCK LOOKOUT

ELEVATION: 4624 ft on Rooster Rock, 4590 ft on Rooster Rock Viewpoint, 4338 ft at Pechuck Lookout; with vertical gains of about 1500 ft for both Rooster Rock and Rooster Rock Viewpoint; about 2500 ft including Pechuck Lookout (2000 ft for the lookout alone)

DISTANCE: 2 mi up to Rooster Rock or Rooster Rock Viewpoint, 4½ mi round-trip for both; plus 3 mi round-trip for Pechuck Lookout spur (5 mi round-trip lookout alone)

DURATION: 1½–2 hours up, 3–4 hours round-trip; plus 2 hours for Pechuck Lookout spur

DIFFICULTY: Mix of strenuous for Rooster Rock Viewpoint or Pechuck Lookout (steady steep with breaks, wide, drop-offs, route-finding, undermaintained and blowdowns possible for lookout with ups/downs) and very challenging for Rooster Rock (Class 4, solid holds, loose rock, brief, slight exposure, drop-offs, scrambling)

The author enjoys the less crowded Rooster Rock for the total solar eclipse while dozens of others experience it from Rooster Rock Viewpoint.

TRIP REPORT: Rooster Rock and its smaller neighbor Rooster Rock Viewpoint to the W (falsely called Chicken Rock by some) are prominent rocky basalt fins on the southern ridge of the Table Rock Wilderness (not to be confused with other pinnacles named Rooster Rock like one in the Menagerie Wilderness and one in the western Columbia Gorge). Here we have two straightforward day hikes with wonderful, far-reaching perspectives, Rooster Rock Viewpoint being the more family-friendly jaunt. Pechuck Lookout and the steeper spur trail have both deteriorated somewhat over the years but not enough to frighten heartier hikers away from visiting the only intact two-story stone structure (built in 1932) in Oregon. Closed more than a half century ago, it's now kept up by the BLM and open to the public (even though vandalized), but may be best served as an emergency shelter only at this point. No fee or restroom.

TRAILHEAD: Rooster Rock TH (Table Rock Wilderness). Take I-205 S from Portland to exit 10 (Molalla) onto OR-213 S 12½ mi, turn left on S Union Mills Road 3¾ mi, turn right on OR-211 S ¾ mi, turn left on S Wright Road 1½ mi, turn right on S Feyrer Park Road ½ mi, stay straight on S Dickey Prairie Road 5¼ mi. Turn right over the Molalla River across Glen Avon bridge and stay left on narrowing S Molalla Forest Road 12½ mi (watching for logging trucks, two outhouses en route, left of fork at 11 mi), fork right on Copper Creek Road over the bridge ½ mi farther, fork left on one lane Rooster Rock Road (small hidden sign, rough gravel, dusty, 2WD okay, AWD preferred) less than 6½ mi to the end in a small lot (55 mi, 1½ hours more or less from Portland).

ROUTE: Begin on the slightly hidden Rooster Rock Trail left of the road, and follow it NNE without difficulty 1 mi and 1000 ft up to the High Ridge Trail intersection. You will ascend the wide, smooth Rooster Rock Trail steeply (with micro-breaks) through the older forest with thinner trees and a few bigger Doug firs for 22 switchbacks and turns to the unsigned juncture. From there, to the right (SE) 1½ mi up and down the ridge is the historic Pechuck Lookout. Turn sharp left (NW) instead on High Ridge Trail 1 mi to the Rooster Rock–Rooster Rock Viewpoint saddle. You will head down right of the ridge slightly, then up, down, and up to the ridge steeper within the first ¼ mi with glimpses to Mount Hood through the woods. Soon traverse left (S) of the ridge easier with shots up to the right of a few tall basalt pillars then the larger Rooster Rock on the high ridge. Pass through a small open meadow with trillium, paintbrush, bear grass, aster, and wild geranium; turn up the switchback just before the trees 100 ft to an unsigned crossroads at the nearby saddle.

From the saddle crossroads, the steep and overgrown Saddle Trail moves straight (NE) back into the woods down and up 1½ mi to a juncture under Table Rock. Tacking on Table Rock would add 4½ mi round-trip of steep hiking and might be best as a separate outing. See Table Rock (hike 49) for more of the description. Turning left at the saddle on the faint spur path in the opening leads NW briefly and steeply 100 ft up to Rooster Rock Viewpoint. Be careful if you scramble boulders up the side pinnacle near the open top. On a clear day you'll see Table Rock to the N across the valley, as well as Mount St. Helens, Mount Rainier, and Mount Adams. To the SW is nearby Rooster Rock above the trees with Mount Jefferson behind, and on a bluebird day Three Fingered Jack, Mount Washington, and even Three Sisters can be made out!

Return to the saddle and bushwhack across the main trail for Rooster Rock through trees 75 ft the to the base of the rocky fin jutting above the forested ridge. Work over rocks and boulders around the right (S) side of the outcrop immediately right of a 12-ft-long chimney. Fight past minimal brush to ledges leading very steeply with decent holds (be sure to check) to the top of the chimney, then carefully follow a long ledge to the right 30–40 ft below (S of) the ridge crest for about 100 ft watching for loose rock along the partially exposed section. A few cairns may help, otherwise pick the best of a few possible choices before the sheer cliff at the SE end of Rooster Rock. Climb cracks and brief ramps 30 ft or so up the rock or cross a bit more brush as you hug the rock ascending very steeply left to a wider rocky gully with some low flora clinging on and better footing. Then scramble N steeply, a bit easier, 40 ft up to the highest ridge. Turn right (SE) to walk 35 ft without trouble carefully over boulders or just right a tad safer to the very top with views to the local Wilderness and everything as seen from Rooster Rock Viewpoint plus Mount Hood, and far more dramatic perched above the cliffs. See the

The Pechuck Lookout in Table Rock Wilderness.

nearby slender rock towers ESE from the E end of Rooster Rock and return down by the same route using caution to the saddle.

From the intersection on the ridge, you make your next decision—the trail right that leads back (SSW) 1 mi to Rooster Rock TH, or the trail straight ahead 1½ mi to Pechuck Lookout. Most of the views from the lookout are now overgrown with trees but there's still a good angle of Table Rock across the valley and the ambling will definitely give seasoned hikers a full day.

For the lookout, continue SE on the undulating High Ridge Trail without any real concern even as you navigate some brushy trail, and then move over or around twenty or so downed trees near a little high point (some TLC on the trail here might make a big difference). The path fluctuates past many rhododendrons from being fairly steep (with flagging as the forest tightens) to fairly level at times including to the next juncture with an older road and an aging kiosk. A small sign for Pechuck Lookout points across the road (about 1 mi from the TH juncture) to the trail. Walk SE up briefly then down to a small tree-covered saddle with your goal seen far above. Climb 8 switchbacks very steeply and then be careful along a cliff-lined open cirque with views back N to Table Rock and even part of Mount Hood to the NE. Pass an old road coming from the left as you climb steeper and wider up right, past an aged open-air composting toilet (on the right). The route becomes very steep again for 2 switchbacks with overgrown rhododendron to the right-hand turn (leaving the ridge trail) onto level ground in the clearing home to the Pechuck Lookout. There is a fire pit, a rusty old single bed frame, and the adorable stone lookout worth exploring respectfully.

51 LITTLE NORTH SANTIAM LOOP TO THREE POOLS

ELEVATION: 1480 ft at Shady Cove Campground (E) TH, with around 1000 ft vertical gain with ups/downs plus the optional bike ride

DISTANCE: 4½ mi one way, 8½ mi round-trip loop with a bike

DURATION: Around 3–5 hours with breaks, 5–6 hours round-trip loop

DIFFICULTY: Mix of moderate for Three Pools Day Use Area or a short walk down Little North Santiam Trail to Three Pools then back up from Shady Cove Campground TH (steep next to trail at times, rocky, slippery when wet) and strenuous (many ups/downs, steep at times, narrow, overgrown, tough bike ride for loop, potholes, gravel, ups/downs, dusty)

TRIP REPORT: Underappreciated is this wonderful trail that parallels one of the most beautiful rivers in Oregon or anywhere for that matter, but doesn't see nearly the number of visitors that nearby more family-friendly Opal Creek Trail receives (hike 53). That said, Three Pools Day Use Area within the Opal Creek Recreation Area is a slightly shorter drive, requires very little actual hiking (brief steep paths), and gets very busy on hot summer weekends (as the amount of trash is sadly noticeable). Little North Santiam Trail is also possible year-round because of its lower elevation with rain, snow, and ice bringing a stunning contrast of colors to the river corridor. Snowshoes may be necessary in winter as you would begin from the Little North Santiam (lower, W) TH and return by the same route after seeing Three Pools from the S side of the river (6½ mi round-trip).

Shuttle a bike (or another vehicle) to the Shady Cove Campground (upper E) TH and begin back down at the Little North Santiam (lower, W) TH for the loop. Begin at the upper E TH (sans the bike ride) and hike down 1¼ mi for a more family-friendly path to visit Three Pools or other rocky beaches for free, and return the same way. Or simply avoid the hiking for a visit to Three Pools and hike the trail another day. There is a separate $5 fee required for Three Pools Day Use Area parking. Northwest Forest Pass is only required at Shady Cove Campground (upper, E) TH, and a restroom is present at Shady Cove Campground and Three Pools Day Use Area.

TRAILHEAD: Three Pools Day Use Area, Shady Cove Campground (upper E) TH, and Little North Santiam (lower W) TH. Take I-5 S from Portland to exit 253 in Salem, turn left for OR-22 E (Detroit Lake/Bend) to Mehama, turn left at the second flashing signal (milepost 23, before bridge over Santiam River) on easy-to-miss Little North Fork Road for 14¾ twisting mi (with ½ mi unpaved dusty section). For Three Pools Day Use Area, follow Little North Fork Road into gravel FR-2209 for 1¼ mi; take the signed turnoff right on FR-2207 ¾ mi to Three Pools Day Use Area. For the Shady Cove Campground (upper, E) TH, continue on FR-2207 another mile beyond Three Pools; cross the bridge just past Shady Cove Campground; park in the pullout on the left with the signed TH on the right. For the optional bike loop, stash and lock your bike to something at this upper (E) TH then drive down to the lower (W) TH. From Shady Cove Campground (upper, E) TH to Little North Santiam (lower, W) TH, drive back to FR-2209, turn left 1¾ mi to Elkhorn Drive, turn left sharply ½ mi by crossing over the bridge into gravel as the road narrows and steepens up to the signed Little North Santiam TH with parking in the pullout on the left (90 mi, 1½ hours from Portland).

ROUTE: For Three Pools Day Use Area only, pay the fee and walk down from the scenic boardwalk, scrambling boulders and rocks steeply to the shoreline. The pools farthest left from the parking lot are easier to access but the sought-after gorgeous spire area is a bit steeper and right of the upper pools. All are worthy of inspecting

Kayakers call this gorgeous area at Three Pools "Thor's Playroom."

carefully. Use caution around the steep rock that slopes to the river and while jumping and diving in from many perches to cool off in summer. And cool off you will in the frigid clear river!

Look ahead for clues if you begin the easy hike down from the Shady Cove Campground TH, otherwise begin from the bottom at the Little North Santiam TH. From there, walk NNE down a few turns on the solid Trail 3338 with exposed tree roots toward the river as you pass narrow, moss-covered pines and ferns with a few bigger Douglas firs mixing in. Cross a tiny creek over a bridge and at ¼ mi in begin to parallel the Little North Santiam River heading E. Walk by more ferns, Oregon grape, salal, and moss-covered everything along the river (muddy when wet) coming to a short spur path on the left to Elkhorn Falls at more than ½ mi in. The angle of your view is improved from the boulders below the falls (as opposed to the view from the main trail) as water curtains down rocks across the entire river (or only the left side during lower flows). The waterfall empties into a large turquoise pool you may be tempted to dive into.

Back on Trail 3338, at nearly ¾ mi from Little North Santiam TH, fork to the right away from the river up steep turns, then walk easier up and down some to a very brief spur path down to the river for a swim (1 mi in). See Henline Mountain across the valley on the main route and move up 2 switchbacks steeper above a short, mossy cliff band. At almost 1¼ mi from this lower TH is a short spur to a poor look at the next falls area. The next immediate spur provides a better vantage point but is very steep; it forks with both short paths in the trees meeting quickly where you stop or scramble even steeper down to the river. From this point, you can see the mostly hidden Triple Falls coming down Henline Creek to the river as well as the much smaller Little North Santiam Falls as they pour into beautiful pools.

Shortly after this area, Trail 3338 becomes a bit rockier and turns uphill to the left; watch your footing while gazing down to the blue-green river. Walk past huge firs as the route steepens continuously up a switchback, turns, and a tight switchback to a rocky flat overlook (1¾ mi in). Then the trail eases but becomes overgrown somewhat as you move down a tad, up, and then down 2 switchbacks. The route turns rockier and steeper, but the trail becomes friendlier as you walk down another switchback to cross a tiny creek over another solid footbridge at about 2 mi from Little North Santiam TH.

Continue down steeper turns and switchbacks as the trail eases a bit past big, mossy boulders, ferns, and a few large Douglas fir closer to the river. At 2½ mi from the lower TH is a short spur path left to a nice rocky beach near a wide, shallow section of river. Soon after is a log bridge leading into the lush forest followed by another footbridge over another small stream. Pass a nice camp (down to the left at 2¾ mi in) with river access, then walk the narrower and slightly overgrown trail along an easy section to a view of the colorful river.

Move down a bit, then up over yet another solid bridge at 3 mi from the lower TH. Continue up, then over more level ground as you begin to hear voices coming from the Three Pools section of the Little North Santiam River. At 3¼ mi in is a small but great overlook from above the river (be careful). The second overlook gives way to a sweet shot of a 30-ft tall rocky pillar rising from the S bank of the brilliant green river between the lower pools. Wow! Shortly after, from the main trail, is the steep rocky spur path down directly to the spire—worth exploring and taking a rather brisk

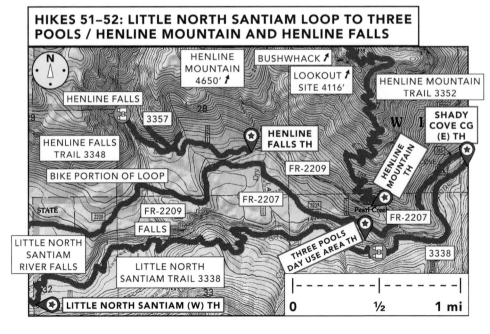

HIKES 51–52: LITTLE NORTH SANTIAM LOOP TO THREE POOLS / HENLINE MOUNTAIN AND HENLINE FALLS

plunge like everyone else on a warm day. You will find a few flatter spots and boulders to hang out on the less crowded side of the stream. There are fantastic views: downriver, below the spire to the lowest of Three Pools, and across to the steep rocky embankment; and up the river to a series of small cascades, the upper pools, and the bottom of Whetstone Mountain!

Return to Trail 3338 whenever you can tear yourself away, and continue left to Shady Cove Campground (upper) TH in a mile without any difficulty. You realize why the loop makes so much sense, as returning back to the lower TH would entail a lot more work with ups and downs. From the Three Pools area walk E down some on Trail 3338 for ½ mi and cross a lovely creek over a nice log bridge. Head up a switchback a bit more before descending slightly with a few tree roots and rocks mixing in, but the widening trail N provides the finest walking all day. The route levels with the river in sight and at 4 mi from the lower TH (almost ½ mi from the upper TH) is a steep spur path down to a secluded pebble beach and large pool. Continue on Trail 3338 through the old growth forest with trees not quite as imposing and views up to the cliffs and mountain above. See Shady Cove Campground across the river at 4¼ mi in with the trestle bridge barely visible ahead. Walk with ease up the wide trail to the nearby Shady Cove Campground TH to finish the hike.

For the 4-mi bike loop option, refer to the last of the TH directions and return to your vehicle at the Little North Santiam (lower) TH remembering you will have a few ups and downs en route. This is accomplished much easier with use of an electric bike (lucky me!), though even with that it's impossible to avoid the dusty road with other vehicles passing.

52 | HENLINE MOUNTAIN AND HENLINE FALLS

ELEVATION: 4116 ft at the lookout site; 4650 ft on Henline Mountain; 1780 ft near Henline Falls; with vertical gains of 2216 ft, 2800 ft, and 200 ft for the falls

DISTANCE: 2½ mi up to the lookout site, 5 mi round-trip; 3½ mi up to the summit of Henline Mountain, 7 mi round-trip; 1 mi up to the falls, 2 mi round-trip

DURATION: 1½ hours to the lookout site, 2½-3 hours round-trip; 2½ hours to the summit, 4-5 hours round-trip; ¼ hour to the falls, ½-1 hour round-trip

DIFFICULTY: Mix of strenuous for the lookout or summit (switchbacks, steeper at times, narrow, scree crossings) and easiest for the falls (family-friendly, wide, brief, drop-off areas near Henline Creek)

TRIP REPORT: Wonderful neighborhood in the Opal Creek Wilderness and often overlooked as most visitors continue to the nearby Opal Creek area. This great mountain with an old lookout site (edifice long gone) still has abundant views with even better vistas from the summit above, and a third option exists to visit nearby Henline Falls. Combine the lookout site or summit hike with a visit to the falls to put the icing on the cake, or come back multiple times to appreciate them all. Traction devices or snowshoes may be required until late spring. Northwest Forest Pass is required at both THs, and there are no restrooms.

TRAILHEAD: Henline Mountain TH or Henline Falls TH. Take I-5 S from Portland to exit 253 in Salem, turn left for OR-22 E (Detroit Lake/Bend) to Mehama, turn left at the second flashing signal (milepost 23, before bridge over Santiam River) on easy-to-miss Little North Fork Road for 14¾ twisting mi (with ½ mi unpaved dusty section), then into gravel FR-2209 for 1¼ mi to the turnoff for Three Pools on right. Stay left ¼ mi to Henline Falls TH (small sign) with a few parking spots on the left, or continue ¾ mi farther to Henline Mountain TH (another small sign) on the left with a small pullout on the right (85 mi, 1½ hours from Portland).

ROUTE: At Henline Mountain TH, fill out the free self-issue Wilderness Permit and proceed up Henline Mountain Trail 3352 steady steep for 4 quick switchbacks. Cross the bottom of a scree field (less than ½ mi from the TH) looking up right to a rocky spire you will soon pass from above. Ascend the first of 8 switchbacks in the next set heading NE. A 30-ft spur right could take you atop the spire you saw from below for views into the Little North Santiam valley across to Elkhorn Mountain. After 2 more switchbacks (1 mi from the TH) is another spur to the right with a somewhat larger and safer perch for a picture or picnic. The trail is easy to follow with a pleasant grade up and is slightly overgrown in places with Oregon grape, bear grass, rhododendron, salal, and ferns. After the eighth switchback, see through the trees to the cliffs ahead (almost 1½ mi from the TH).

Hike N up 3 switchbacks a bit steeper and cross the S ridge to a somewhat steep and narrow traverse. See rocky pinnacles left on the ridgeline and the top of Mount Jefferson to the right. Move down some and around a corner in the woods before the route becomes steeper and rockier up to a switchback at the bottom of the next scree field (2¼ mi from the TH). Continue along rocky turns W up the scree field, and after the fourth switchback cross the ridgeline back to the left easier with improved views back to Mount Jefferson. Hike up shortly to 4 quick switchbacks, then traverse W of the high ridge along the steep slope to 1 more switchback leading to the unsigned juncture on the high ridge. To the left at the sharp turn heads to Henline Mountain while continuing straight leads 75 ft out to the open lookout site.

From the rocky plateau where the old lookout used to be (careful as only some rebar remains), see up the continuation of the ridge to the tree-covered summit of Henline Mountain with a cliffy little pinnacle along the other ridge to the NE. Also see the square-topped Battle Ax Mountain, Mount Jefferson, the other local mountains to the S, and even Marys Peak toward the coast on a clear day! Return down the same route to the TH or press on for a slightly more challenging route a mile to the summit with worthwhile payoffs.

Take a right on Trail 3352 at the nearby fork you passed to the lookout site; the path descends the narrow ridge surrounded by little pines, rhododendrons, and wildflowers with a good view of your goal ahead before reaching a saddle. Follow the tacky trail with good footing, as it's not too steep up the left side of the ridge to a switchback taking you back to the E side of the ridge. Ascend 6 switchbacks more up the steeper and narrower trail with a thinning ridgeline to a bump short of the true summit.

Walk down a tiny bit, then hike steeper N to the nearby

Clear pool below fascinating Henline Falls.

nondescript summit area of Henline Mountain (not on map included). This is simply a thin section of trail next to a steep opening with trees blocking all views to the W and the trail continuing down into the woods. One tree is roughly carved with slightly inaccurate summit elevation indicating the top. You do however have humbling views from the opening of Mount Hood, Olallie Butte, Battle Ax, Whetstone Mountain, Mount Jefferson, Three Fingered Jack, Mount Washington, Black Butte, others, and even the white-capped Sisters Range through the trees on a clear day!

For Henline Falls, fill out a free self-issue Wilderness Permit at the Henline Falls TH and walk without any difficulty W up stony Henline Falls Trail 3348 (and Ogle Mountain Trail 3357). It's wide through the lively, thick forest with a ton of ferns and a few bigger Douglas fir and Western hemlock ½ mi to the first of two quick junctions. Keep left at both, the second being Ogle Mountain Trail 3357 indicated by a big X posted high on a tree above the thin path. The easier wide Trail 3348 left leads nearly another ½ mi to the falls; you descend a tad on the narrowing path between some cement foundations that used to be part of the Silver King Mine. Be cautious of the exposed rebar.

The mossy amphitheater is very picturesque indeed as the water drops and cascades 126 ft down the rock into a beautiful shallow blue-green pool. Further down from the logjam and the big boulders in the creek are more pools with multiple vantage points of the falls. These are worth investigating carefully and also for a possible dip (or at least your feet in the chilly, chilly water). To the right of the good-looking falls is a thin path leading into an old mine shaft and locked cage about 20 ft in.

53 OPAL CREEK

ELEVATION: 2075 ft at Opal Pool, with around 300 ft vertical gain including ups/downs

DISTANCE: 3¾ mi one way to Opal Pool, 7½ mi round-trip loop

DURATION: 2 hours one way to Opal Pool stopping at Sawmill Falls first, 4–5 hours round-trip loop with Opal Creek/Mike Kopetski Trail

DIFFICULTY: Mix of easiest to Opal Pool without Sawmill Falls or a loop (wide, ups/downs not difficult) and moderate for Sawmill Falls, the loop, and/or the upper pools (steeper, bushwhack, tree roots, narrow, rocky)

TRIP REPORT: One of the cleanest watersheds in the Pacific Northwest, unmolested by logging or mining activities, has got to be Opal Creek on the Little North Santiam River between Salem and Detroit Lake. The absolute clarity of the water lives up to its colorful namesake. A few quality waterfalls drop along a narrow gorge with a family-friendly grade and several excellent pools. You'll find plenty of spots to enjoy an icy plunge while being surrounded by flatter rocks for drying out amongst the ancient-growth Douglas fir and red cedar! Avoid weekend crowds if possible, but don't expect you'll ever be alone for very long on a hot summer day at this popular easy-access location. Northwest Forest Pass required, and an outhouse is present.

TRAILHEAD: Opal Creek TH. Take I-5 S from Portland to exit 253 in Salem, turn left for OR-22 E (Detroit Lake/Bend) to Mehama, turn left at the second flashing signal (milepost 23, before bridge over Santiam River) on easy-to-miss Little North Fork Road for 14¾ twisting mi (with ½ mi unpaved dusty section), then into gravel FR-2209 for 5½ mi to the end (many potholes, 90 mi, 2 hours from Portland).

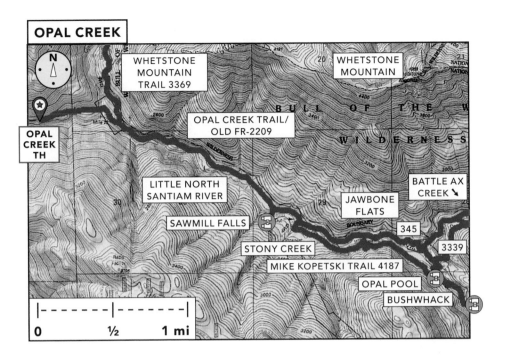

OPAL CREEK

WHETSTONE MOUNTAIN TRAIL 3369

WHETSTONE MOUNTAIN

OPAL CREEK TH

OPAL CREEK TRAIL/ OLD FR-2209

BULL OF THE W

WILDERNESS

LITTLE NORTH SANTIAM RIVER

BATTLE AX CREEK

JAWBONE FLATS

SAWMILL FALLS

345

STONY CREEK

3339

MIKE KOPETSKI TRAIL 4187

OPAL POOL

BUSHWHACK

0   ½   1 mi

ROUTE: Begin past the gate; the trail undulates along the wide, private road (Opal Creek Trail/old FR-2209) that ends in 3½ mi at Jawbone Flats, a tiny "active" neighborhood with a mix of old and new. After the first ½ mi from the TH, cross the bridge high over the clear Gold Creek. At 2¼ mi in, take a detour to the right on the spur path 100 ft or so past what remains of the Merten Mill (what appears like an old, open wooden garage). Be careful with children as the best viewpoints of Sawmill Falls (30 ft high and twice as wide) is seen by steeply navigating tree roots then a narrow rocky fin down to the creek itself. Travel as far as you are comfortable and then indulge in a freezing swim below the falls if you wish.

Continue on the main trail ¼ mi more to the return route on the right (Mike Kopetski Trail 4187) for a clockwise loop from Opal Pool. Stay straight instead on old FR-2209 a mile to Jawbone Flats; be respectful by staying between the buildings and down right briefly to cross Battle Ax Creek over a newer bridge. Move up a bit and through an open pasture, then down right on the narrowing trail back into the old trees to a juncture. Turn right down to the nearby creek with a deeper gorge below the footbridge and Opal Pool just above it. The luminous green water is enticing with a little cascade falling off the main pool and also just above it.

Return the same way back across the newer bridge for the most straightforward route to the TH. It would be more interesting, however, for the loop or the bushwhack up higher. For the upper pools, turn left (SE) on the bushwhack path along Opal Creek toward Cedar Flats more than ½ mi and a hundred feet up to about 2200 ft in elevation as the rougher overgrown path crosses the creek again. Work your way down

Just off the beaten path is the captivating Sawmill Falls into crystal-clear water.

left 30 ft or so around a cable on the ground, then cross the creek carefully to see the pool below (or pools, depending on water levels), or pick your own spot. Return the same way to Opal Pool, but stay on the left (S) side of the main creek on Mike Kopetski Trail for the clockwise loop. The path is narrow but fun, with more beach options as you pass Stony Creek along the 1½ mi back to the main trail finishing over the solid footbridge. Turn left (NW) on old FR-2209 for 2½ mi easily to the TH.

54   WHETSTONE MOUNTAIN

ELEVATION: 4969 ft, with vertical gains of 3400 ft, 3200 ft on a loop from Opal Creek TH, 1120 ft from Whetstone Mountain TH

DISTANCE: 5½ mi up, 11 mi round-trip; 15 mi round-trip loop; 4¼ mi round-trip from Whetstone Mountain TH

DURATION: 3–4 hours up, 5–7 hours round-trip (loop or not); 2 hours round-trip from Whetstone Mountain TH

DIFFICULTY: Mix of very challenging from Opal Creek TH (steep several miles, many switchbacks, overgrown, less maintained but recognizable, longer loop) and moderate from Whetstone Mountain TH (brief, steady steep, narrow, peaceful, signed).

TRIP REPORT: Less traveled and underrated is Whetstone Mountain that passes back and forth between Opal Creek Wilderness and Bull of the Woods Wilderness. You will have views from Mount Jefferson, Mount Washington, and Three Sisters to Mount Hood, Mount St. Helens, and Mount Rainier. The longer and more scenic trek from Opal Creek TH provides far more of a workout than from the cheating Whetstone Mountain TH. And the Opal Creek TH has the option of looping down to Opal Pool, or others, to take a dip in the beautiful freezing waters. Late June or so may be best for this while rhododendrons are in full bloom, but huckleberries choke the upper trail in autumn when the bugs are gone so it's a tough choice. Northwest Forest Pass required, and an outhouse is present at Opal Creek TH. No pass or restroom for Whetstone Mountain (upper) TH.

TRAILHEAD: Opal Creek TH or Whetstone Mountain TH. See hike 53 for directions to Opal Creek TH. For Whetstone Mountain TH (high-clearance AWD recommended, steeper at times, one lane, slightly rough, gravel), take OR-224 E less than 50 mi from Portland (and past Estacada) into FR-46 on the winding road 3½ mi, turn right on FR-63 (Bagby Hot Springs) 3½ mi, turn right on FR-70 (unsigned, roughly paved) 7¼ mi, turn sharp left on FR-7020 (small old sign, gravel, one lane) 5¾ mi to an intersection with FR-7030 (closed, overgrown, washed out) on the right. Stay straight ½ mi, then take the rougher narrow fork down to the left (small, old, unreadable sign FR-028) very briefly to the large lot in the trees with a sign for Whetstone Trail 546 (90 mi to Opal Creek TH; 75 mi to Whetstone Mountain TH, 2 hours from Portland).

ROUTE: Jump to the end for the description from Whetstone Mountain TH. For the

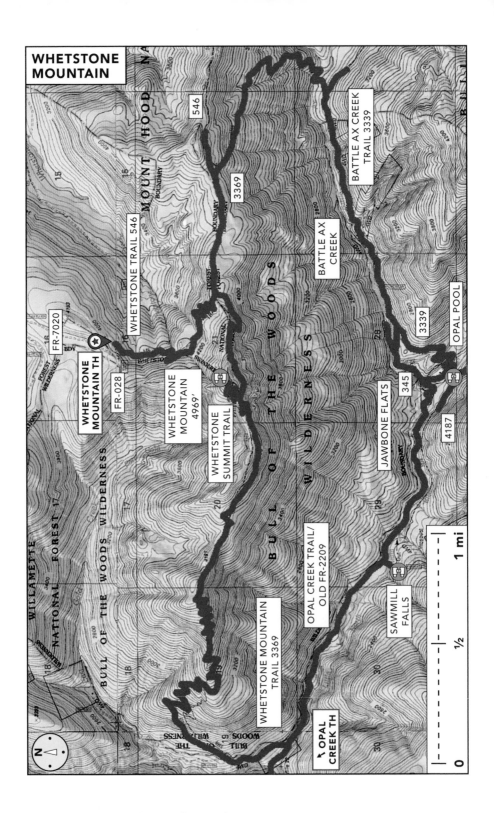

WHETSTONE
MOUNTAIN

WHETSTONE TRAIL 546

546

3369

MOUNT HOOD

BATTLE AX CREEK
TRAIL 3339

BATTLE AX
CREEK

3339

OPAL POOL

FR-7020

FR-028

WHETSTONE
MOUNTAIN TH

WHETSTONE
MOUNTAIN
4969'

WHETSTONE
SUMMIT TRAIL

BULL OF THE WOODS WILDERNESS

JAWBONE FLATS

345

4187

WILLAMETTE
NATIONAL FOREST

OPAL CREEK TRAIL/
OLD FR-2209

WHETSTONE
MOUNTAIN
TRAIL 3369

SAWMILL
FALLS

OPAL
CREEK TH

BULL OF THE WOODS WILDERNESS

N

0   ½   1 mi

Battle Ax Mountain to Mount Jefferson from a butterfly's point of view on Whetstone Mountain.

primary route begin past the gate easily on Opal Creek Trail (old FR-2209) past huge old Douglas fir and western hemlock ½ mi (including down a tad) to cross the bridge 60 ft above Gold Creek with waterfalls and clear pools visible below. Walk another ¼ mi up to a signed juncture and turn left (N) on Whetstone Mountain Trail 3369 after filling out a free self-issue Wilderness Permit.

The old road narrows to a nice trail traversing, then ascending, tiresomely E for a steep 40 switchbacks to the historic lookout site on the small summit. There is a decent shot of Mount Hood from the first little saddle, then a glance of Mount Jefferson through the forest filled with various hemlock, fir, cedar, bear grass, and rhododendron on the endless climb 3 mi up to the high ridge before the route levels and eases somewhat. There may be some fallen trees and brush to navigate around but it's usually not a major problem unless snow-covered in winter or early spring. Head down briefly to a small saddle, then hike up S of another ridge bump and down to another saddle. Continue right (S) of the high ridge nearing the summit block of Whetstone Mountain and proceed up to a signed intersection.

Turn sharp left (N) on Whetstone Summit Trail ¼ mi steeper but not bad or overgrown on the final 6 switchbacks to the open top where the trees finally give way to better than expected views. See all the mountains mentioned, the local mountains in the Bull of the Woods Wilderness, Broken Top, Coffin Mountain, Three Fingered Jack, Battle Ax Mountain, and Olallie Butte. Only some rebar remains from the lookout site on the flatter top. Return down to the juncture S of the summit and turn right (W) on Trail 3369 for the one-way trip option without the longer but somewhat easier loop.

For the less arduous loop, turn left (E) from the summit path on Trail 3369 for ¾ mi (with a couple steeper switchbacks near the ridge) without difficulty through the overgrown woods (with plenty of rhododendrons and huckleberries) to the next juncture. Continue E on Trail 3369 for ½ mi past the signed Whetstone Trail 546 (left, N to Whetstone Mountain TH more than 1 mi away) along the high ridge to another connection. Turn right off the ridge, down Trail 3369 almost 2 mi (SE then S) to Battle Ax Creek past big old trees and tiny creeks; the grade is steeper but very workable. The trail is unmaintained with some fallen trees to negotiate most of the time, but it's usually not too bad.

After minimal switchbacks arrive at Battle Ax Creek, which can be more difficult to cross with high water earlier in the season (spare dry socks?), otherwise use logs or rocks that can be slippery to hop over. Then follow the switchbacks near campsites up to an old road. Turn right (SW) on Battle Ax Creek Trail 3339, more than a mile down easier, but somewhat rockier, with mining evidence near crossings of Blue Jay and Ruth Creeks to a clear fork. Heading right (W) on Trail 345 at the sign moves steeply and more directly ½ mi to a solid bridge over Battle Ax Creek. From there you would walk up to nearby Jawbone Flats and stay (right, NW) 3½ mi easily to the TH. Hike steeply left (SW) at the fork instead for least a mile down slightly overgrown and rockier turns on old FR-2209 to Opal Pool.

For Opal Pool pass the return trail at a junction on the right, just before the footbridge over Opal Creek nearest Opal Pool. The beautiful clear water is located just above the footbridge. Take a dip in the colorful pools between cascades. Return over the same bridge when you are ready and take a left (NW) at the three-way juncture on old FR-2209 briefly up, then down, past a meadow to cross the bridge at Battle Ax Creek. Continue up a few feet to the old community of Jawbone Flats and then finish 3½ mi leisurely up and down the wide Opal Creek Trail (FR-2209) to the TH.

From the upper Whetstone Mountain TH, take the only trail narrowly down S, fairly steeply, to begin about 100 ft to an old Wilderness Permit sign-in box; continue down through the thick forest with big Douglas fir, rhododendron, bear grass, salal, and wild berries. Cross a few downed trees without difficulty and head up 3 steeper switchbacks before an easier traverse where the trail is slightly overgrown. Pass a tarn pond at the bottom of the scree field in a small clearing (¾ mi from the TH) as you move between. The route becomes a bit steeper with shots of Mount Hood through the trees, and then you ascend 6 switchbacks and moderate turns. Traverse up, down a hair, and then up easily to the high ridge and intersection with the trail overrun with huckleberries in season.

Turn right for the summit on Trail 3369 climbing the narrow ridge steadily as it opens up a bit to 2 steeper switchbacks. Continue up the ridge, then traverse left (SW then W) through the forest under the summit to the last juncture. Turn right (N) on Whetstone Summit Trail ¼ mi to the top like above and return to Whetstone Mountain TH in no time at all.

<table>
<tr><td>**55**</td><td>**DOME ROCK**</td></tr>
</table>

ELEVATION: 4859 ft, with 3260 ft vertical gain

DISTANCE: 5 mi up, 10 mi round-trip

DURATION: Around 3 hours up, 5–6 hours round-trip

DIFFICULTY: Strenuous. Steady steep and even steeper at times, narrow, switchbacks, overgrown at times, rocky near top, drop-offs

---

TRIP REPORT: Opposite the bustling Detroit Lake State Recreation Area is this wonderful workout to outstanding views of the lake and Mount Jefferson up Tumble Ridge with a superb payoff from the treeless peak! Dome Rock is the highest summit close to Detroit Lake and the second highest summit in a rather picturesque little cirque surrounding Tumble Lake. The hike to the very top is more difficult in winter with snowshoes but tempts locals, as the first couple miles usually remain snow-free. No fee or restrooms.

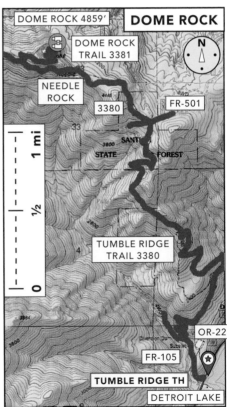

TRAILHEAD: Tumble Ridge TH. Take I-5 S from Portland to exit 253 in Salem, turn left for OR-22 E (Detroit Lake/Bend) 46 mi, and turn left into the sleepy, small pullout immediately after crossing over the bridge signed for Tumble Creek (just W of milepost 48; 95 mi, 1¾ hours from Portland).

ROUTE: Left of the sign warning about algae blooms in the creek and lake is the sign for Tumble Ridge Trail 3380, Dome Rock Trail 3381, and Tumble Lake Trail 3379. Walk past the old green gate N along Tumble Creek as the overgrown old FR-105 road is easy less than ½ mi to a fork. Hike to the right (NE) on Trail 3380 steeper up the apparent narrow trail clogged with salal and Oregon grape. After 5 switchbacks and turns through the old

Mount Jefferson, Three Fingered Jack, and Coffin Mountain beyond Dome Rock.

forest of Douglas fir, vine maple, hemlock, and cedar, see Detroit Lake and Mount Jefferson (¾ mi up).

Traverse ½ mi NE on a friendlier grade as the route is a bit overgrown through the thick woods to another switchback. Notice the burn areas above and below the trail. In ¼ mi more, turn right (N) up the ridge past additional burned trees. Ascend 2 switchbacks (USGS maps off here) with views opening past rhododendron steadily steeper. Hike NW up 2 more switchbacks before the trail eases some on a high traverse at 2 mi from the TH. See Detroit Lake and radio towers across the valley on the lowest part of Hall Ridge, which comprises the W side of the cirque around Tumble Lake to Dome Rock.

Trail 3380 becomes steeper again as you cross a tiny creek (that dries up) to a switchback at less than 3 mi up. Climb the wide ridge N up 2 turns where it's somewhat overgrown into a clearing, then move back into the woods to an old road junction. An aged wooden sign denotes that OR-22 is 4½ mi away, but it's really a little more than 3¼ mi from the intersection to the TH. Walk right 25 ft, then left (NW) at the tree blockage up the continuation of the solid Trail 3380.

Travel up 2 quick switchbacks, then follow the steeper, rockier, narrow ridge trail. You see rhododendron, bear grass, paintbrush, and Mount Jefferson on a traverse E and N of a bump before the trail finally mellows and evens descends a few feet on the ridgeline. Walk up some more, and then at 4 mi from the TH leave the high ridge on a traverse left (S) of Dome Rock with a quick shot left to Needle Rock along the way.

In ¼ mi, hike a few feet down very steeply crossing a rocky, boulder-filled area, then climb up past little cliffs on the right under Dome Rock. Be mindful as the path is narrow and overgrown. You see back to Detroit Lake, Mount Washington, and Three

Above the woodland down to Tumble Lake.

Sisters. Then it's super-easy through the trees to the juncture with Dome Rock Trail 3381 on the right (newer sign embedded into a tree next to an old sign at 4½ mi from the TH).

Turn right on Trail 3381 nearly ½ mi to the summit. For this, walk up to a nearby saddle on the ridge crest and turn right (E) at a switchback. Continue much steeper through the woods with less flora and some views from the rockier path down to Tumble Lake right (E) of Elephant Rock. Comically S of Tumble Lake is Tumble Rock with Tumble Falls on Tumble Creek, accessible from Tumble Lake Trail and/or Tumble Ridge Trail down very steeply E of Tumble Lake! Finish the summit block instead up 5 quick switchbacks as you suddenly break out into the wide open above tree line to an old cement lookout foundation slab surrounded by broken glass.

You will find plenty of nice picnic perches along the wide-enough summit plateau with wildflowers and a nice breeze to cool off and keep the flying bugs at bay. To the N you've got Bull of the Woods Wilderness, N of the nearby French Creek valley. The tip of Mount Hood can be seen to the NE just left of Battle Ax Mountain. To the E are Olallie Butte and Mount Jefferson. Farther SE is Three Fingered Jack just left of Coffin Mountain, with Mount Washington, and Three Sisters. Marys Peak on the coast can be seen as well.

Locally we have the radio towers up Hall Ridge to Whitman Rock, Water Tower Mountain, and Sardine Mountain. Dome Rock down Tumble Ridge completes the cirque above Tumble Lake. If you walk a few more steps NW to the end of the summit you see the Forest Service road moving past the upper TH to Dome Rock. The winding, dusty, longer drive cheats you out of almost all of the hiking, shortening it to only 1½ mi each way with very little elevation gain. Return the same way.

ELEVATION: 5526 ft on Big Slide Mountain; 5523 ft on Bull of the Woods Mountain, with 2810 ft vertical gain (3430 ft if you count ups/downs in both directions between summits)

DISTANCE: 5½ mi to Big Slide Mountain, more than 11 mi round-trip loop

DURATION: 2 hours to Big Slide Mountain, 5–6 hours round-trip loop

DIFFICULTY: Strenuous. Long, tiring ups/downs, biting bugs June into August, recognizable trails, brief scramble, GPS device helpful

TRIP REPORT: In the heart of the Bull of the Woods Wilderness is its most rugged-looking summit with a fun little rocky scramble to finish. And then you can view Big Slide Mountain (with so much more) from the Bull of the Woods Lookout on a wonderful double-summit loop hike! From the lookout, Mother Lode and Silver King Mountains are also seen in the Wilderness to the SW with Mount Jefferson not far SE, and Mount Hood lies to the NE. Some families with younger ones are happy with Pansy Lake alone or a jaunt to the lookout without a loop. No pass or restroom.

TRAILHEAD: Pansy Lake TH. Take OR-224 E 32 mi from Portland to Estacada, continue on OR-224 E winding 25 mi into FR-46 for 4 mi, turn right on FR-63 (no more signs) more than 5½ mi, fork right on FR-6340 (at almost 1800 ft in elevation) 7½ mi, fork right on FR-6341 (only paved portion) 3½ mi to the TH on the left with ample parking (75 mi, less than 2½ hours from Portland).

ROUTE: Begin past the signage on Pansy Lake Trail 551 S a mile easily through old growth trees with tiny creek crossings and rhododendrons to a juncture on the left (end of counterclockwise loop, Dickey Lake Trail 549). Stay S on Trail 551 for ¼ mi to Pansy Basin at another junction (the brief spur right (W) moves down briefly to Pansy Lake and is worth checking out). Continue

Lake Lenore within an older burn between Big Slide Mountain and Knob Peak.

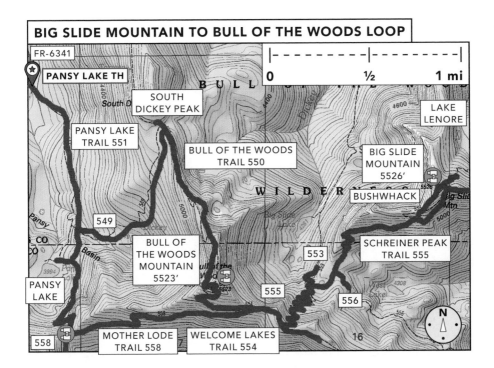

BIG SLIDE MOUNTAIN TO BULL OF THE WOODS LOOP

S almost a mile on the main trail only a bit steeper up switchbacks to a saddle juncture with views down to Pansy Lake and straight ahead SW to Pansy Mountain and Mother Lode Mountain.

Turn left (E) on Mother Lode Trail 558 at the saddle traversing easily more than 1¼ mi with only a couple switchbacks to the juncture SE of Bull of the Woods Lookout. See that mountain and Mount Jefferson en route to the turnoff (counterclockwise loop for later). Stay E momentarily (now on Welcome Lakes Trail 554) to the next crossroads at a little ridge saddle; turn left on Schreiner Peak Trail 555 and hike less than a mile down 17 tight switchbacks (and 500 ft to return up after summiting Big Slide Mountain). Stay on Trail 555 past Dickey Creek Trail 553 (N, left for Big Slide Lake) leveling past a tarn and West Lake Way Trail 556 (toward Welcome Lakes) on the right. Then ascend steeper up switchbacks NE less than 1½ mi—this includes traversing the overgrown trail under the rocky summit to a tiny saddle just E of Big Slide Mountain.

Instead of continuing down the path steeply to pretty Lake Lenore or bushwhacking right (NE) farther to Knob or Schreiner Peaks, turn left and scramble without too much difficulty or a solid trail up rocks and boulders to the top of nearby Big Slide Mountain. See Mount Jefferson, Mount Washington, Three Sisters, and Mount Hood above Lake Lenore and Schreiner Peak (5710 ft) at the end of the ridge (highest summit in the Wilderness) above an old burn area. Also see Mount St. Helens, Mount Adams, and Mount Rainier on a clear day. Observe your next goal (Bull of the Woods Lookout, 1½ hours away) and return E to the trail when you are ready, or

Bull of the Woods Lookout is one of the bests locales for the view the Wilderness!

descend the rocks SW along the high ridge less than ¼ mi to the end of the steeps and meet the main trail again.

Hike down past wildflowers on Trail 555, then climb up the switchbacks again, turning right on Trail 554 (to Trail 558 briefly) along the ridge to the right-hand turn for Bull of the Woods Mountain. For the worthwhile second summit of the day, ascend (for the last time) N ½ mi up on Trail 554 around a half-dozen switchbacks easily to the wildflower- and grass-covered top breaking out of the trees. Enjoy many of the same views seen from Big Slide Mountain as you survey the intact lookout before moving on.

Continue the loop N on Bull of the Woods Trail 550 down the high ridge from the top without any trouble 1¼ mi with views to a saddle juncture just S of South Dickey Peak. Turn left on Trail 549 (SSW) 1¼ mi steeply down past Dickey Lake (seen through the trees) to Pansy Basin at the end of the loop. The trail fades in this section and may be overgrown and slightly more difficult to follow. Turn right (N) at the last junction on Trail 551 about a mile down to the TH.

57 | LOWER SODA CREEK FALLS

ELEVATION: 1360 ft, with 460 ft vertical gain

DISTANCE: 1½ mi round-trip

DURATION: 1 hour round-trip

DIFFICULTY: Easiest. Wide, muddy when wet, possible drop-offs
near viewing area

TRIP REPORT: Combine with one or more of the upcoming waterfall jaunts on your spring tour to catch the best flows! Lower Soda Creek Falls slows to a trickle by the end of summer. Cascadia State Park does not charge a day use fee, but some fees do apply for camping. The only pay station is a few feet along the middle fork after crossing the river bridge toward the campgrounds, and restrooms are plentiful.

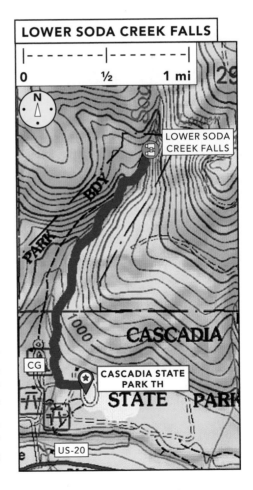

LOWER SODA CREEK FALLS

TRAILHEAD: Cascadia State Park. Take I-5 S from Portland 70 mi to exit 233 (Albany), merge onto US-20 E 40 mi, turn left into Cascadia State Park (past milepost 41) crossing the S Santiam River over the bridge to a parking lot. Park immediately or take the farthest road to the right briefly to another sizable lot on the right with the signed trail in between the two lots (110 mi, 2 hours from Portland).

ROUTE: From either parking area, walk down the road a few feet toward Soda Creek and turn onto the signed trail for Soda Creek Falls ¾ mi away (also called Lower Soda Falls). Follow the creek N without any difficulty and cross a couple solid footbridges early on as the wide gravel trail (with spurs

The fascinating triple-tiered ribbon that is Lower Soda Creek Falls!

to the campground) turns back to dirt, mud, and rock but with very few trees roots to navigate. Pass endless ferns and a few big old trees through the pretty mossy forest that only steepens a bit near the falls.

After walking over a few boulders, arrive at the main viewpoint near a fairly large boulder. The falls drop in three narrow tiers for 134 ft total (49 ft, 39 ft, and 54 ft respectively) into a beautiful, mossy grotto. Many people work left of the big boulder down a few feet carefully with no trouble to the base of the falls when the spray isn't pushing back! Return the same way S to the TH.

IRON MOUNTAIN LOOKOUT TO CONE PEAK LOOP

ELEVATION: 5455 ft on Iron Mountain; 5646 ft on Cone Peak; with vertical gains of 755 ft to the lookout from Civil Road TH, 1400 ft from Iron Mountain TH; 1500 ft for Cone Peak directly; 2500 ft for both summits

DISTANCE: 2½ mi round-trip from Civil Road TH, 3½ mi round-trip from Iron Mountain TH; 5½ mi round-trip for Cone Peak from Tombstone Pass TH, 7¾ mi round-trip loop with both summits (6¾ mi round-trip loop with only Iron Mountain)

DURATION: 1–2 hours round-trip from Civil Road, 2–3 hours round-trip from Iron Mountain TH; 3–4 hours round-trip from Tombstone Pass TH; 5–6 hours round-trip loop with both summits

DIFFICULTY: Mix of strenuous for all routes to Iron Mountain including the loop (switchbacks, steady steep, drop-offs, signed, not long, ups/downs, family-friendly) and very challenging for Cone Peak (very steep, route-finding, bushwhacking, minimal drop-offs)

TRIP REPORT: The wildflower show seems to continue for months, with late June into July being the very best time when more than 300 species bloom over the season, making this unique region the most prolific in Oregon! There are also at least seventeen varieties of trees, the most diversity in one place within the state. And then there's the hiking! Northwest Forest Pass required at all THs, and there are restrooms or portable outhouses at all THs.

TRAILHEAD: Tombstone Pass (Cone Peak) TH for the loop. Take I-5 S from Portland to exit 253 in Salem, turn left for OR-22 E (Detroit Lake/Bend) 80 mi, turn right toward US-20 W 50 ft, turn right on US-20 W 10½ mi, turn left on FR-060 (Tombstone Pass, milepost 63½) with parking immediately in the gravel.

Alternately from farther S for Tombstone Pass TH (taking the same time driving from Portland with more winding roads), take I-5 S to exit 228 (Lebanon/Corvallis), turn left on OR-34 E 5¼ mi, exit onto Denny School Road 1¼ mi into Airport Drive 2 mi (look for a Safeway), turn right on US-20 E 48 mi (15 mi to Sweet Home Ranger Station), turn right on nondescript FR-060 and park in the long pullout. For Iron Mountain or Cone Peak alone you can save ½ mi of hiking near Tombstone Pass to the trails directly. See below for the shortest route to Iron Mountain. For Cone Peak alone park off US-20 about ½ mi E of Tombstone Pass in a long pullout with a simple "Trail"

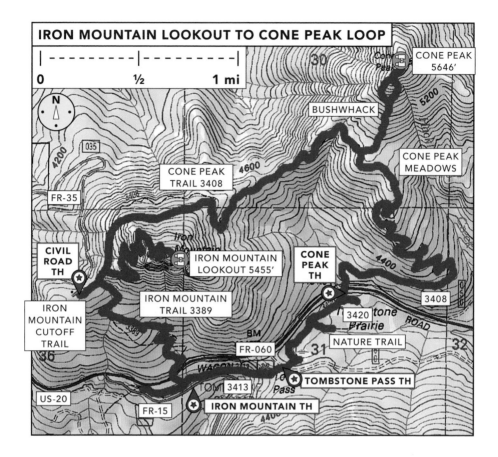

IRON MOUNTAIN LOOKOUT TO CONE PEAK LOOP

sign. Across the highway 40 ft up is a big yellow highway sign warning of the downgrade ahead with the signed Cone Peak Trail 3408 to the right.

For Iron Mountain TH, from the Tombstone Pass TH, turn S on FR-15 more than ½ mi W of Tombstone Pass on US-20. Follow signage on FR-15 less than ½ mi to a pullout on the right.

The Civil Road TH is a more difficult drive but the shortest hike for Iron Mountain Lookout. Drive 1½ mi W of Tombstone Pass, N of US-20, on FR-35 (Civil Road) more than 2½ mi winding up the rough gravel road to the signed TH at 4700 ft (140 mi roughly, 2½ hours from Portland).

ROUTE: Pick up clues in this section for the routes from all the THs and feel free to hike to your goal or try the loop counterclockwise. For the sake of brevity we will hike the loop clockwise from Tombstone Pass and include both summits. At the Tombstone Pass TH, cross the parking driveway to the narrow trail left of the Tombstone Pass sign and head W up a few feet before walking down a switchback. Traverse the wider trail through the jungle-like setting below the highway passing a few large Douglas firs about ½ mi to a three-way juncture (left moves down briefly to

Iron Mountain's rocky obelisk appendage.

Iron Mountain TH). Turn right at the signage for Iron Mountain (exaggerates mileage to both locales by around ½ mi) and cross the highway with caution.

Hike N up the first of 5 well-graded switchbacks on Iron Mountain Trail 3389 with more impressive Douglas fir. The now steeper trail turns up over a rise and narrows after 1 mi from Tombstone Pass. After a solid switchback see the rocky cliff face directly ahead. Move up another switchback more through a meadow to a signed three-way intersection where left leads easily down Iron Mountain Cutoff Trail to the Civil Road TH in ¼ mi. Turn right on the wide trail instead (3389) briefly to another juncture (continuation of the loop); at 1½ mi from Tombstone Pass turn sharply right for Iron Mountain Lookout.

See the cliff face of Iron Mountain, as the route becomes steeper and rockier E 5 switchbacks and a turn up the ridgeline passing steep meadows and wildflowers. See a little rock arch while ascending 4 dusty true switchbacks (drop-offs near) to a nice flat perch left a few feet. See Cone Peak, Cone Peak Meadows, and Mount Jefferson. Finish briefly to the visible platforms (with info signage) on the open summit and enjoy the expansive views from a safe overlook.

Return down to the first juncture from the summit and turn right (N) on Cone Peak Trail 3408 for the clockwise loop. Follow the much easier wide traverse that skirts N of Iron Mountain with a few minor ups and downs through low flora and mossy trees in the beautiful forest. The terrain begins to open a bit with a shot to Cone Peak and the nearby saddle as you approach the saddle from the right (S) side of the ridge via 1 switchback. Stay S of the ridge a while, as the wide saddle is 1 mi from the

Iron Mountain Lookout juncture and more than 1 mi from Cone Peak. Continue up steeper for 2 switchbacks and turns where it's overgrown, and then hike somewhat easier across mostly dry mini creeks through the jungle with a few wildflowers to improved views. The trail turns SE in the thicket at a larger runoff creek SW of Cone Peak and then moves briefly through thinning trees across sloped pastures to a more open area at the top of Cone Peak Meadows (4925 ft).

Stay on the trail, immediately heading down through the colorful steep rocky meadows on the return loop without Cone Peak; or bushwhack left (N) up 720 ft in ½ mi for more solitude with a steep scramble to the summit. There are a few discernible paths that become more distinct a hundred feet or so from the main trail bearing up the center of the wide SSE shoulder past tall bushes, grasses, and small trees to the even wider wildflower-covered super-steep slopes. Then work N up the steep hill without a trail, zigzagging back and forth, angling just left of the little cliffy area with steep rock (SW of summit). Scramble up the rock ledges (perhaps using hands for balance) aiming for the high ridge and find the user path that moves left (W) of a natural rock wall blocking the ridge crest. Then walk easier along the open wide ridge to the rocky top a few feet away.

A few small snags don't block the 360-degree views, superior to the views from Iron Mountain. See Iron Mountain down the ridge with its huge spire to the left, and other local mountains, Three Sisters, Mount Washington, Three Fingered Jack, Mount Jefferson, Mount Hood, and Mount St. Helens. When returning down, it is possible once you are past the rock wall blocking the ridge to move left (S) off the high ridge quite steeply down dirt, gravel, and rocks on faint paths to the sloped meadow below ending the tiny summit loop. Work steeply and slowly back to the main trail seen below.

Turn left onto Cone Peak Trail 3408, down the open rocky meadow with phlox, larkspur, paintbrush, scarlet gilia, penstemon, and cat's ear, to name a few. Wind down over a shoulder (S ridge of Cone Peak) back into the forest to the first of 12 fairly easy switchbacks to the highway. Pass towering Douglas fir again after the fifth switchback and traverse a mostly level, long stretch that becomes slightly overgrown after the tenth switchback. Finish with 2 quick turns and cross US-20 carefully near a big yellow sign. Walk left 40 ft down to find the "Trail" sign on the right (at Cone Peak TH) at 7¼ mi from the start of the loop (if you began at Tombstone Pass and included Cone Peak).

From Cone Peak TH, walk easily down toward a tiny creek with 1 switchback and then cross it over a footbridge to a signed juncture. Turn right (SW) on Tombstone Prairie Trail 3420 past a big wooden kiosk explaining the old Santiam Wagon Road and Tombstone Prairie. Stay right at a little fork on Trail 3420 (opposite the Nature Trail) as the path narrows and becomes overgrown at times up through the wonderful forest with big old firs. Ascend the final switchback to the nearby info kiosk with a map and day use fee instructions at the Tombstone Pass TH.

ELEVATION: 6229 ft, with 2460 ft vertical gain

DISTANCE: 5 mi up, 10 mi round-trip

DURATION: 2 hours up, 3–4 hours round-trip

DIFFICULTY: Strenuous. Steady but never too steep, straightforward, many blowdowns probable, switchbacks, rocky near top

---

TRIP REPORT: The Maxwell Butte Trail rises from the lava field SW of Three Fingered Jack and provides outstanding views up and down the Cascades once you are above the forest near the summit of the old lookout and volcano. The seemingly abandoned trail entails navigating little paths around, over, and under at least 175 fallen lodgepole pines until some serious maintenance occurs. Happily none are too huge or dangerous unless snowshoeing (before they are all well covered). The amble is thus a nice workout without a lot of hoopla away from other more congested day hikes. No pass required at the official TH, and there is a restroom nearby.

TRAILHEAD: Maxwell Butte TH. Take I-5 S from Portland to exit 253 in Salem, turn left for OR-22 E (Detroit Lake/Bend) 76 mi, turn left on FR-80/Maxwell Butte Road (gravel, between mileposts 79/80) passing an outhouse and a long pullout on the left for Maxwell Sno-Park as the road becomes one-lane gravel ¼ mi more, turn left down a short driveway to the signed TH with a tiny parking lot (125 mi, 2½ hours from Portland).

South past local buttes to a snowy **Mount Washington** and others from **Maxwell Butte.**

ROUTE: Begin E, past the faded sign for Maxwell Butte Trail 3391 and the free self-issue Wilderness Permit station, through the old growth fir, hemlock, and pine 2¼ mi to a signed intersection at Twin Lakes; highway sounds quickly dissipate. Ignore the initial three junctures (snowshoe trails) to stay straight the first 1¼ mi, and then almost ¼ mi farther is a Mount Jefferson Wilderness sign. There are around twenty small blowdowns to the sign and eighty more after (twenty before the trail levels a bit) to the intersection.

Turn right (E) to stay on Trail 3391 passing the shallow Twin Lakes easier with a shot up to Maxwell Butte through the bear grass and thinning trees. There are about seventy-five more fallen trees to steer by for the next 1¼ mi or so through the woods and small meadows to the very first switchback. Then enjoy a long traverse with Mount Washington and Three Sisters Range finally popping largely into view. Rise up another switchback and a quick turn as the route becomes a bit steeper and rockier up a couple more switchbacks and another traverse S of Maxwell Butte. See down S to Diamond Peak and ESE to Black Butte.

Hike the last ½ mi and 5 switchbacks to the summit steeper and narrower up the rocky trail with views and wildflowers rapidly improving. Follow the high ridge or just right (S) for a ways after the fourth switchback before the final turn left 30 ft to the top. The boulder-filled summit above most of the trees holds rebar from the old lookout as well as a USGS benchmark. On the last switchback you are greeted with sweet views to the nearby craggy Three Fingered Jack and Mount Jefferson with Mount Hood behind to the N. To the S is Santiam Pass and of course Mount Washington over Hoodoo and Hayrick Buttes with Three Sisters and Broken Top behind. Between Maxwell Butte and Three Fingered Jack to the N are Santiam, Duffy, and Mowich Lakes, with Upper and Lower Berley Lakes visible just S.

60 THREE FINGERED JACK LOOP

ELEVATION: 6400 ft, with about 1850 ft vertical gain

DISTANCE: 12 mi round-trip loop

DURATION: 4–5 hours round-trip

DIFFICULTY: Strenuous. Not a summit hike or the super-long loop, route-finding, lingering snow, bushwhacking, long, mosquito swarms until late August or so above 6000 ft

TRIP REPORT: This ancient volcano between Mount Jefferson and Mount Washington is a crumbling basaltic mass of gorgeous rock worth scrutinizing from a safe distance. Wildflower-covered meadows dotted with small colorful lakes amid a recovering burn area give way to impressive views for most of the day. The summit of Three Fingered Jack is a technical climb that's not at all inviting and quite airy at the tiny top. This is a shorter version of the 22 mi loop that encompasses Three Fingered Jack. See the next jaunt (61) as the Porcupine Rock Loop makes for another solid day hike to cover the entire NE side of Three Fingered Jack. Northwest Forest Pass required, and an outhouse is present.

Wildflowers and grasses work up through the old burn.

TRAILHEAD: Santiam Pass (PCT) TH. Take I-5 S from Portland to exit 253 in Salem, turn left for OR-22 E (Detroit Lake/Bend) 80 mi into OR-126 E/US-20 E 5½ mi, turn left after Hoodoo Ski Area at Santiam Pass on the access road signed for the Pacific Crest National Scenic Trail (FR-845). Drive less than ½ mi to the end with plenty of parking in the traffic circle (135 mi, 2½ hours from Portland).

ROUTE: Begin farthest to the right (E) from the restroom and parking circle, and fill out a free self-issue Wilderness Permit before heading left (N) on the spur trail briefly to the PCT. Take PCT 2000 left (N) past more burned and downed trees ¼ mi with Summit Lake Trail 4014 intersecting from the right (odd name for this long trail that doesn't go near that lake). This is the return trail for the clockwise loop finishing near the not-so-Square Lake. Continue straight on the PCT without trouble for most of the hike through the 2003 B&B Complex Fire that took out 90,000 acres of forest. In present times, colorful undergrowth and great views S through the blackened trees to Mount Washington make the walk quite enjoyable right from the TH!

After a mile or so is another signed juncture, this one just past a nice little tarn near a boulder-covered bump. Hiking left at this juncture would put you on Santiam Lake Trail 3491, but continue right (NE) instead, still on the PCT, up 2 mi steadily to what becomes the S ridge of Three Fingered Jack. After following the W side of the ridge for a bit you finally catch up to it and proceed a bit easier ¼ mi through unburned trees with Martin Lake less than ½ mi down to the right (E) and Booth Lake barely visible below (with Black Butte in the background). You will have to bushwhack without any clear trail, but quite easily, down to the lake later for the loop, so scout the easiest and least rocky steep route as you pass from the PCT.

For the very best views of the day, you should continue to follow the PCT for at least another ½ hour and 1½ mi to the W side of the ridge (about 6400 ft) directly below Three Fingered Jack. Climb up a few switchbacks through the woods on the ridge before moving left (W) of it for the remainder on a steady, rockier traverse. Walk out of most of the trees with greatly enhanced shots of the Three Sisters Wilderness Area and nearby Maxwell Butte. Work across massive boulder fields (carefully if snow/ice remain) past wildflowers as you come around to outstanding views straight up the right to the entire W face of Three Fingered Jack in all its glory! Turn around from the rock field before the forest thickens when you are ready and return down S to a lower perch on the ridge (5850 ft) directly above Martin Lake. Return to the TH for a 10-mi or so day without a loop, as many do, or press on for more of an adventure.

From the lower perch on the ridge above Martin Lake, turn left (E) off the PCT fairly steeply down through the grass and charred trees with no trail or difficulty to the colorful shallow lake. Follow its right (S) side briefly to a nice open meadow with views from the blue-green lake to the living forest and surrounding rocky cirque. Take the suddenly appearing path on the E side of the lake ½ mi E down through the burn; the route fades again but is simple to the more solid Summit Lake Trail 4014. Then turn right (S) easiest around ¼ mi to Booth Lake (ground zero for the big fire).

You may be pulled more to the right (SE) directly to Booth Lake from Martin Lake too, but the bushwhack is a bit more tedious ending on the left (N) side of that somewhat larger lake.

Stay on Trail 4014 SE 1¾ mi past Booth Lake to the much bigger Square Lake; meander up a bit and through a notch before descending to the lovely lake, suitable for a swim on a hot day. Turn right at the faint juncture near the water to stay on Trail 4014 and finish the loop past the lake's W side, through the burn with easy ups and downs, 2¼ mi S then W to the PCT intersection near the TH. Enjoy the last superb views rising above Square Lake to Mount Washington, Three Sisters, Black Butte, and Three Fingered Jack. Turn left once on the PCT ¼ mi finding the spur path on the right to the nearby parking circle.

Subalpine spirea splash some color near a small tarn.

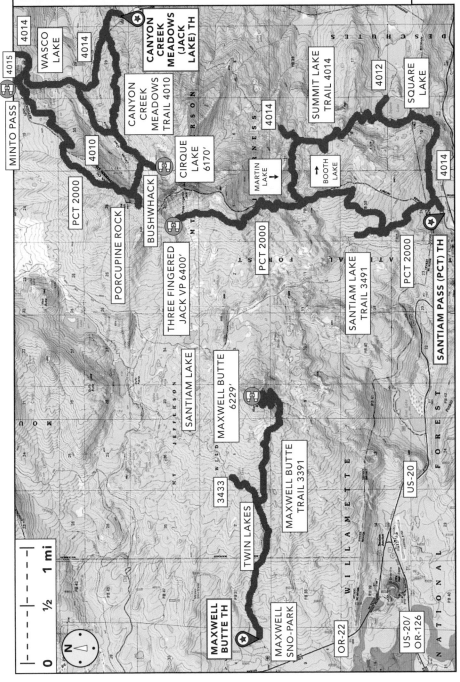

WASCO LAKE

4014

4014

4015

MINTO PASS

CANYON CREEK MEADOWS (JACK LAKE) TH

DESCHUTES

SUMMIT LAKE TRAIL 4014

4012

SQUARE LAKE

CANYON CREEK MEADOWS TRAIL 4010

CIRQUE LAKE 6170'

4014

4014

J E F F E R S O N   W I L D E R N E S S

BUSHWHACK

4010

PCT 2000

PORCUPINE ROCK

MARTIN LAKE

BOOTH LAKE

THREE FINGERED JACK VP 6400'

PCT 2000

M T   J E F F E R S O N   N A T I O N A L   F O R E S T

SANTIAM LAKE TRAIL 3491

PCT 2000

SANTIAM PASS (PCT) TH

SANTIAM LAKE

MAXWELL BUTTE 6229'

3433

TWIN LAKES

MAXWELL BUTTE TRAIL 3391

W I L L A M E T T E   N A T I O N A L   F O R E S T

US-20

M T   J E F F E R S O N   W I L D E R N E S S

MAXWELL BUTTE TH

MAXWELL SNO-PARK

OR-22

US-20/ OR-126

N

0   ½   1 mi

ELEVATION: 6200 ft, with vertical gains of about 2500 ft for Porcupine Rock loop, and 1300 ft for Canyon Creek Meadows to Cirque Lake loop

DISTANCE: 10 mi round-trip Porcupine Rock loop; 6¾ mi Canyon Creek Meadows to Cirque Lake Loop

DURATION: 5–6 hours round-trip longer loop; 4 hours round-trip for the shorter loop

DIFFICULTY: Strenuous. Porcupine Rock loop holds a very steep bushwhack over somewhat loose rock and ground, otherwise only occasionally steeper including last bit to Cirque Lake, scree, perceptible, ups/downs not bad, bugs July into August, crowds on shorter loop in summer, lingering snow into August at Cirque Lake

TRIP REPORT: Here's a couple great loops that cover the best of the rest that the previous hike (60) doesn't cover from the shadows of the old volcano's sharp pinnacles. You could also easily call this Wasco Lake Loop, Canyon Creek Meadows Loop, or Three Fingered Jack N Loop. If you go July into August the wildflowers will be exceptional, but there will be very little shade and mosquito swarms will keep you from hanging out for very long. You could use Deet like everyone else or try September through nice days in October before the snow settles back in. Northwest Forest Pass required, and an outhouse is present.

TRAILHEAD: Canyon Creek Meadows (Jack Lake) TH. Take I-5 S from Portland to exit 253 in Salem, turn left for OR-22 E (Detroit Lake/Bend) 80 mi into OR-126 E/ US-20 E 13 mi, turn left after Suttle Lake (milepost 88) on Jack Lake Road (FR-12) 4¼ mi, turn left on Jack Lake Road (FR-1230) 1½ mi into gravel almost 6 mi more (washboard, rougher last miles, AWD preferred) to the end with ample parking near a small primitive campground (150 mi, 3 hours from Portland).

ROUTE: See Three Fingered Jack from the TH and fill out a free self-issue Wilderness Permit at the signage, beginning farthest to the right (N) of the parking lot. Take the fork in a few feet to the right on Summit Lake Trail 4014 around the E side of quaint Jack Lake with a possible reflection of Three Fingered Jack looking W. It's less than ½ mi from the TH easily up to a juncture in the middle of the burn zone (2003 B&B Complex Fire) on a small saddle. The signed Canyon Creek Meadows Trail 4010 moves up left (W) and is the possible return trail for the long counterclockwise loop that includes Wasco Lake and the Pacific Crest Trail to the bushwhack under Porcupine Rock.

For the direct route to Cirque Lake and Canyon Creek Meadows as part of the recommended shorter clockwise loop, proceed left (W) on Trail 4010 up quite easily a mile over the wide, dusty trail past a few low pines creeping up through the burn. Pass a couple decent little tarns before rounding a shoulder then descending, steeper at times with turns and ups and downs, ¾ mi (and past smaller tarns and wildflowers) to the three-way intersection in Canyon Creek Meadows. Turn right for the continuation of the recommended clockwise loop on Trail 4010 reading below for the description.

For Upper Canyon Creek Meadow beneath Cirque Lake, take the easygoing spur left across the creek ¾ mi SW. Walk through lupine-blanketed meadows then move through the woods on the main spur trail or on the narrower path nearest Canyon Creek to the wide-open upper meadow directly under the very distinctive Three Fingered Jack (near the confluence of another creek). Enjoy the scenery under the NE face of Three Fingered Jack from the flatter meadow littered with lupine, paintbrush, and others, and return down or take the path left of the meadow (¼ mi up to Cirque Lake) easily for a moment. Then hike left (E) of the rocky moraine ridge and cirque surrounding the lake as the route becomes abruptly steep with a few observable choices that work well. At the top of the steepest part near larger boulders, move right a few feet over the rocks and snow to the rim above Cirque Lake, a stunning milky green pool receiving snow melt from the only lasting glacier on the mountain directly above. See Porcupine Rock on the NE ridge and the top of Mount Jefferson over the moraine and valley below. Some people scramble ¼ mi and 300 ft more very steeply up to a saddle for even more views. Return back down steeply then quite easily through the meadows.

From the intersection in Canyon Creek Meadows near the babbling brook take the steeper branch of Trail 4010 more directly to the right (E) back to Trail 4014 near the TH, or stay on the creek (also Trail 4010) for the clockwise loop (easier but ½ mi longer to the TH). For the direct trail right (E) move by tarns and wildflowers in and out of unburned trees with easy ups and downs before the trail becomes steeper up 2 quick switchbacks. Continue up through the woods before rounding the shoulder beginning a stress-free descent a mile to the last major juncture near Jack Lake, turning right on Trail 4014. For the loop in Canyon Creek Meadows on Trail 4010, continue following the creek with some small cascades about a mile NE without any trouble down past ample wildflowers and a marshy area halfway to a

Canada thistle in bloom.

four-way juncture with Trail 4014. Turn right (SSE) on Trail 4014 for 1¼ mi to the end of the loop, first noticing the waterfall area on Canyon Creek; then walk with easy ups and downs through mostly old burned trees to the juncture with Canyon Creek Meadows Trail. Continue straight (left) on Trail 4014 less than ½ mi to the TH at Jack Lake.

For the long Porcupine Rock Loop and bushwhack continue straight from the first juncture (less than ½ mi from the TH) on Summit Lake Trail 4014 with ups and downs NW 1¼ mi easily to the confluence with the N end of Trail 4010 on the left at Canyon Creek. Stay straight on Trail 4014 again rocking hopping the creek, then walk without difficulty more than ½ mi N down through the burn area past a couple smaller lakes to Wasco Lake. Walk around the left (W) side of the pretty blue-green Wasco Lake past steep rocky terrain with burned trees and wildflowers to its N end (past a lake spur) in to living trees near a juncture, where you leave Trail 4014 (continues briefly around to Minto Lake). Turn left (N) instead on Minto Pass Tie Trail 4015 up the switchback less than ¼ mi to its termination at PCT 2000 on Minto Pass. It's fairly open up steeper with only 1 more switchback to the pass near a four-way intersection (less than 2¾ mi from the TH).

Turn left (SW) on the PCT with a couple quick switchbacks easier up the widening ridge. Wasco Lake is revealed below with countless tarns, ponds, and small lakes soon appearing off the trail. See Black Butte in the distance SE and Three Fingered Jack up the ridge. Hike through trees, mostly scorched but some not, before you turn to the N side of the ridge after a switchback, crossing a wide saddle 1½ mi from Minto Pass. Continue traversing 1¼ mi SW through the burn on the PCT around the forested ridge bump (looking back to Mount Jefferson) as the route becomes a bit steeper then mellows after a switchback through unburned forest and paintbrush to the ridge again.

Move through the trees SW up the narrower ridge briefly and easily as the PCT soon traverses left (S) of the ridgeline, and scout one of at least two steep bushwhack routes with no lasting trails down to the left, the first one (almost 1 mi to the main spur trail for Upper Canyon Creek Meadow and Cirque Lake, GPS helpful) SE down through a few rocks to the nearby trees where the going will be very steep through the thin forest to begin. Then descend through lupine-covered steep meadows as you track left (E) then right (SE) slightly less steep, then eventually bushwhacking across Canyon Creek moving steeper up a few feet to the main spur trail. It's around ½ mi more to the right up to Cirque Lake.

From the PCT (under Porcupine Rock, almost 6300 ft), it's also possible to walk up to the edge of the forest less than 100 ft farther on the PCT past the first bushwhack option. You would then hike ¾ mi very steeply left (S) following the edge of the trees on the rocky bushwhack path down SSE to Upper Canyon Creek Meadow near the confluence of creeks at the main spur trail for Cirque Lake or Canyon Creek Meadows. See above for details on the remainder of the hike to Cirque Lake and the loop options on Trail 4010.

62 | UPPER DOWNING CREEK FALLS

ELEVATION: 3000 ft, with 300 ft vertical gain

DISTANCE: 2 mi round-trip at most

DURATION: 1½ hours round-trip

DIFFICULTY: Moderate. Trail-finding, narrow, no signs, overgrown, not popular

---

TRIP REPORT: Here's one of the most interesting waterfalls in the OR-22 corridor, off of most people's radar. The access road and trails are underdeveloped and wonderfully raw, even for the Pacific Northwest's tourist-driven economy! Perhaps combine with nearby Triangulation Peak (hike 64) or other brief waterfalls walks. No fee or restroom.

TRAILHEAD: Take I-5 S from Portland to exit 253 in Salem, turn left for OR-22 E (Detroit Lake/Bend) 67 mi, turn left very carefully (with no designated turning lane on a fast stretch of highway) onto a one-lane, overgrown, hidden driveway (FR-161, unsigned). This is exactly 3 mi E of Marion Creek and just past Straight Creek Road (signed on the right after milepost 69). If there is traffic behind you, seriously consider turning right on Straight Creek Road (FR-11) to allow vehicles to pass then continue less than ¼ mi on OR-22 E to the overgrown drive on the left (E side). In 100 ft, park in a pullout on the right with room for only a couple of vehicles. For a larger pullout, the only option is to continue around ¼ mi steeper up the old road to a juncture. It's even more overrun with pine branches and undergrowth, but if you're not worried,

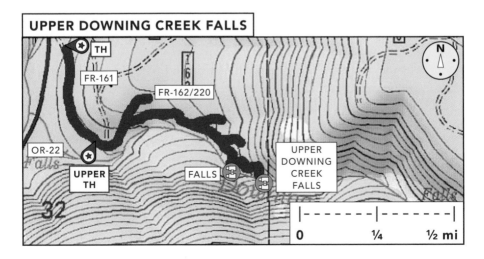

Just another sumptuous PNW waterfall in an emerald setting!

have at it to shorten the already brief walk (115 mi, 2 hours from Portland).

ROUTE: Walk SSE up the narrow road from the lower TH steeper more than ¼ mi to the upper TH at a crossroads. Take the fork right past the post (FR-162/2200) along the wide old road almost ¼ mi NNE to the next fork moving over or under a few rather large fallen trees with minimal effort for most. Then stay right (E) at the faint fork toward the creek easily a hundred yards or so on the narrowing, mossy, rocky road to a faint juncture marked with a cairn.

Turn right (SE) at the cairn onto a thin level path overgrown with rhododendron a few feet to Downing Creek, as the views of the creek and mossy forest become the focus for the remainder. There is a small cascade worth checking out down to the right if you like, otherwise stay on the main trail to Upper Downing Creek Falls just above. See the waterfall first as you creep up to it through the old growth, then have many wonderful vantage points near the pretty creek surrounded with mossy rocks, boulders, and trees. The falls split across a small mossy cliff falling 35 ft or so and continue to cascade along the mossy wall in the woods. It's utterly alluring after recent rains or rapid snowmelt! Be cautious as spray peeling away makes mossy rocks and logs closer to the base slippery, and it may be best to keep a few feet away just to be safe. Return briefly and enjoyably by the same route.

63   GRIZZLY PEAK

ELEVATION: 6799 ft, with 2700 ft vertical gain

DISTANCE: 5½ mi up, 11 mi round-trip

DURATION: 3 hours up, 5 hours round-trip

DIFFICULTY: Strenuous. Rather long, steady steep above Pamelia Lake, mostly forested, snow near the summit until July

---

TRIP REPORT: This lovely day hike leaves the mobs at Pamelia Lake and rises up above the majestic old firs and others to fantastic views only a few miles SW of Mount Jefferson. The summit was not named for the oversized brown bears roaming the area but because the climb was a terribly steep "grizzly" of a hike. Perhaps that was true before a wonderfully well-graded trail was laid, but it's actually quite tame compared to many others in the Pacific Northwest. A Limited Entry Area Permit is required and can be purchased up to a month in advance (https://www.fs.usda.gov/detail/willamette/passes-permits/recreation/?cid=fse_005446) or on the way at the Detroit Ranger Station. Northwest Forest Pass is required, and an outhouse is present.

TRAILHEAD: Pamelia Lake/Grizzly Peak TH. Take I-5 S from Portland to exit 253 in Salem, turn left for OR-22 E (Detroit Lake/Bend) 62 mi, turn left on Pamelia Road (FR-2246, after milepost 62) 3¾ mi to the end with parking on the left (110 mi, 2½ hours from Portland).

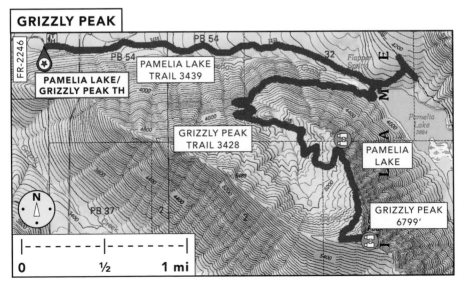

Unreal look at Mount Jefferson more than 6600 ft above Pamelia Lake from Grizzly Peak.

ROUTE: Take Pamelia Lake Trail 3439 E for 2¼ mi and almost 800 ft up to Pamelia Lake. You will hike along Pamelia Creek through a mossy, timeworn forest with fir, cedar, hemlock, and rhododendron, and then past a rocky, aged mudslide en route to a four-way intersection just before the lake. You will eventually turn right here (opposite the trail up to the PCT) on Grizzly Peak Trail 3428, but first take the spur straight to see the lake for a moment. From the spur, if you work right a bit from the water's edge there's a nice reflection of Mount Jefferson. The water level drops throughout the summer into fall here.

From the signed lake juncture (now on Grizzly Peak Trail 3428) traverse without difficulty steadily up W, then S and SE, past plenty of bear grass to a nice viewpoint at a switchback on the ridge (almost 2¼ mi and 6 switchbacks from the lake). See Mount Jefferson towering over Pamelia Lake below. Continue less than a mile SE to the summit through thinning pines with glimpses out. After a final switchback, the trees finally begin to break up just enough to give way to great views of the mountain and Cathedral Rocks along Mount Jefferson's S ridge, plus Three Fingered Jack and Three Sisters Wilderness looking S. And on a clear day, the top of Mount Hood can be made out to the N. Return the same way to the TH.

64 TRIANGULATION PEAK

ELEVATION: 5434 ft, with 700 ft vertical gain

DISTANCE: 2¼ mi up, 4½ mi round-trip

DURATION: 1 hour up, 2 hours round-trip

DIFFICULTY: Moderate. Very brief, steeper near the top, slender summit block, rocky, drop-offs, fairly family-friendly

---

TRIP REPORT: Obscure short steep walk to an old lookout site with distant shots to many high Cascade volcanoes and one not-so-distant one to Mount Jefferson only 6 mi SE. Perhaps combine with Upper Downing Creek Falls (hike 62). Check www. fs.usda.gov/recarea/willamette/recreation/recarea/?recid=4269 for conditions as the nearby Whitewater Fire forced this trail closed until cleanup concluded in spring 2018. No fee or restroom.

TRAILHEAD: Triangulation TH. Take I-5 S from Portland to exit 253 in Salem, turn left for OR-22 E (Detroit Lake/Bend) 55 mi, turn left (opposite Coopers Ridge Road, between mileposts 56/57) on McCoy Creek Road (FR-2233, one lane into gravel) 7¾ mi, turn right on FR-650 for 1¼ mi with the small TH parking on the right

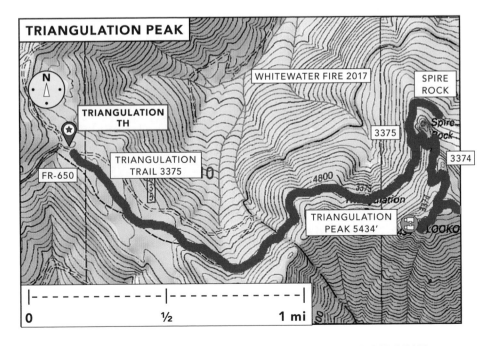

Mount Jefferson plus much more under prime summer conditions.

(110 mi, more than 2 hours from Portland).

ROUTE: Take the signed Triangulation Trail 3373 to the right (SE) briefly to a free self-issue Wilderness Permit station and continue without any difficulty more than 1½ mi traversing through Douglas fir, cedar, and hemlock to an unsigned juncture. Fork right on Triangulation Peak Trail 3374 ascending 3 quick switchbacks under the tall monolith known as Spire Rock to a small saddle before continuing S directly toward the summit. Wildflowers, bear grass, and blooming rhododendron into late June and early July enrich the hike.

After around ½ mi from the lower juncture and 2 more switchbacks, the solid steeper trail brings you to a tiny saddle just E of the rocky summit with vastly improving views. Be careful climbing the steepest last stretch W up the narrowing rocky high ridge to the very top where you will be greeted with fabulous vistas. See Mount Hood looming to the N over Spire Rock with high Cascade Mountains visible in Washington. See Olallie Butte, a few more minuscule spires locally, Three Fingered Jack, Mount Washington, North Sister, Middle Sister, Diamond Peak, and of course Mount Jefferson over the summit and old lookout site. Excellent!

65   BEAR POINT

ELEVATION: 6043 ft, with 3000 ft
   vertical gain

DISTANCE: 4¼ mi up, 8½ mi round-trip

DURATION: 2 hours up, 3–4 hours
   round-trip

DIFFICULTY: Strenuous. Steady steep,
   switchbacks, overgrown at times,
   narrow, scree

Barrett's penstemon and rebar from the summit of Bear Point gazing SE.

TRIP REPORT: Here's another noteworthy little gem of a day hike (best late June through September) with plenty of exercise and terrific views toward Jefferson Park and Mount Jefferson only 5 mi to the SE. Several local lakes can be seen as well as Olallie Butte, Mount Hood, Three Fingered Jack, and others once you break out of the thick forest to the rocky summit block. No fee or restroom.

TRAILHEAD: S Breitenbush TH. Take I-5 S from Portland to exit 253 in Salem, turn left for OR-22 E (Detroit Lake/Bend) almost 49 mi, turn left in Detroit on FR-46 for 11 mi, turn right past Breitenbush Hot Springs on gravel FR-4685 over the bridge and then 4½ mi more. Park to the right before a big corner on the road at a "Trailhead" sign (110 mi, more than 2 hours from Portland).

ROUTE: Fill out a free self-issue Wilderness Permit and begin right (E) past the small sign for S Breitenbush Trail 3375 (and Crag Trail 3374 very briefly) more than 2 mi gradually up to the turnoff for Bear Point. Cross a number of little creeks through the jungle of a green forest filled with bear grass, rhododendron, avalanche lilies, and more. The last ½ mi will be steeper and rockier after a switchback to the juncture.

Turn left (N) on Bear Point Trail 3342, following older signage, up much steeper steadily for 21 switchbacks to the (removed) old lookout. You'll cross a creek, see your goal, and then grind up with thinning flora and better than average views of nearby Mount Jefferson. Finish the narrow path over scree, boulders, and rock to the wide-open summit with rocky wind walls for the occasional camper. Be careful if snow lingers near the top into July. Look SE over Bear Lake to Dinah-Mo Peak, Park Ridge Summit, and Mount Jefferson, even seeing into Washington's high Cascades on a clear day.

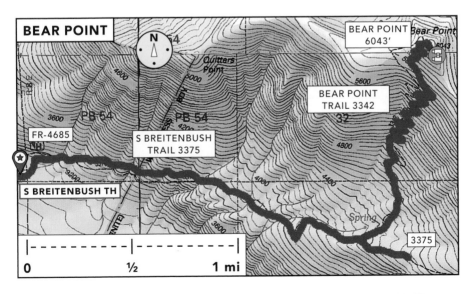

<table>
<tr><td>**66**</td><td>**PACIFIC CREST TRAIL TO PARK RIDGE SUMMIT**</td></tr>
</table>

ELEVATION: 7018 ft, with 1518 ft vertical gain plus 150 ft with Point 6989 too

DISTANCE: 3½ mi up, 7 mi round-trip; 7¾ mi round-trip with Point 6989 too

DURATION: 2 hours up, 3–5 hours round-trip

DIFFICULTY: Strenuous. Steady steep, not hard, loose and steeper briefly to very top, scree, more difficult with snow until August, bugs July through August, Point 6989 is a bushwhack, route-finding, brief scramble, rocky

TRIP REPORT: The easiest and shortest route to this summit and to view Jefferson Park from above is from the PCT TH near Breitenbush Lake. The only problem is that the roads to access the lake are only open a few months a year and require a high-clearance AWD. For the easiest drive but the longer hike, see Jefferson Park to Park Ridge Summit (hike 67). Since the PCT TH is at 5500 ft the views become increasingly grander in no time at all, which is perfect for families trying to get the most out of a short hike. No pass required, and an outhouse is present.

TRAILHEAD: Breitenbush (PCT) TH. Take OR-224 E 32 mi from Portland to Estacada, continue on OR-224 E winding 25 mi into FR-46 for 28 mi, turn left on gravel FR-4220 almost 6½ mi (where two driveways meet, green gate at 1 mi up, high-clearance AWD only, one lane, rocky, few pullouts, potholes, worsens after a couple bridges), turn right (opposite Breitenbush Campground), and right again into a large parking circle, with red gravel, to the end (87 mi, less than 2½ hours from Portland).

ROUTE: Begin slightly right (SW) from the parking area on the spur that quickly meets PCT 2000 arriving at a free self-issue Wilderness Permit station. Continue ¼ mi and stay right on PCT 2000 at an older fork (near faded signs for the PCT and Jefferson Park), walking through pines with wildflowers on the narrow but easygoing trail. See nearby cliffy Pyramid Butte through the trees and ascend 2 quick switchbacks before you soon traverse across a boulder field with an open shot to Pyramid Butte across a burn area. Olallie Butte also dominates the skyline. Hike steeper before easing to cross a saddle at less than 1½ mi from the TH. Look back N to Pyramid Butte, Mount Hood, and Olallie Butte.

Move down a tad, then traverse easily through the woods. See the high ridge from Park Ridge Summit to Park Butte through another burn zone. The wider trail will only be a bit rockier at times through thinning trees with openings and colorful meadows around scree fields. The top of Oregon's second tallest mountain emerges above Park Ridge. Hike up the center of an open meadow following large cairns without difficulty (unless snow covered). The rocky route steepens past several fumaroles as the landscape evolves splendidly to the high ridge. Around 2½ mi from the TH begin passing several small tarn ponds, and then ascend the rock and scree world somewhat steeper using the cairns along conspicuous route winding up to Park Ridge. Strangely, from both sides on the PCT, the high ridge you are aiming for appears closer than in reality.

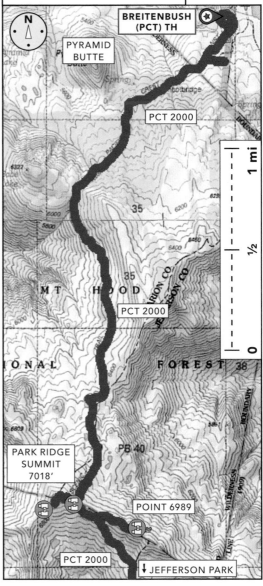

PACIFIC CREST TRAIL TO PARK RIDGE SUMMIT

The second you reach Park Ridge at a rather large rock cairn, the whole of Mount Jefferson stands solidly in your face just 3 mi away. See Russell Lake below 2 mi away in Jefferson Park. An option is to visit the lake, vast meadow, and several more lakes out of eyeshot from the saddle area. This would tack on 4½–7 mi roundtrip (1000 ft in elevation to reclaim) and still be easier than by other routes. See the next hike (67) for more of the description in Jefferson Park. Turn right (W) for Park Ridge Summit less than ¼ mi away for views far surpassing those near the saddle area.

At the somewhat confusing high ridge and saddle area (where most people stop ascending, sadly) the PCT continues left (SE) along the ridge for a moment before traversing down S of Park Ridge to Jefferson Park. For nearby Park Ridge Summit turn right (W) near the large cairn on the path and head up the rocky ridgeline, perhaps a

few feet left around trees to begin finding the solid track. Most families can make it no problem a little more than a hundred yards up the steeper, narrower, looser slope, finishing on the right (N) side of the ridge crest to the wider summit area. Ta-da! Right?! From the boulders among the short pines on the very top, a living postcard presents itself in Mother Nature! At least three USGS benchmarks are embedded in the rock as well as other delightful revelations including a small

Mount Jefferson rears its head in the high country from one of many tarns on the PCT.

colorful tarn below you toward Mount Jefferson. Return down the ridge when you are ready, and consider hiking to Point 6989 for more of a challenge and exercise if you are not descending steeply toward Russell Lake.

From the large cairn at the saddle turn left (N) on the PCT down to Breitenbush TH. For the curious few continuing SE along the high ridge less than ½ mi to Point 6989, stay high on the PCT for a moment as it begins to dip to the right about 100 ft more before you leave it to the left. There will be no trail, so just walk across the rocks in the clearing a few feet back to the ridgeline and follow it or very close to it. Pass old snags and short pines up the black rock and pumice. Perhaps notice cairns around the only blockage, a short rocky gendarme, that may be climbed or passed carefully as you bushwhack to the right across loose pumice and a few obstacles on the steep slope. Then steeply gain the ridge crest again. Scramble up the narrow ridge easily to the top of the bump and finally see part of Scout, Rock, and Park Lakes between Park Butte and Mount Jefferson. Tragically, the largest and prettiest, Bays Lake, is just out of sight. See several more lakes and ponds on both sides of Park Ridge as well as down to Pyramid Butte and over to Mount Hood and Olallie Butte. The 360-degree breathtaking views and solitude say it all!

ELEVATION: 7018 ft, with about 3000 ft vertical gain from Whitewater Creek TH

DISTANCE: 5 mi to Jefferson Park, 12–13 mi round-trip including lakes spurs without the summit; 7½ mi directly to summit, 16-plus mi round-trip including brief lakes spurs

DURATION: Less than 2 hours to Jefferson Park, 4 hours or so round-trip without the summit; 3–4 hours to summit with lakes spurs, 6–8 hours round-trip to summit with lakes spurs

DIFFICULTY: Strenuous. Not that steep until the end, very long, scree, wide, switchbacks, family-friendly to Jefferson Park

---

TRIP REPORT: The absolute crown jewel of Mount Jefferson lies just N of the big Cascade volcano within the flats of Jefferson Park. Great campsites surround several beautiful high alpine lakes and ponds, of different sizes and colors, close in proximity on a large plateau, giving campers and day hikers incredible views of Mount Jefferson and Park Butte. Most people explore the lakes region and return down without the longer and more difficult summit bid. The Breitenbush Lake Campground TH cuts the hiking mileage in half, but the road is one of the most problematic in the state and not recommended without a 4WD if at all, and so the route is not mentioned here.

See Pacific Crest Trail to Park Ridge Summit (hike 66) for a much better but also difficult drive to the same TH area. Listed here is the easiest of the drives, with the best views throughout on the fairly simple and straightforward hike. Northwest Forest Pass required, and an outhouse is present.

TRAILHEAD: Whitewater Creek TH. Take I-5 S from Portland to exit 253 in Salem, turn left for OR-22 E (Detroit Lake/Bend) 58 mi, fork left on Whitewater Road (near milepost 61, gravel FR-2243, slight washboard, slower last 1½ mi), staying on the main road less than 7½ mi to the end at the

Tall Doug firs entertain through the lush forest to Jefferson Park.

Vibrant Bays Lake to Park Butte within Jefferson Park.

sizable parking area (115 mi, more than 2 hours from Portland).

ROUTE: Begin on the wide, and sometimes rocky, Whitewater Creek Trail 3429 after filling out a free self-issue Wilderness Permit. Work easily NE up 5 nicely graded switchbacks through large old growth Doug fir 1½ mi to a ridgeline intersection where you follow the sign to the right. Traverse SE without any difficulty as views of Mount Jefferson improve at every glimpse; descend a bit before crossing a solid bridge over Whitewater Creek. Work up 4 quick steeper switchbacks to the juncture with PCT 2000 at around 4 mi and 1½ hours from the TH. Continue left on the PCT over smaller branches of Whitewater Creek through the thinning woods with wildflowers appearing almost a mile to the wide-open Jefferson Park plateau.

At the immediate junctions you'll have several quality options. One is to stay straight on the PCT NNE a mile farther to the good-sized Russell Lake (to investigate) en route to Park Ridge Summit. The more immediate options in Jefferson Park might entice you into bailing on Park Ridge for another day hike. For the local stroll, take one of at least two quick left-hand paths (Bays Lake Trail and Scout Lake Trail) W toward Scout, Bays, Rock, or Park Lakes. Then head left (W) on Bays Lake Trail once past the S side of Scout Lake (Scout Lake Trail moves N around the lake, then splits to go in

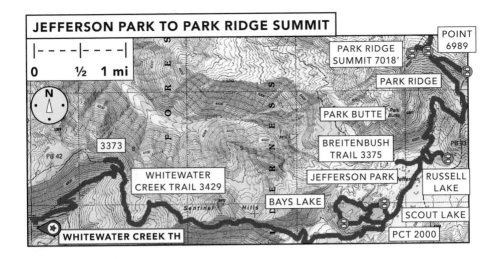

POINT 6989

PARK RIDGE SUMMIT 7018'

PARK RIDGE

PARK BUTTE

BREITENBUSH TRAIL 3375

3373

WHITEWATER CREEK TRAIL 3429

JEFFERSON PARK

RUSSELL LAKE

BAYS LAKE

SCOUT LAKE

WHITEWATER CREEK TH

PCT 2000

0   ½   1 mi

several directions to the other lakes) and a small pond to the even prettier Bays Lake with many great angles. Continue longer clockwise on Bays Lake Trail around the interestingly shaped lake as the path becomes Scout Lake Trail with superb reflections of Mount Jefferson, or come back from the S side of Bays Lake briefly to walk left (N, clockwise) around Scout Lake and meet the PCT again (1 mi or less totally worthwhile excursion). Rock and Park Lakes are close, (signed) smaller, and also deserving of a side visit, especially if you are not climbing to Park Ridge (Summit) on a day hike.

Pass the first of two spurs on the right leading E to Russell Lake just past the left-hand turn W on Breitenbush Trail 3375. The ½-mi-long easy spur from the PCT to the sizable pretty lake is yet another option within the vast meadow of Jefferson Park. You might skip the lake to view it from above on Park Ridge and to save mileage. It's 2 mi from the PCT at the Russell Lake junctures to Park Ridge Summit.

The PCT to Park Ridge climbs the high basin steeper than any of the trails leading up to it and the basin contains rockier sections as well. After crossing the creek in a clearing with views of Mount Jefferson, Park Butte, and the tiny semi-tree-covered Park Ridge Summit, enter the thinning woods for only a couple more turns total as you traverse up a bit steeper near the high ridge. The landscape will be dramatically diverse from Jefferson Park. Follow the dusty PCT up briefly once you reach Park Ridge, NW to a fork near a huge rock cairn. PCT 2000 continues down steeply to the right from the cairn (N) but stay on the narrow, steeper high ridge path instead less than ¼ mi WNW to the summit. From the rocky top see nearby Olallie Lake/Butte, Dinah-Mo Peak, Bear Point, others, and Mount Hood to the N. Down the ridge S toward Park Butte (6851 ft) from the scenic summit, you see Russell Lake, a colorful small pond and others, Jefferson Park, and Mount Jefferson's summit tower! Return the same way.

THREE SISTERS WILDERNESS AND SOUTH

68 Mount Washington....................211

69 Sahalie–Koosah Falls Loop.......214

70 Tamolitch (Blue) Pool...............216

71 Belknap Crater...........................219

72 Black Crater..............................221

73 No Name Lake to
Broken Saddle.........................223

74 Broken Top................................226

75 South Sister..............................230

76 Mount Thielsen.........................232

77 Crater Lake, Watchman Peak
Lookout, and Garfield Peak 234

68 | MOUNT WASHINGTON

ELEVATION: 7794 ft, with 3100 ft vertical gain

DISTANCE: 6¼ mi up, 12½ mi round-trip

DURATION: 3½–4 hours up, 7 hours round-trip

DIFFICULTY: Expert only. Ultra-steep finish, route-finding, Class 5 move 12 ft straight up with slight overhang, Class 4 above/below on summit block, significant exposure, steep ledges, cliffs, bouldering, rope and gear not mandatory but preferred by many, helmet recommended, GPS device helpful

---

TRIP REPORT: One of Oregon's most difficult scrambles challenges seasoned climbers and hikers for the nearly vertical summit. The ancient volcanic plug rises from the plains in the Mount Washington Wilderness as a protuberant steeple between Mount Jefferson and the Sisters Range. Here is the detailed description for the more traveled N ridge route. Pick a nice bluebird day August through October. No pass required, and restrooms are along FR-2690 near the TH.

TRAILHEAD: Pacific Crest TH at Santiam Pass. Take I-5 S from Portland to exit 253 in Salem, turn left for OR-22 E (Detroit Lake/Bend) 80 mi into OR-126 E/US-20 E 5 mi, turn right on FR-2690 (near Santiam Pass) 1 mi, turn left (past Hoodoo Ski Area, FR-2690) 2 mi, turn left before Big Lake on gravel FR-811/Old Santiam Wagon Road ½ mi to the Pacific Crest TH on the right with ample parking (135 mi, 2½ hours from Portland).

ROUTE: Fill out a free self-issue Wilderness Permit and begin S without any trouble on PCT 2000 for an hour and 2½ mi through an old burn area to some living trees, catching a glimpse of Mount Washington along the way. Continue SE ½ mi slightly steeper to the climber's trail marked by an obvious cairn after a large boulder at about 5100 ft. Turn left (E) 150 ft to a fork and stay left up the main bushwhack route steeper almost 2 mi to reach the N ridge at 6300 ft. You'll have to steeply ascend the NW shoulder through the woods as the dirt trail turns to scree and rocks.

Views of the menacing mountain improve on the well-flagged path from the PCT, but the trail is easy to

Butterfly inspects the wildflowers more closely.

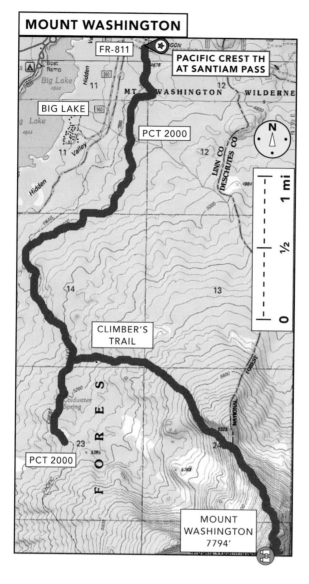

MOUNT WASHINGTON

FR-811

PACIFIC CREST TH AT SANTIAM PASS

BIG LAKE

PCT 2000

CLIMBER'S TRAIL

PCT 2000

MOUNT WASHINGTON 7794'

lose at times on the route down from the summit. You might be pulled left (W) from the ridgeline ¼ mi or so from the end while descending (at a little point/ outcrop). Bushwhack paths entice you through the woods and easy enough over a few small blowdowns to meet the main path again at around 5800 ft.

Scramble a mile up on or near the N ridge to tree line and above with views out to Black Butte, Three Fingered Jack, Mount Jefferson, and Big Lake. Avoid super-steep loose scree paths on the right (W) used as an alternate rapid descent—and avoid that route on the way down too. It's more difficult and you lose most of the grand vistas from the wonderful high ridge. Slowly ascend red pumice and rock past small outcrops and gendarmes. Lastly there's a huge obstacle you will pass on the right, up very steeply to a notch directly under and N of Mount Washington's precipitous summit block. The serious climbing clearly begins from there for the last ¼ mi or so to the peak.

Scout the route, put your helmet on, and begin a Class 4 traverse from the right of the notch and ridge crest. Scramble the third faintly visible ramp with a bit of loose rock back left to a very small landing on the nose of the ridge, with high rock surrounding it, only about 50 ft up from the notch. Another Class 5 route heads straight up and slightly right from the ramps instead to avoid the main crux. Rope and gear should be mandatory for that. From the small landing on the ridgeline it is possible to free-climb up (and down) 10–12 ft for the most difficult portion of the

Nearing the notch under the summit, climbers contemplate the harrowing route...

entire hike, working over a slight overhang fairly narrowly (low Class 5) with good holds. Thankfully, the rock is pretty solid here and for most of the N ridge route, as opposed to other areas on the summit block. Above the crux, the climbing remains ultra-steep with much exposure for 25 ft more to a sizable flat spot.

There are several possibilities to the summit from the flat landing, but working left (SSE) on short traverses very carefully may be best. After more super-steeps (check all holds) the scramble eases only somewhat as you boulder the last stretch enjoyably to the small, but larger than expected, top. The 360-degree views of the Cascades including Three Sisters down S are nothing less than striking! Return by the same route to the N attentively and respectfully after you've had your fill.

ELEVATION: 3000 ft, with 400 ft vertical gain

DISTANCE: 2½ mi round-trip loop

DURATION: Around 2 hours round-trip loop with many breaks

DIFFICULTY: Moderate. Rougher trail at times, tree roots, rocks, some guard rails, easy grade, drop-offs, brief, ups/downs, more difficult and dangerous with snow, traction devices required in winter

---

TRIP REPORT: The next two jaunts will be vastly different from the surrounding summit hikes. The only way to see the brilliant McKenzie River is not from a lofty peak but close up on the river itself! Combine with Tamolitch Pool (hike 70) to maximize your day if coming from the Portland area. May through October works best although flow diminishes somewhat. No pass required, and a restroom is present.

TRAILHEAD: Sahalie Falls TH. Take I-5 S from Portland to exit 253 in Salem for OR-22 W (Detroit Lake/Bend), turn left on OR-22 W 80 mi, turn right 50 ft and right again on US-20 W 3 mi, turn left on OR-126 W more than 5 mi, turn right slowly into the parking circle (135 mi, 2½ hours from Portland). If the lot is full do not park along the highway but drive ¼ mi farther on OR-126 W to the quieter Koosah Falls TH (no

Hikers feel the power and the spray from Sahalie Falls.

pass or restroom) on the right; drive an additional ¼ mi or so down a brief driveway, and begin the hiking loop from there.

ROUTE: For Sahalie Falls alone, begin right past the kiosk and left at the juncture only 50 ft down to the most popular overlook of the raging water blasting 73 ft over an ancient lava dam. A narrower stream plummets just right of the main plunge under the best conditions. Be careful near any viewpoints in the waterfall corridor, whether they are fenced in or not.

For the counterclockwise loop, however, begin to the right from the Sahalie Falls TH signage on Waterfall Trail 3503 for 100 ft up to another overlook with some wooden fencing, just off the trail to the left. Again, be cautious leaning over for that perfect picture. Stay on the main thin trail (right of other immediate spurs) N through the old-growth forest, navigating tree roots and snow

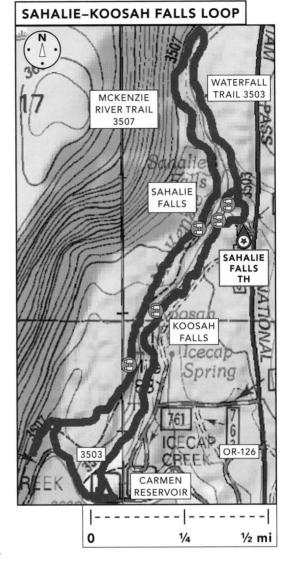

or mud depending on the season, ½ mi up to a signed juncture in a little clearing. Turn left on McKenzie River Trail 3507 crossing the solid footbridge over the gorgeous McKenzie River, then head left (S) on Trail 3507 again heading downstream. Pass a few pretty large fir and cedar with mossy flora as the path undulates easily over more roots and rocks. Notice several small cascades down the fast-moving blue-green river as you arrive at the top of Sahalie Falls almost a mile from the TH. The first spurs end abruptly at the very top at the falls, while somewhat safer and better viewpoints lie closer to the main trail moving down (although none have guard rails). See the rainbow effect near the falls on a sunny day. And notice pockets of cooler and windier air that exist on the loop, which are much different from the air of the warmer TH.

After winding down the steepest part of the trail, arrive at the top of Koosah Falls more than 1¼ mi on the counterclockwise loop from Sahalie Falls TH. During high water these roar even more than Sahalie Falls as the curtain spreads out to 70 ft wide while dropping 64 ft into a colorful pool. Watch for drop-offs along the trail while gazing to the falls and river, then walk more to the SW away from the water to a signed crossroads. Move left on Trail 3503 at a giant tree; walk 100 ft to a parking area, outhouse, and short gravel road; then walk left (SE) at Carmen Reservoir.

Cross the bridge over the river on the road and turn sharp left (N) back into the woods on the Waterfall Trail at 1¾ mi from Sahalie Falls TH (on the loop). Walk easier ¼ mi to a steep spur path down left that very few people follow to some calmer water with a shot up to Koosah Falls. Continuing on Trail 3503, the views to Koosah Falls up in the valley only improve at several railed (with stone) overlooks, the least favorite being the one nearest the top of the waterfall (2¼ mi from the TH on the counterclockwise loop). Hike easier as the trail follows close to the river, then moves up several steps to a cool cascade just off-trail. Be careful there, then continue up more steps and mud (or snow) to the first views and overlooks of Sahalie Falls near the TH at the end of the loop.

70   TAMOLITCH (BLUE) POOL

ELEVATION: 2400 ft, with around 350 ft vertical gain

DISTANCE: 2 mi one way, 4¼ mi round-trip

DURATION: ½–1 hour up, 2–4 hours round-trip with lingering

DIFFICULTY: Moderate. Roots, sharp rocks, mud, magma, drop-offs near pool, ups/downs

TRIP REPORT: The mighty McKenzie River completely disappears underground through an old lava flow from Carmen Reservoir almost 3 mi to Tamolitch Pool. There the water resurfaces as a spring (almost unnoticed during drier months) into a large and remarkably crystal clear, luminous blue pool! Only a phantom (dry) waterfall flows over the top of the rocky end of the stunning and peaceful glassy pool most of the time, but as a bonus a real cascade emerges from the lava in the form of a short and wide curtain from the basalt fissure springs when the river is at 900 cfs or more at least 4 days in a row (waterdata.usgs.gov/or/nwis/uv/?site_no=14158500 &PARAmeter_cd=00065,00060). Under rare, high water, a full-on 60-ft waterfall pours over the old lava with smaller cascades and seepages visible flowing into the pool farther right all the way around. Combine with hike 69 if you are coming from the Portland area. No pass required, and portable outhouses may be present.

TRAILHEAD: Tamolitch TH. Take I-5 S from Portland to exit 253 in Salem for OR-22 E (Detroit Lake/Bend), turn left on OR-22 E 80 mi, turn right 50 ft and right again on US-20 W 3 mi, turn left on OR-126 E more than 10½ mi (exactly 5½ mi down S of Sahalie Falls TH), turn right on FR-730 (brown sign for Trailbridge CG/Smith Boat Launch), cross the bridge over the river, fork right on gravel FR-655 with a few potholes less than ½ mi to the long pullout on the right at the signage before the road continues up to the left (140 mi, 2½ hours from Portland).

ROUTE: Begin left past the kiosk with a map of the Tamolitch Valley Section of the McKenzie River National Recreation Trail. Otherwise there are no signs for somewhat hidden Tamolitch TH/Pool/Falls or Blue Pool. Head up the road 30 ft and turn right (N) on McKenzie River Trail 3507, which is fairly wide and easy to follow, but can be more difficult closer to the pool with jagged volcanic rock taking over the route at times (ankle breakers). Follow the tranquil trail above the river through a lovely, old, mossy forest with some good-sized fir and step aside for the occasional mountain biker. Cross a little bridge after moving down a bit, then at ¾ mi up you walk across a longer and very charming footbridge over a colorful little side creek through the emerald landscape.

Continue over roots, rocks, and mud on the more rustic trail, and after 1 mi up the pitch steepens with more rocky magma covering the path. Look to a short rocky cliff area across the river, then at more than 1¾ up you get a faraway shot of Tamolitch Pool (and possible waterfall). Walk over more pumice, watching for twisted ankles, and see the steep rocky cliff band again on the opposite side of the river before arriving

Bridge over scenic mossy creek to Blue Pool.

above the amazing pool at 2 mi from the TH. Remind children not to run in the pool region and to be mindful.

The azure water is surrounded by sharp, steeply sloped lava as a cliffy area up to 70 ft or so above the pool. During drier times it is possible to work around the rocky trails above the basin to the far right then down steeply to a flatter area by the water to find your picnic spot or even take a very quick dip into the 37-degree water! From wherever your vantage point, its clarity is astonishing—more than 30 ft deep to the bottom in places. Fair warning, however: cliff jumping is not at all recommended as many accidents and even multiple fatalities have occurred from people jumping, falling, or tripping from the rough rocks into the icy water. Return S on the same trail when you can peel yourself away from what normally appears to be the birth of a beautiful river!

ELEVATION: 6872 ft, with 1850 ft vertical gain including Little Belknap Crater

DISTANCE: 3¾ mi up, 8 mi round-trip including Little Belknap Crater

DURATION: 2½ hours up, 4 hours round-trip total

DIFFICULTY: Mix of strenuous for Belknap Crater (lava fields, solid shoes required, not recommended for pets, very little shade, route-finding, steep a short time, pumice, longer to combine both craters) and moderate for Little Belknap Crater (brief, obvious paths, rough on feet for some, family-friendly)

TRIP REPORT: This is a delightful and relatively easy day hike with beautiful, otherworldly scenery from the TH through vast lava fields and meadows to a shield volcano between Mount Washington and North Sister with a bonus for dessert in Little Belknap Crater! Check ahead (oregon.gov/ODOT/Regions/Pages/McKenzie-Highway.aspx) as roads remain closed to McKenzie Pass in winter well into spring. No pass required, and restrooms are located nearby at Dee Wright Observatory.

TRAILHEAD: Pacific Crest TH on McKenzie Pass. Take I-5 S from Portland to exit 253 in Salem, turn left for OR-22 E (Detroit Lake/Bend) 80 mi into OR-126 E/US-20 E 22 mi, turn right at milepost 96 on FR-1012, a mostly gravel shortcut bypassing the town of Sisters and signed for Cold Springs Cutoff/Graham Corral. Stay on FR-1012 for 3 mi, turn right on OR-242 W 11 mi to the TH on the right (past milepost 77) with plentiful parking ½ mi W of the Dee Wright Observatory atop McKenzie Pass (160 mi, 3 hours from Portland).

ROUTE: Walk E from the parking lot past the signage and free self-issue Wilderness Permit station onto PCT 2000 heading N between islands of small forests amid huge lava fields. Leave the edge of the second island of trees for the magma trail with very few trees left for shade. The sharp loose volcanic rock requires your attention but is never very steep as you wind up the worn trail less than 2 mi more to the juncture with Little Belknap Crater.

Remember decent hiking shoes for the magma trails near Belknap Crater.

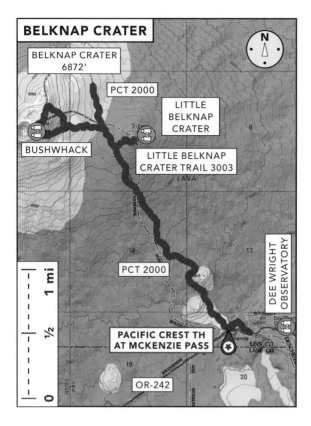

BELKNAP CRATER

BELKNAP CRATER
6872'

PCT 2000

LITTLE
BELKNAP
CRATER

BUSHWHACK

LITTLE BELKNAP
CRATER TRAIL 3003

LAVA

PCT 2000

1 mi

½

0

PACIFIC CREST TH
AT MCKENZIE PASS

DEE WRIGHT
OBSERVATORY

LINN CO
LANE CO

OR-242

See Mount Washington, Black Crater, Belknap Crater, North Sister, Middle Sister, and The Husband along the path.

It's 2½ mi total on the PCT (about an hour from the TH) from the juncture to reach the less than ½-mi-long spur to Little Belknap Crater on the right (5¾ mi round-trip and 1065 ft vertical gain as its own hike). Families skipping Belknap Crater should read ahead for the description, otherwise continue another ¼ mi to the end of the lava. Then leave the PCT, or soon thereafter, for faint paths heading left (W) through meadows toward a long thin row of trees between you and Belknap Crater. Once through the trees you see several awfully steep traverses with very loose rock coming down from the summit; best worth saving this for the descent.

For the main route from the tree line, hike N up the path zigzagging to a small rise; continue in the same direction to the right around the steeps (and possibly lingering snow) for the N ridge of Belknap Crater. See Dugout Butte to the NE and find the more pronounced trail left (S) straight up the fairly steep ridge with loose pumice and stones to the vague and wide summit of the crater rim. It's only from here when you finally see the cliffy breadth of the crater bowl with reddish rock to the right (SW). And of course you can see all the mountains mentioned with Mount Washington in your face plus Little Belknap Crater, Three Fingered Jack, and Mount Jefferson!

For the slightly more challenging, interesting, and quicker loop from the summit, hike ½ mi and 500 ft down to the tree line juncture; continue S almost 100 ft along the high ridge toward the crater but turn sharp left (NE) on a path that soon divides into two. They parallel each other as you scree ski the very steep slope to the main trail in no time at all.

Walk easier back up to the signed juncture for Little Belknap Crater Trail 3003 and turn left (E) less than ½ mi to the tiny summit. It's not without its own charm and surprises as the lava trail changes texture and turns to red pumice and larger rock. Work steeper winding up to the very top. Enjoy the lighting later in the day. Return to the TH after relishing countless views, and remember to stop at Dee Wright Observatory for another bonus!

72   BLACK CRATER

ELEVATION: 7251 ft, with 2400 ft vertical gain

DISTANCE: 4 mi up, 8 mi round-trip

DURATION: Less than 2 hours up, 3 hours round-trip

DIFFICULTY: Strenuous. Steady steep grade, even steeper finish, scree, volcanic pumice and stones, only trail, switchbacks, drop-offs from summit boulders

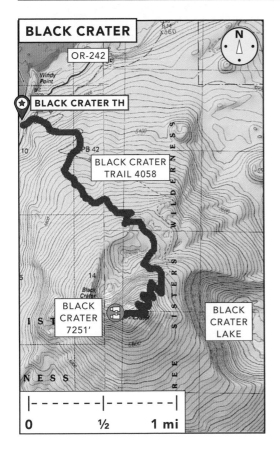

TRIP REPORT: Great under-valued day hike rising above an unburned forest to the top where Ice Age glaciers carved out two huge craters worth checking out; the one E of the summit holds Black Crater Lake. The summit boasts unsurpassed views of the Oregon Cascades N and S. Later in July through October work best as OR-242 closes for several months in winter. No pass required, and a restroom is present.

TRAILHEAD: Black Crater TH. Take I-5 S from Portland to exit 253 in Salem, turn left for OR-22 E (Detroit Lake/Bend) 80 mi into OR-126 E/US-20 E 22 mi, turn right at milepost 96 on FR-1012, a mostly gravel shortcut bypassing the town of Sisters and signed for Cold Springs Cutoff/Graham

Twisted bark and red pumice from a fish-eyed view atop Black Crater.

Corral. Stay on FR-1012 for 3 mi, turn right on OR-242 W less than 8 mi to the TH (after milepost 80 and Windy Point) with parking on the left (155 mi, 3 hours from Portland).

ROUTE: Fill out a free self-issue Wilderness Permit and take Black Crater Trail 4058 moderately steeply without any trouble SE through thick hemlock, pine, and fir. After a couple miles up a handful of switchbacks views begin to open somewhat as trees thin a bit through wildflower-dotted meadows on the N slopes of Black Crater.

Head up another shoulder through the forest with switchbacks moving SW toward the high point, finally breaking out above most of the trees for the last mile. Views expand with every step steeper up the wide-open summit plateau passing some pretty sweet old Whitebark pines along the loose red pumice path to the very top. Be cautious scrambling larger boulders 40 ft to the summit with some rebar from an old lookout present. See Three Fingered Jack, Black Butte, and even Mount Adams on a clear day.

ELEVATION: 8200 ft at No Name Lake; 8388 ft above Broken Saddle; with vertical gains of 1100 ft, and 1288 ft from Broken Top TH

DISTANCE: 2¼ mi to No Name Lake; less than 2¾ mi above Broken Saddle, 5½–6 mi round-trip

DURATION: 1½ hours up, 3–5 hours round-trip with many breaks

DIFFICULTY: Strenuous. Wide trail, sometimes steeper, rocky, scree, pumice, creek crossings more difficult in early summer or with snow, steeper brief loop at top, windy

TRIP REPORT: One of Central Oregon's hot spots no longer a secret is this stunning high alpine glacial lake (not for swimming) within one of the craters off of Broken Top. The Crook Glacier fills the smaller crater bowl directly S of the summit and the Bend Glacier extends E from Broken Top down to the basin containing No Name Lake. The hike is rather long from the Todd Lake TH (at least 14 mi round-trip) so here we slog up to Broken Top TH in a high-clearance AWD vehicle past Todd Lake for the much easier hike to No Name Lake (or Green Lakes to Broken Top). Check ahead for road and trail conditions as snow lingers at higher altitudes until late July into August (www.fs.usda.gov/recarea/deschutes/recarea/?recid=38810). Snow and icebergs may still cover the lake and trails as late as September while wildflowers pop up later as well. Northwest Forest Pass required, and an outhouse is present.

TRAILHEAD: Broken Top TH. Take US-26 E from Portland 103 mi into US-97 S (in Madras) 38 mi to exit 135A in Bend, continue on US-26 E 1½ mi, fork right on NE Division Street ¾ mi, turn right on NW Revere Avenue 100 ft, turn left on NW Wall Street 1¼ mi, turn right on SW Colorado Avenue/Cascade Lakes Nation Scenic Byway (Mount Bachelor) 1½ mi more through Bend, then 21½ mi W, turn right on gravel FR-370 ½ mi to the Todd Lake Day Use Area with pullout parking (no restroom), and continue (high-clearance AWD only, rutted, steep at times, obstacles, one lane) past the green gate if open (usually late July through September, but check ahead; no suitable roadside camping) for 3½ mi, turn left on FR-380 for 1¼ mi (even rougher, or more fun depending how you look at it) to the end at a larger parking lot that fills up on weekends (190 mi, 4 hours from Portland).

ROUTE: Begin NW past the sign for Broken Top Trail 10 to the nearby free self-issue Wilderness Permit station and resume easily through a few trees down ½ mi to an unsigned juncture (old post as a landmark). Fork to the right (N) on the unofficial No Name Lake Trail (opposite the trail that continues to traverse down to Green Lakes) and proceed up through the open pumice meadow. The wide trail vacillates between being rather steep and moderately mellow 1½ mi to a rockier slightly confusing area below No Name Lake. You will cross small creeks without any difficulty, enjoying views of Mount Bachelor to the S, the small summit of Broken Hand ahead to the N (layers of cliffs to a table top summit), as well as the many sharp pinnacles and gendarmes of Broken Top to the left (W).

The terrain is unearthly above most trees and flora into a boulder-filled basin with trails splitting at times to avoid melting snow. They join for a moment in the semiflats before splitting again directly under the rocky gullies. One narrow path, visible from farther away, continuing N is a much steeper option up a narrow, rocky gulch that eschews the direct route to the lake for those avoiding snow and ice. It's also an express route towards Broken Saddle or Broken Hand, but the direct route is preferred with its dramatic entrance to the lake basin. For this direct route, from the slightly confusing area, turn more to the left (W) and discover steep, rocky paths (in a narrow gully) on either side of the small creek coming from the outlet of nearby No Name Lake. Perhaps start up the left side for the best tread, then switch to the right partway up when you encounter looser rock, but either way it's not too tough when it's dry.

Entering the lake basin and crater area for the first time is a phantasmagoric experience! The area is completely spectacular and beats most locales in the entire state, crowds aside. Try to stay on established trails to prevent erosion, as there are plenty to fully explore the region. Walk easier, but carefully, on the thin trail right of the lake and try not to fall in as you gaze into your surroundings. The bright turquoise water only reveals itself for a month or so a year (late August into September), other times being more milky from the glacial flour or frozen over. The lake is a bit larger than first revealed as you meander to the wildflower-covered meadow adjacent the water. You can finally see the summit of Broken Top farthest right (N) of the 9000-ft towers and this view will only improve should you continue ¼ mi to nearby Broken Saddle or above.

Look up the open crater at the many scree paths and take the most pronounced one directly, and a bit steeper, to the saddle where all Three Sisters come into view, as well as Mount Washington, Three Fingered Jack, Mount Jefferson, and Mount Hood. Luckily there are several choice picnic spots for folks to spread out. There are many hiking path options from the saddle. Most people head right to the top of a small bump for the best view of the day, but first take the brief spur to the left (SW) toward Broken Top for a delightful surprise in a small, colorful tarn pond just as bright as No Name Lake when thawed. A small rise just left of the ridge or the ridge itself descends a few feet toward the pond. Another path descends to the bigger lake from there, but hike up to the high point instead.

Unbelievable color from the trail at No Name Lake.

Passing bright red and colorful rock along the ridge, be mindful near the edge and the high point itself (usually quite windy on the ridge). Return down to No Name Lake by the same route or take a more difficult brief loop to the lake by continuing E along the ridge past stunted snags toward another ridge bump before the even more challenging Broken Hand. Leave the ridge almost immediately from the next saddle on a downward traverse S, then move very steeply and briefly down loose rock and pumice to a fork. Left is the fastest route out of the basin toward the TH, while moving right heads down a bit rougher over boulders and snow to the main trail just above No Name Lake. Head left in the brilliant basin past the lake then E down steeply from the outlet creek.

ELEVATION: 9175 ft, with vertical gains of 3735 ft from Green Lakes TH, and 3185 ft from Broken Top TH

DISTANCE: More than 4 mi to Green Lakes from either TH; 6½ mi to the peak, 13 mi or more round-trip from either TH; 16 mi round-trip long loop around Green Lakes including the summit from either TH

DURATION: 1½ hours to Green Lakes, 3–4 hours round-trip; 3–4 hours up, 6 hours round-trip; 6–8 hours round-trip long loop including summit

DIFFICULTY: Expert only to the summit (strenuous to Green Lakes basin or thereabouts). Super-steep, narrow ridge, brief low Class 5 crux, Class 4 above crux at times to peak, highly exposed summit block, narrow catwalk, possible brief scree (foot) ski on descent, mountaineering gear mandatory with snow coverage

---

TRIP REPORT: Broken Top is an extinct complex stratovolcano with extensive erosion and only two glaciers remaining. It is also one of the most picturesque volcanoes from all perspectives and holds the very best views of all Three Sisters a thousand feet higher just to the NW. Some are satisfied omitting the peak to explore the vast and beautiful Green Lakes region with astounding shots up to Broken Top and South Sister. Avoid busy summer weekends if possible. The challenging free-climb up the NW ridge is great for aspiring and seasoned climbers alike with exhilarating (or white-knuckle) exposure for most of the summit block. Northwest Forest Pass required for both THs, and restrooms are present at both THs.

TRAILHEAD: Green Lakes/Soda Creek TH or Broken Top TH. For Green Lakes/Soda Creek TH, take US-26 E from Portland 103 mi into US-97 S (in Madras) 41 mi to exit 138 in Bend (Mount Bachelor) into Cascade Lakes National Scenic Byway (closed in winter) 28 mi, turn right ¼ mi (no sign, across from Sparks Lake, 4 mi past Mount Bachelor Ski Area) along the driveway and large parking circle (overflow lot opposite the highway). For Broken Top TH see hike 73 for directions (around 190 mi, 4 hours from Portland to either TH).

ROUTE: From the N end of the parking area at the very popular Green Lakes TH, begin past the signage and free self-issue Wilderness Permit station on Fall Creek Trail 17 (also called Green Lakes Trail), crossing over a log bridge then easily winding up scenic Fall Creek with several small waterfalls almost 2 mi N to the first major

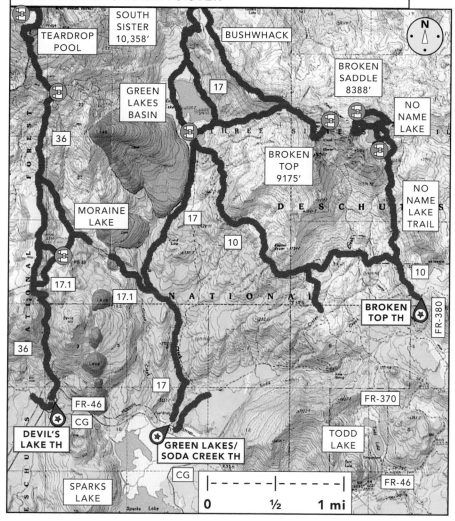

HIKES 73–75: NO NAME LAKE TO BROKEN SADDLE / BROKEN TOP / SOUTH SISTER

SOUTH SISTER 10,358'

TEARDROP POOL

BUSHWHACK

BROKEN SADDLE 8388'

NO NAME LAKE

17

GREEN LAKES BASIN

36

BROKEN TOP 9175'

NO NAME LAKE TRAIL

MORAINE LAKE

17

10

17.1

17.1

10

BROKEN TOP TH

FR-380

36

17

FR-46

CG

DEVIL'S LAKE TH

GREEN LAKES/ SODA CREEK TH

TODD LAKE

FR-370

CG

FR-46

SPARKS LAKE

0   ½   1 mi

juncture. Stay right (opposite Trail 17.1 to Moraine Lake) N on Trail 17 more than 2 mi without any difficulty to the next intersection in Green Lakes basin. You will cross the creek over another solid footbridge and proceed N up the E side of the creek. You pass a couple substantial lava flows on the W side of Fall Creek en route to the high basin.

Several options arise from the three-way intersection in the flats of the basin. To the left is the fading Green Lakes Trail moving left (W) of the largest lake. To the right, 40 ft, is another three-way juncture just W of a small lake. From there, Broken Top Trail is to the right coming from Broken Top TH, Todd Lake, or Soda Spring. Straight and then left of the small lake (great reflection into Broken Top) would take you S of the largest lake to the direct route up Broken Top Trail or the option around the entire

lake on the more pronounced Green Lakes Trail for a nice counterclockwise loop without a summit bid. Many people swim, picnic, and explore the basin without ever attempting Broken Top.

From Broken Top TH, begin NW past the sign for Broken Top Trail 10 to the nearby free self-issue Wilderness Permit station and resume easily through a few trees down ½ mi to an unsigned juncture (old post as a landmark). Fork to the left (W) on Trail 10 (opposite the trail that goes up to No Name Lake—hike 73) and continue to traverse down about 500 ft less than 4 mi to Green Lakes. Cross several little creeks with views out to Mount Thielsen and Diamond Peak and easily walk through some trees, finally opening up again to a three-way juncture in Green Lakes basin. For the primary route, turn right on Trail 10 past a small lake to the S side of the largest lake.

For the direct route up Broken Top Trail, look for the climber's path to the right of the main trail as you reenter the forest briefly near the S lakeshore of the largest lake. Hike ENE very steeply and continue to follow the dirt and scree path 1½ mi with turns to a low spot on the high NW ridge of Broken Top. A few paths take off right (E) up higher, but ignore those as they are best saved for the super-steep scree ski on the descent, if at all. See below for the remainder of the route from the ridge at about 7900 ft.

For the longest and most scenic route up Broken Top you will begin from the saddle at the base of the NW ridge and then complete the clockwise loop by descending one of the routes above back to Green Lakes. For this route, move left or straight (N) on Green Lakes Trail from the first three-way intersection (if coming from Green Lakes TH) through the flats of the basin on the left (W) side of the largest colorful lake (or take the main trail right around the E side a bit easier). Follow the faint trail 2 mi without trouble to the saddle through mostly open terrain and lowlands with great shots back to Mount Bachelor and continuous views of Broken Top and South Sister. You arrive at the juncture with the lake loop and move left (N) on Green Lakes Trail steeper past the brightest green smaller lake into the woods up

Incredible panorama from Broken Top on a lovely fall day.

to the fairly open saddle.

Use your route-finding skills to leave the trail a bit into the flats turning right (SE) with only few faint paths discernible as the ridge defines itself a few feet farther. Pass a few small tarns and begin to ascend steeper up the wide NW ridge. It's about 2 mi more to the summit as you work sharper up the wonderful ridge past small snags with improving vistas of the lakes under South Sister, and with Middle Sister, North Sister, Three Fingered Jack, and Mount Jefferson also in sight. The route steepens over the rocky trail but is easy to follow past the main ridge juncture (about 7900 ft) up to the main crux, a sheer basalt band (with a lot of red) blocking easier travel on the ridgeline.

There are two main choices from the Class 5 section and although most of the rock here is fairly solid, remember to check your holds carefully first and take your time for the rest of the climb. To the left from the ridge crest is a visible crack 12 ft or so up with some looser rock that most people climb. Straight up actually holds a more solid route, with good foot ledges for a possible descent too, covering the same height to better ground.

The rest is so fun (even though mostly Class 3 and Class 4 with much exposure) that you might forgo the super-steep scree ski, S of the ridge SW into the valley much quicker on the descent, to stay on the high ridge with its never-ending wild views. Follow the narrow scree and red pumice path on or near the ridge to the catwalk just W of the peak. Take this exposed ledge to the right (S) cautiously over to a notch below the summit block. Turn left (NNE) up the highest ridge where you must navigate over ledges very steeply the final 20 ft or so, paying attention and finding some solid holds up the exposed rocky red top.

See several lakes from the peak including Green Lakes to the W and a piece of No Name Lake down to the E. Unequivocally the very best angle of all the Three Sisters, and you can also see Mount Washington, Three Fingered Jack, Mount Jefferson, and Mount Hood. Descend with care from the summit to Green Lakes.

75 SOUTH SISTER

ELEVATION: 10,358 ft, with 4900 ft vertical gain (plus 250 ft with Moraine Lake loop)

DISTANCE: 6 mi up, 12 mi round-trip (12½–13 mi round-trip with Moraine Lake)

DURATION: 2½–4 hours up, 6–8 hours round-trip

DIFFICULTY: Very challenging. Long, sustained steeps last miles, windy on top, no protection from storms, solid trails, scree, crowded on weekends, mountaineering gear in winter

TRIP REPORT: Oregon's third highest mountain is a nontechnical climb and thus very popular with both weekend warriors pushing their bounds and with experienced hikers who have hiked the volcano multiple times. The route described here is the most common, being straightforward up the S ridge. South Sister is the highest and broadest of all Three Sisters, the most active of the three volcanoes, and holds the state's largest glacier, the Prouty Glacier, as well as the state's highest lake (when thawed) in Teardrop Pool. August into October works best and only on completely bluebird days as weather changes rapidly around the summit crater. Northwest Forest Pass required, and restrooms are present.

TRAILHEAD: Devil's Lake TH. Take US-26 E from Portland 103 mi into US-97 S (in Madras) 41 mi to exit 138 in Bend (Mount Bachelor) into Cascade Lakes National Scenic Byway (closed in winter) 30 mi, turn left (small brown TH sign) ¼ mi passing the Devil's Lake Campground with parking in or near the circle (190 mi, 4 hours from Portland).

ROUTE: Begin N of the parking circle on South Sister Climber's Trail 36 after filling out a free self-issue Wilderness Permit. Walk over a footbridge above Tyee Creek before crossing the highway and hiking steep steadily almost 1½ mi N up through thick hemlock on the wider horse trail with switchbacks and not much for views to a four-way intersection in a partial clearing. To the right is Moraine Lake on the return trail for the optional miniloop later.

Continue straight (N) instead on the sandy climber's trail 3 mi up to pass a little green cirque lake, the last half being much steeper and rockier than the flats above Moraine Lake. Views will open immediately above Moraine Lake over to Broken Top topping the last shrubs and wind-blown small pines; several other lakes and mountains are visible. A few paths take off right (E) down (steeper briefly) to the lake, including one near the top of (N) the Moraine Lake valley, but save this one or the others for the loop to the lake on the return for even better reflections and scenery on a great side trip.

The pitch mellows for a moment thankfully passing above (8900 ft) the pretty cirque lake at the bottom of the Lewis Glacier to the N as the ridge to the left becomes more defined a long mile very steeply to the crater rim. The loose scree and red pumice is tedious and unrelenting. The trudge

From the super-steep climber's trail looking toward Mount Bachelor and countless lakes.

N finally gives way to the mellow glory walk once you crest the volcano's snow-filled crater. Finish less than ½ mi and almost 30 minutes around the rocky rim trail to the right without any difficulty to the actual summit. Some people cross straight over the crater when the snow is safe. Walk a bit beyond the summit for more angles of turquoise Teardrop Pool (only seen in September and October most years, if at all).

The sights are overwhelming from the rim, to say the least. Gaze out to Middle Sister, North Sister, Three Fingered Jack, Mount Jefferson, Mount Hood, and even Mount Adams on super clear day, as well as endless nearby colorful lakes and tarns of different sizes. And of course there's also Broken Top, Mount Bachelor, Mount Thielsen, and Mount McLoughlin to the S.

Return down from the rim and super-steep loose trail; consider hiking one of the more moderate pumice trails left (E) down to Moraine Lake along the top half of that valley. From E of the lake itself, near the outlet, are some cool cascades down Goose Creek for another little side spur. Otherwise, traverse up SW easily under a mile on the main trail S of Moraine Lake to the end of the little loop at the four-way intersection. Turn left on South Sister Climber's Trail steadily down 1½ mi to Devil's Lake.

76 MOUNT THIELSEN

ELEVATION: 9182 ft, with 3782 ft vertical gain

DISTANCE: Almost 5 mi up, less than 10 mi round-trip

DURATION: 2½–3 hours up, 4–6 hours round-trip

DIFFICULTY: Very challenging. Ultra-steep summit block, Class 4 last bit, airy, decent rock, well liked, ropes not mandatory when dry, bugs late July through August, loose scree

---

TRIP REPORT: The Mount Thielsen Wilderness stretches almost 55,000 acres out including up to Crater Lake, a very different kind of volcano. Mount Thielsen is an extinct shield volcano that rises like a pinnacle thousands of feet above the landscape as historic glaciers eroded the mountain and carved the sheer walls. So much so that the peak attracts lightning rods if storm clouds move in, so be aware! Although technical routes do exist, there actually is one route quite feasible and popular. Try this wonderfully challenging free-climb on a sunny summer day to stay on your game if visiting the flourishing Diamond Lake Recreation Area or nearby Crater Lake. Many hiking enthusiasts make it with some effort to the notch known as Chicken Ledge, before the last 80 ft of ultra-steeps below the peak, and are quite satisfied without a summit bid. Northwest Forest Pass required, and a restroom is present 30 ft onto the trail.

TRAILHEAD: Mount Thielsen TH. Take I-5 S to exit 188 (Oakridge/Klamath Falls), merge onto OR-58 E 80 mi, take the ramp onto US-97 S 18 mi, turn right on OR-138 W 19 mi, turn right into the signed small parking lot off the highway (235 mi, 4 hours from Portland).

ROUTE: Begin from the end of the parking lot 30 ft along the trail to the signage and free self-issue Wilderness Permit station next to an outhouse. Walk all too easily winding up Mount Thielsen Trail 1456 (with equestrians) through lodgepole pine and hemlock almost 4 mi to the intersection with the PCT. Only about 30 minutes and 1¾ mi from the TH are the first shots of your goal (which looks rather menacing from every angle) near a juncture with Trail 1458 heading left (N, down longer to Diamond Lake). Stay on Trail 1456 more than 2 mi up the wide trail with 4 switchbacks and turns through the woods and clear-cut section as the W ridge of Mount Thielsen defines itself clearly to the PCT (at 7350 ft).

The imposing peak only appears impossible without gear for most day hikers!

Hike straight (E) on Trail 1456 at the intersection with the PCT onto the rougher climber's path mostly just to the right (S) of the ridge or on it through quickly thinning trees. You will see the remainder of the sometimes Class 3 ridge (some wear helmets) better above timberline, as you traverse up semiloose scree and pumice very steeply, but not too bad. Head right (E) under the summit block over rocky ledges to an obvious SW-facing gully route. Watch your holds and carefully ascend the steep, wide gully with looser rock to the little notch called Chicken Ledge (9100 ft) below the final climb to the peak. From the notch, enjoy the views across Diamond Lake to Mount Bailey with the rim of Crater Lake visible to the S. Return slowly down the summit block back to the W ridge or continue upwards.

To reach the summit, turn left (N) from Chicken Ledge to scramble up the S face of the highest ridge; find reasonably solid rock up ramps and ledges to the left of the ridgeline with considerable exposure. Some use protection and rope in. Test all holds and then climb to the right and straight up before the vertical rock and overhang. Find some better footing nearest the larger-than-expected peak with far reaching views from the Sisters Range to Mount Shasta. Be mindful of others and the wind while on the narrow summit area, then hike down to relative safety.

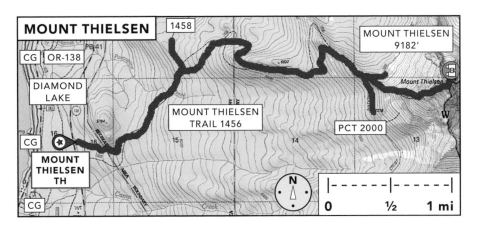

77 CRATER LAKE, WATCHMAN PEAK LOOKOUT, AND GARFIELD PEAK

ELEVATION: 6173 ft at the lake (from Cleetwood Cove Trail); 7100 ft average viewpoint from loop roads; 8013 ft at Watchman Peak Lookout; 8054 ft at Garfield Peak; with vertical gains of 650 ft for Cleetwood Cove Trail, around 100 ft for brief trails to various viewpoints around the lake, 400 ft for Watchman Peak Lookout, 1100 ft for Garfield Peak

DISTANCE: 2¼ mi round-trip for Cleetwood Cove Trail; 1 mi one way to Rim Village from a pullout for Discovery Point Trail; 1¾ mi round-trip for Watchman Peak Lookout; 3½ mi round-trip for Garfield Peak

DURATION: 1–2 hours round-trip for Cleetwood Cove Trail; less than 1 hour round-trip for brief viewpoint spurs or Discovery Point Trail; 1 hour round-trip for Watchman Peak Lookout; 1½–3 hours round-trip for Garfield Peak

DIFFICULTY: Mix of moderate for Watchman Peak, Mount Scott, most roadside stops, viewpoints, and short rim trails (paths can be simple but border cliffs thousands of feet into the crater without fencing or guard rails for most of it, similar to the roads) and strenuous for Cleetwood Cove Trail, Garfield Peak, and others (steep switchbacks down the only legal trail to the lakeside, drop-offs for Garfield Peak with snow, ice, mountaineering conditions near the top until July or later)

TRIP REPORT: Oregon's only national park is not big at all, as national parks go, and is more or less underdeveloped, underfunded, and understated, and therefore mostly a delight to visit. That is, during midweek, or late in the season when there are fewer crowds on the slender roads and trails. Although the park is open year-round, the roads around the crater rim do not open until late June or July when the snow finally melts (road from the S entrance plowed to Steel Visitor Center); the crater receives almost 45 ft of the white stuff per winter! Be sure to check ahead for current conditions (craterlakelodges.com/lodging/mazama-village-campground/). E Rim Drive on half of the loop as well as the Pinnacles Road are slow to open. The national park fee for passenger vehicles ($25) is good for 7 days, and there are plentiful restrooms throughout the park.

TRAILHEAD: Take I-5 S from Portland to exit 188 (S of Eugene), merge onto OR-58 E (Bend/Klamath Falls) 84 mi, merge onto US-97 S (Klamath Falls) 17 mi, turn right on OR-138 W 14¼ mi, turn left on Crater Lake Highway less than 1 mi to a pay

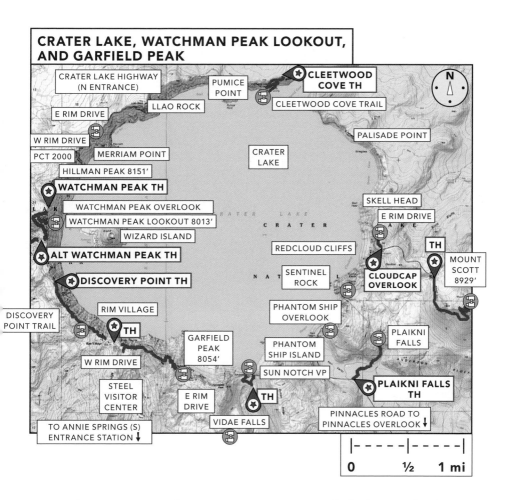

CRATER LAKE, WATCHMAN PEAK LOOKOUT, AND GARFIELD PEAK

CRATER LAKE HIGHWAY (N ENTRANCE)

PUMICE POINT

CLEETWOOD COVE TH

CLEETWOOD COVE TRAIL

LLAO ROCK

E RIM DRIVE

PALISADE POINT

W RIM DRIVE

PCT 2000

MERRIAM POINT

CRATER LAKE

HILLMAN PEAK 8151'

WATCHMAN PEAK TH

SKELL HEAD

E RIM DRIVE

WATCHMAN PEAK OVERLOOK

WATCHMAN PEAK LOOKOUT 8013'

WIZARD ISLAND

REDCLOUD CLIFFS

TH

ALT WATCHMAN PEAK TH

MOUNT SCOTT 8929'

DISCOVERY POINT TH

SENTINEL ROCK

CLOUDCAP OVERLOOK

DISCOVERY POINT TRAIL

RIM VILLAGE

PHANTOM SHIP OVERLOOK

TH

W RIM DRIVE

GARFIELD PEAK 8054'

PHANTOM SHIP ISLAND

PLAIKNI FALLS

STEEL VISITOR CENTER

E RIM DRIVE

SUN NOTCH VP

PLAIKNI FALLS TH

TH

TO ANNIE SPRINGS (S) ENTRANCE STATION ↓

VIDAE FALLS

PINNACLES ROAD TO PINNACLES OVERLOOK ↓

N

|- - - - -|- - - - -|

0   ½   1 mi

station, then 8 mi more to the crater rim at a juncture with the loop road and many options. Rim Drive is 33 mi winding around the crater's mountains; many people take a couple days to explore the area's trails more thoroughly, although it can be driven in a single day (240 mi from Portland to the rim, more than 4 hours driving). Crater Lake Lodge provides the only accommodations near the crater with camping a few miles away. Diamond Lake Recreation Area is nearby for visitors coming from the N, offering three campgrounds and several nearby hiking options to combine with Crater Lake (diamondlake.net). From the S entrance (Annie Springs Entrance Station) for those coming from Grants Pass or Medford on State Highway 62, many camp at the also quite large Mazama Village Campground just inside the park (craterlakelodges. com/lodging/mazama-village-campground/). The rest of the driving and hiking tour follows.

ROUTE: From the N entrance to the park, the natural and far more dramatic progression for the loop takes visitors counterclockwise (right) around Crater Lake

Magnificent shot near a cornice on Garfield Peak to Wizard Island in Crater Lake.

on W Rim Drive. If Cleetwood Cove Trail is your first goal, however, then turning left (clockwise), on E Rim Drive from Crater Lake Highway will bypass Llao Rock before giving any lake views more than 4½ mi to the Cleetwood Cove TH (leading hikers down to the tour boat landing). The large parking lot for Cleetwood Cove Trail is on the left, with the trail across the road next to a map and info kiosks. You would take the wide trail down S from the main road quite steeply for 8 switchbacks and a mile to the actual shoreline of the unbelievably clear blue lake. This is the only lake level area in the park for visitors.

Stay right instead at the first juncture on the rim from Crater Lake Highway 2 mi to the Watchman Overlook with a small lot on the left (being very careful along the narrow road). Families can easily walk up a few feet to the fenced overlook closest to Wizard Island in Crater Lake. The lighting into the super-deep clear blue lake changes radically throughout the day and year. It is the deepest lake in the United States at 1949 ft with no stream running in or out of the caldera and so completely depends on snowmelt (and rain)! To the left (N) from the saddle is Hillman Peak, the highest summit on the crater rim itself at 8151 ft. Some people scramble to the top from the Pacific Crest National Scenic Trail (PCT Spur Trail). To the right (S) is the signed trail for the more popular Watchman Peak. If you're lucky you might even spot the Old Man of the Lake lurking around Wizard Island. The 30-ft-long hemlock log has been somehow floating vertically in the lake since before 1896 with more than 4 ft jutting above the water and remaining dry.

For Watchman Peak, take the trail that parallels above the road SW easily (unless still covered by snow and ice) before leaving the PCT at a fork left for the summit trail to the Watchman Peak Lookout (8013 ft). There are 8 moderately steep switchbacks up the wide, rocky trail to the old fire lookout. From the short rock wall around the lookout is the very best view of Wizard Island directly below. Many people seek Watchman Peak as one of the park's best locales for sunset gazing. Like the saddle below, Mount McLoughlin can be seen as well as Mount Shasta to the S and to the N over the lake left of Mount Thielsen are Three Sisters!

For an alternate Watchman Peak TH and for the rim loop, continue the twisting drive 1½ mi from the Watchman Overlook parking lot (see nearby prominent Union Peak) to a small nondescript driveway on the left. There you'll find picnic tables near the woods and the PCT on the left providing a slightly longer and quiet route NW to a signed trail (right) for Watchman Peak.

Less than 5 mi on the drive from the N juncture for the rim loop is the long pullout for Discovery Point (Trail) on the left. Enjoy the local splendor and consider taking an easy, short walk SE along the rim; there are great perspectives from several viewpoints, but use caution around some precipitous drop-offs next to the trail. Walk right from the pullout to the sign for Discovery Point Trail to Rim Village (1 mi); go as far as you like and come back, or arrange for a pickup. The simple trail moves up and down a tad and follows the actual rim so be extra cautious, especially with younger ones. And leave the selfie-stick in the car or at home! Peer into the deep blue lake from several perches including a few looking past a huge rock spire well below about ½ mi in. Watch for deer and elk in the meadows. Soon after that the trail descends a bit to Rim Drive where you follow the road to the adjoining path briefly to Rim Village.

At 5¾ mi drive from the N juncture for the rim loop, or 2½ mi from Steel Visitor Center S of the crater, is the signed intersection for Rim Village. Within the tiny hamlet are Rim Village Café and Gift Shop, Sinnott Memorial Overlook, Rim Visitor Center, and Crater Lake Lodge (with a restaurant). The TH parking for Garfield Peak is W of the lodge anywhere you can find a spot in the various areas. For Garfield Peak, walk E past the lodge in front or behind it on the paved path with a short rock wall down briefly to a big sign with a map for Garfield Peak.

Walk left onto the wide and dusty trail and ascend 10 reasonably steep switchbacks along the S side of the mountain and on the ridge itself bordering Crater Lake to the summit. Keep in mind that just like Rim Drive (without any guard rails) the trails here have no safety fences to protect you when you approach the crater's edge for endless panoramas. Traction devices might help in July as the last of a short steep pitch after 8 switchbacks finally melts off. Later in the day the snow warms up and isn't as much a problem. There is even a brief and deep glissade chute next to the steeper snow trail. The snowy trail traverses right a moment, and then heads left up the ridgeline again. See your goal and the big snow cornice hanging from it (until late summer), and remember to keep your distance once on top if snow and ice remain. Otherwise, wildflowers pop up along the rocky path where there isn't snow, and after a couple more switchbacks you climb to the top of the mound with very few trees

No mediocre viewpoints of sunset near Oregon's only national park!

around. The views of the lake and surroundings are similar to Watchman Peak, only even more intense! Some people find the bushwhack continuing SE along the rim without difficulty over to Applegate Peak and back, but most return down for more pronounced trails around the park.

Leaving Rim Village, continue driving straight at the loop juncture 2½ winding miles to the Steel Visitor Center on the right (the S entrance is straight 4½ mi from the visitor center). Turn left a few feet past Steel Visitor Center for the crater loop on E Rim Drive (if open) 3 mi to the Vidae Falls pullout. The three-tiered, 115-ft cascade can be seen from the car and has a nice flow in early summer but nearly dries out by autumn. At more than 4¼ mi on E Rim Drive from Steel Visitor Center is the Sun Notch Viewpoint on the left. Take this easy, wide pumice trail to stretch your legs if for no other reason as views are relatively minimal. Walk a 1-mi loop with many confusing variations, but just stay on the most worn path if you're concerned. All paths lead to a shot of Phantom Ship Island below the sheer cliff band surrounding the lake.

Drive 4 mi more on E Rim Drive to an intersection with Pinnacles Road near the Phantom Ship Overlook, also known as Kerr Notch, accessible from a pullout on the left, with a great view of the cool tiny island below Garfield Peak. Turn sharp right (S) on Pinnacles Road for Plaikni Falls TH a mile down on the left. This easy trail climbs less than 200 ft up a mile through a lush forest with openings and wildflowers to a picturesque little 25 ft or so cascade and drop.

From Plaikni Falls TH, drive 5 mi more down to the end of Pinnacles Road for the Pinnacles Overlook and trail away from Crater Lake (not on map included). This area would be anticlimactic and could easily be skipped if you've ever been to Bryce

Canyon in Utah, but it's still interesting. From the TH, with less fanfare walk left, then back right (E) to several overlooks along a rim of several volcanic fumarole chimneys ranging 30–60 ft high. After ½ mi or so of little elevation change on the wide sandy trail you reach the old TH in another nondescript area where most people turn around from there or soon after.

From the Phantom Ship Overlook, continue counterclockwise on E Rim Drive past more viewpoints to the 1-mi-long side road left to Cloudcap Overlook (at about 12 mi from Steel Visitor Center). Check out the nearby Redcloud Cliffs from the driving circle or from a brief spur trail heading right along the steep rim. This is another superior viewpoint area for the crater but even more so for sunrise. About ¼ mi farther is the long pullout on the right for the Mount Scott Lookout, technically the park's highest summit at 8929 ft, although it sits back from the crater rim. The 4½-mi round-trip hike with 1250 ft vertical gain along gradual switchbacks isn't snow-free until August or so but gives visitors a grand perspective in the early morning light.

At 18½ mi from the Steel Visitor Center is the extensive parking lot on the right for Cleetwood Cove Trail. See the first paragraph for the description. Finish the driving loop 4½ mi to the juncture with Crater Lake Highway where you turn right to the N entrance station and exit the park.

OREGON NORTHERN COASTAL RANGE

78 Clatsop Spit Loop..................... 241

79 Saddle Mountain 243

80 Clark's Mountain (Tillamook
Head Summit)............................ 245

81 Cannon Beach to
Silver Point 248

82 Neahkahnie Mountain.............. 250

83 Rogers Peak.............................. 253

84 Kings Mountain Loop 256

85 Elk Mountain............................. 260

86 Marys Peak 262

ELEVATION: Sea level, with maybe 10 ft vertical gain

DISTANCE: 4 mi round-trip loop plus less than ½ mi with Wildlife Viewing Bunker miniloop from Lot D TH

DURATION: 2 hours round-trip

DIFFICULTY: Easiest. Route-finding, flat, much sand, few trails, windy, more difficult at high tide, road walking

TRIP REPORT: Fort Stevens State Park, located at Oregon's farthest most NW corner at the edge of the Columbia River on the Pacific, was the primary military defense installation from the Civil War to WWII. It's now a huge 4200-acre park with a museum and gun battery, camping, fishing, freshwater swimming and boating, a jetty, several THs, wildlife viewing, biking and hiking trails, and an old shipwreck to visit.

For this jaunt we skip the tourist attractions and get right to the best of the best with the Clatsop Spit Loop, a huge sand spit spreading out at the end of the peninsula, which formed from river sediment brought after the last Ice Age. A special day use fee is required and available near the beginning of the park, and outhouses are located at every TH.

TRAILHEAD: Lot D TH. Take US-26 W from Portland 75 mi, exit right onto the ramp for US-101 N 13 mi, turn left on OR-104 N 2¼ mi, turn left on Ninth Avenue 1 mi, turn right on NW Ridge Road 2 mi, turn left on Jetty Road (day use area entrance) 4¾ mi to the end at a very large parking lot (100 mi, 2 hours from Portland).

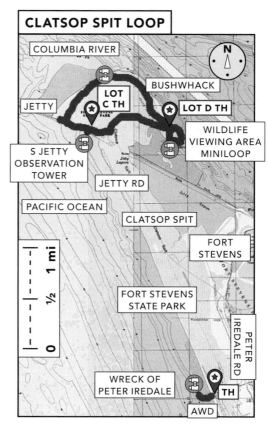

CLATSOP SPIT LOOP

COLUMBIA RIVER

BUSHWHACK

JETTY

LOT C TH

LOT D TH

WILDLIFE VIEWING AREA MINILOOP

S JETTY OBSERVATION TOWER

JETTY RD

PACIFIC OCEAN

CLATSOP SPIT

FORT STEVENS

WRECK OF PETER IREDALE

FORT STEVENS STATE PARK

IREDALE RD

PETER IREDALE RD

TH

AWD

1 mi ½ 0

ROUTE: It is possible to drop bikes off at the Lot C TH (South Jetty, en route to Lot D) to complete the counterclockwise loop almost 1½ mi over pavement, or simply walk on the shoulder of the safe roads the same distance to finish. Instead of being enticed by the large sign for the Wildlife Viewing Bunker and wooden walkway to the beach on the right, head left of the outhouse (end of the Wildlife Viewing counterclockwise miniloop trail at the NE corner of the parking lot). See below for the miniloop trail after the main walk.

Begin the main walk down steeply 6–8 ft where possible from the NE corner of the parking lot to the beach immediately. Turn left (NW) along the water. It's 1¼ mi to round the corner to the wider beach at the tip. During high tide at times of the year, this section may require navigating small trees, bushes, and vines near the water's edge. From the tip, continue SW 1 mi to reach the South Jetty. The flat expanse of sand at lower tides with nice lighting is optimal for viewing the Pacific Ocean at the mouth of the Columbia River! As you see, then walk, easily up to the jetty near some huge boulders lodged on it, you very quickly realize whether or not you are able to walk along the jetty itself (left to Lot C). If giant waves are crashing over the top (winter through spring) you may prefer more solid ground left of the giant rock wall less than ½ mi on sandy paths SE. You will move across a little creek and over a rocky, wide path, sauntering slightly left at a faint fork near the end, moving away from the jetty (leading to Lot C).

Check out the South Jetty Observation Tower for unobstructed views before completing the loop, then walk the paved driveway E around ¼ mi to the end. Turn left on Jetty Road more than a mile around the bend and a long straightaway between high brush and trees to Lot D. Check out the Wildlife Viewing Area miniloop trail by walking over the boardwalk to the brushy path in Trestle Bay. Follow the most pronounced sandy trail left around the corner and back to the parking lot through trees to finish.

Wreck of Peter Iredale from Fort Stevens State Park.

To visit the Wreck of Peter Iredale, take Jetty Road back 3½ mi from Lot D, turn right on Burma Road 1¼ mi, turn right on Peter Iredale Road ½ mi to the end. Those with AWD can drive down to the beach at many times of the year, but the interesting shipwreck frame remnants are only a few feet down the beach from the official TH. The four-masted steel barque was headed for Portland and ran aground in 1906; all on board somehow survived. Leaving the area, turn right at the stop sign onto Peter Iredale Road ¾ mi to the end, passing the campground, and turn right on NW Ridge Road.

ELEVATION: 3283 ft, with about 1885 ft vertical including Humbug Mountain

DISTANCE: 2¼ mi up, 4½ mi round-trip; plus less than ½ mi round-trip for Humbug Mountain Spur Trail

DURATION: 1½–2 hours up, 3 hours round-trip

DIFFICULTY: Strenuous. Brief but steep in places, ups/downs, chain trail near top, rocky, more difficult with snow/ice when traction devices necessary, drop-offs, very popular

TRIP REPORT: One of the highest points in the Northern Coastal Range boasts impeccable views past Astoria to Cape Disappointment and Long Beach, Washington,

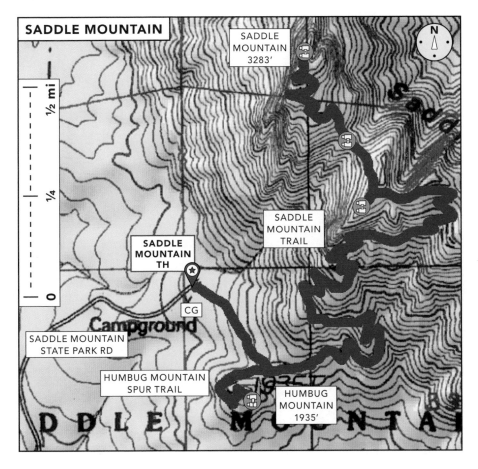

as well as all of the major Cascade Mountains from Mount Rainier, Mount Adams, and Mount St. Helens to Three Sisters Range on a clear day. Although open year-round it is very popular from late May into June or later for some of the best wildflower displays on the North Coast. No fee required, and restrooms are present.

TRAILHEAD: Saddle Mountain TH. Take US-26 W from Portland 65 mi (milepost 10½), turn right at the bottom of the hill for Saddle Mountain (State) Natural Area on roughly paved Saddle Mountain State Park Road 7 mi narrowly to the end with parking all around (75 mi, 1½ hours or so from Portland).

ROUTE: Begin right of the parking lot past the signage and little campground SE up ¼ mi through the emerald forest with maple, alder, and salmonberry bushes to a juncture. Take the signed Humbug Mountain Spur Trail right (S) steeper and narrower less than ¼ mi S and 100 ft up to an outcrop and open knoll (1935 ft) with the best overlook of your distinctive goal in Saddle Mountain. Return down and turn right (E) steeply up the wide Saddle Mountain Trail through Douglas fir and spruce including 8 solid switchbacks to the accurate 1 mi post (without Humbug Mountain).

On the ninth switchback is an old picnic table and near the eleventh switchback you get a taste of the chain-covered trail, which is odd but actually easier to walk on as opposed to avoiding it; and it helps prevent erosion. Views begin opening from the fourteenth switchback. Pass another picnic table on the sixteenth switchback (avoid short-cutting) as the trail becomes slightly overgrown along a traverse E. It's 5 switchbacks more, a bit easier, N to the high ridge (holding several rocky summits) near another picnic table (less than 2 mi from the TH without Humbug Mountain).

Walk W on the undulating trail and stay right in the clearing at a viewpoint spur fork to traverse steep meadows NW toward the summit, finally dropping quite steeply to a small saddle before the final climb. Enjoy views and wildflowers from the saddle area, being careful. Then hike up the chain-covered trail cautiously, against the green hillside with the steepest pitch of the day—11 switchbacks to the very top, which is a railed-in flat area with a picnic bench. Take in the sights near and far from the old lookout site before descending, and return to enjoy the Natural Area at various times of the year.

Narrow mossy stretch toward Saddle Mountain in the spring.

ELEVATION: 1253 ft, with vertical gains of 1000 ft or more directly from Seaside, and 1400 ft from Ecola State Park (Indian Beach)

DISTANCE: 2¼ mi up, 5¼ mi round-trip; 3½ mi up from Indian Beach, 7-plus mi round-trip

DURATION: 1 hour up, 2–3 hours round-trip; 1½–2 hours up from Indian Beach, 3–4 hours round-trip

DIFFICULTY: Strenuous. Muddy often, misty, slippery, tree roots, uneven boardwalks, route-finding, drop-offs, steeper briefly, GPS device helpful for summit

---

TRIP REPORT: Tillamook Head is the cliffy section of land with rolling hills and dense lush forests that rises 1200 ft above sea level between Seaside and Cannon Beach. Clark's Mountain may only be a bucket list item as there are no views from the nondescript summit and the route will most likely be quite muddy. After all, the area receives over 6 ft of rain per year! The majority of people begin from Indian Beach and settle for a few very average tiny viewpoints out to the Pacific Ocean just S on the summit plateau or a better-than-average look from Tillamook Rock Lighthouse Viewpoint. Some people even shorten the hike without the rougher summit bid for the Clatsop Loop Trail (almost 3 mi round-trip) from Indian Beach to the lighthouse viewpoint. No fee or restroom from Tillamook Head TH in Seaside. Day use fee required in Ecola State Park, and restrooms are present.

TRAILHEAD: Tillamook Head TH or Indian Beach TH. For Tillamook Head TH in Seaside take US-26 W from Portland 75 mi, exit right onto the ramp for US-101 N 3 mi, turn left at the first traffic signal on Avenue U ¼ mi, turn left 1¼ mi on Edgewood Street (into Ocean Vista Drive into Sunset Blvd) to the end (82 mi, more than 1½ hours from Portland).

For the primary TH at Indian Beach in Ecola State Park take US-26 W from Portland 75 mi, merge onto US-101 S 3 mi,

Tillamook Lighthouse from a hidden trail near Clark's Mountain.

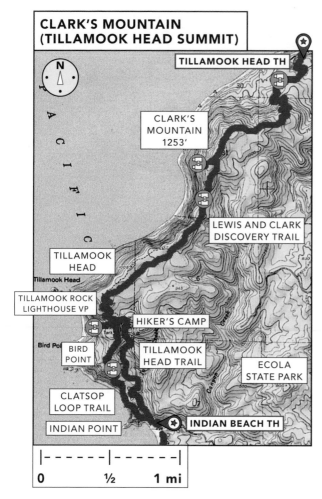

CLARK'S MOUNTAIN (TILLAMOOK HEAD SUMMIT)

N

TILLAMOOK HEAD TH

CLARK'S MOUNTAIN 1253'

P A C I F I C

LEWIS AND CLARK DISCOVERY TRAIL

TILLAMOOK HEAD

Tillamook Head

TILLAMOOK ROCK LIGHTHOUSE VP

HIKER'S CAMP

Bird Po

BIRD POINT

TILLAMOOK HEAD TRAIL

ECOLA STATE PARK

CLATSOP LOOP TRAIL

INDIAN POINT

INDIAN BEACH TH

|- - - - -|- - - - -|

0   ½   1 mi

exit right in Cannon Beach (signed for City Center/ Ecola State Park/Visitor Info), quickly turn right on E Fifth Street, turn right on Ecola State Park Road 1½ mi to the entrance booth, turn right at Ecola State Park TH 1½ mi on Ecola Park Road to plenty of parking on both sides near the end at a small traffic circle for Indian Beach (85 mi, 1¾ hours from Portland).

ROUTE: You could always shuttle an extra vehicle to either TH to hike the trail almost 6 mi one way but this is not the norm. For the less traveled route directly to Clark's Mountain from the N, begin left of Sunset Blvd in Seaside across the bridge and under the wooden arch stamped "Tillamook Head" entering the Elmer Feldenheimer Forest Preserve. Walk a mile and 2 switchbacks up through hefty old Sitka spruce, with plenty of hemlock, alder, and salal on the Lewis and Clark Discovery Trail to the only view outward (until after the summit) following a large downed spruce.

Continue up 15 more switchbacks and turns another mile, navigating under and around trees, tree roots, and most likely the muddy trail; the route will be steeper nearest the mossy summit plateau area. Level out, and then head up to a narrow spur leading 50 ft right to the actual high point in a thicket of trees with one large one at the top and not much outward to see. Return to the N TH or continue S for somewhat better vistas. In less than ¼ mi down from the summit is a brief and hidden spur right, to a nice shot of the old Tillamook Lighthouse on a tiny island. It is around 2 mi more to the Tillamook Rock Lighthouse Viewpoint and Hiker's Camp trudging up and down with only a few looks through the trees to the ocean.

From Indian Beach within Ecola State Park, find the wide Lewis and Clark

Oregon's North Coast from Ecola State Park.

Discover Trail (old road to lighthouse viewpoint, also known as Tillamook Head Trail and Clatsop Loop Trail) N of the parking circle 1¼ mi and 700 ft upwards through the coastal rainforest with hulking spruce and hemlock. After the first 100 ft is the end of the Clatsop Loop Trail on the left. Save this rougher and more scenic path for the return (counterclockwise) loop. After slogging N up past Bird Point the canopy reveals a bit of sky near the open structures at Hiker's Camp. Turn left (W) on Tillamook Rock Lighthouse Trail at the intersection with the continuation of the Lewis and Clark Discover Trail moving past the log shelters. Walk ¼ mi losing a couple hundred feet down the trail for Tillamook Rock Lighthouse Viewpoint with a decent shot of the historic storm-pounded miniscule island a mile out.

Return up and turn left past the shelters more than 2 mi NNE for Clark's Mountain on Lewis and Clark Discover Trail. Climb 8 quick switchbacks before undulating somewhat closer to the high cliff (past Tillamook Head) over the muddy trail and tree roots with only a fraction of the route covered by much-needed boardwalks and walkways as the trail is rarely dry. Eventually arrive at a dangerous little perch, left, just off-trail between a large, cut, downed tree and a huge tree stump with a tight shot down the sheer cliff to the pretty sea. The true summit is more than ¼ mi more on the upper ridge plateau as you hike down, then up, finding one more little hidden spur, left a few feet to a good look of the lighthouse through the trees. Find the uneventful high point at the next spur, left to the top at a giant tree with no views.

Look for the W side of the Clatsop Loop Trail once you are back down near Tillamook Rock Lighthouse Viewpoint past Hiker's Camp to the right, as opposed to taking the Lewis and Clark Discover Trail left (E side of the loop). Follow the narrow, overgrown path 1½ mi to Indian Beach, at first through more rather large spruce, then with thicker grasses mixing in down switchbacks. Look S along the coast to Neahkahnie Mountain. Be cautious along the cliff band closer to Indian Point, with even better views of the long beach below, as you descend to cross Indian Creek over a footbridge to end the loop. Turn right a minute to the TH. Feel free to check out the beautiful beach or even the scenic trail that continues from the SE corner of the parking circle 1½ mi through the forest, past Bald Point to Ecola Point near Ecola State Park TH.

ELEVATION: Sea level, with perhaps 10 ft vertical gain if any

DISTANCE: 2½ mi one way, 5 mi round-trip

DURATION: 1 hour one way, 2–3 hours round-trip

DIFFICULTY: Easiest. Beach walk, obvious, windy, sandy, over rocks, no trail or signs, stormy in fall, winter, and spring

TRIP REPORT: Oregon's North Coast has many highlights and the whole of Cannon Beach with Haystack Rock is no exception. Here is a simple jaunt along the beach past several monoliths to Silver Point opposite a couple seasonal little waterfalls. No fee required, and restrooms are found locally and at Visitor Information (207 N Spruce Street).

TRAILHEAD: Haystack Rock TH. Take US-26 W from Portland 75 mi, merge onto US-101 S 4¼ mi, exit right in Cannon Beach for Sunset Blvd and stay right ¼ mi, turn right on S Hemlock Street three blocks to a sign and day use lot on the right for Haystack Rock Public Parking (80 mi, 1½ hours from Portland).

ROUTE: Begin W from the

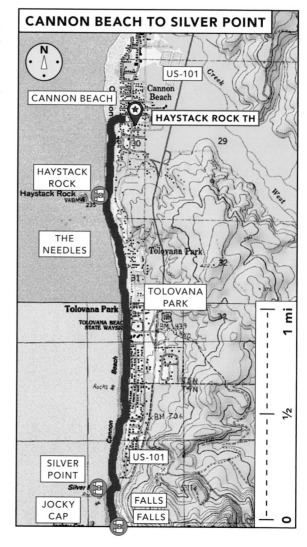

CANNON BEACH TO SILVER POINT

ROUTE: Begin W from the N end of the parking lot on E Gower Avenue to the end, then left on Ecola Court a few feet to the signage for the beach access. Cross the little creek to the left immediately once past the buildings and walk left (S) down the beach toward nearby heavily photographed Haystack Rock. More than 200,000 people visit this attraction per year. It's even possible to venture to the base of the rather large 235-ft sea stack at low tide to examine the rock and interesting tide pools more closely. It is, however, a part of the Oregon Islands National Wildlife Refuge and is a state-protected Marine Garden, so climbing is prohibited. Just beyond to the S and SW are smaller monoliths called The Needles.

Keep walking along the expansive beach almost 2 mi to the next set of big monoliths near or on the shore at Silver Point. There will be boulders to walk past as the beach narrows, and you either move around or over much larger rock (depending on the tide) at Silver Point on the corner. You may also have to navigate over boulders (at high tide) just past the first large pillar to see the long slender monolith (Jockey Cap) a bit better. Continuing the walk, see a thin waterfall coming down the steeper rock as soon as the grasses end and the little cliff band begins. A bit farther is a larger seasonal cascade that drops beneath an old pipe, but spreads out down the sheer rock to the shrubs near the beach in a pleasant fashion with Silver Point as the backdrop. Return the same way whenever you are ready, perhaps close to sunset with wonderful lighting.

Haystack Rock directs your attention on Cannon Beach as the fog burns off.

ELEVATION: 1600 ft, with vertical gains of 870 ft from the S TH, and 1200 ft from the N TH or for the loop with Pacific Coast Scenic Byway (US-101)

DISTANCE: 3 mi round-trip from the S TH; 4 mi round-trip from the N TH; 3½ mi one way end to end plus 1¼ mi along US-101 and ½ mi Neahkahnie Trailhead Road for the loop (with or without a mountain bike)

DURATION: Less than an hour up from the S TH, more than an hour up from the N TH; 2–3 hours round-trip

DIFFICULTY: Moderate. Straightforward, family-friendly for avid hikers, narrow at times, overgrown June through August, switchbacks, tree roots common, steep rocky knob at top, longer loop with highway travel

---

TRIP REPORT: Underhyped but well traveled are the two options to the top of Neahkahnie Mountain. Well, not so much the very top, but the most visited little summit (with the best views) on a mountain with several tiny pinnacles. Consider the loop in either direction even without a bike as there is a sidewalk, berm, or scenic pullout for much of the distance along the W side of the busy highway; hint—for another reason, the bike loop is in this counterclockwise direction (5¼ mi total round-trip loop). And since the THs are only 1¾ mi apart it seems too close to use an additional vehicle for drop-off unless you live in the area. The trails will be tedious and more difficult when wet or muddy. And don't forget the bonus in Treasure Cove Overlook, a short walk to scenic cliffy viewpoints from the N TH described at the end. No pass required at either TH (day use only), and there are no restrooms.

Cliffs under Treasure Cove Overlook.

TRAILHEAD: Take US-26 W from Portland 75 mi, merge onto US-101 S 15 mi to the N TH (milepost 40½) at a large gravel pullout on the right with a brown Oregon Coast Trail sign pointing across the highway (within Oswald West

State Park). Drop a bike and lock it here for the counterclockwise loop (may be preferred for many reasons) and drive 1¼ mi farther S, turn left at the small brown sign for Neahkahnie Mountain Trail (1½ mi N of Manzanita) up the steep gravel road ½ mi to the TH on the left, with parking on the sides and the pullout on the left before the gate (95 mi, less than 2 hours from Portland).

ROUTE: For the route from the N TH, see the second-to-last paragraph and reverse the description.

From the S TH ½ mi E of the Pacific Coast Scenic Byway, take the signed trail up a mile N to a ridgeline saddle and intersection. You rise up 4 switchbacks through the respectable old growth Sitka spruce and Douglas fir with a floor of endless ferns to the first views of the Pacific Ocean and Nehalem Bay. Continue up 5 switchbacks moving into the thicker forest on the wide trail loaded with occasional tree roots and lined with trillium, sorrel, and nettle. Finish only a tad steeper the last 5 switchbacks to the saddle at the four-way intersection with a dirt road. Almost no one climbs the wide road left to the radio tower station (with limited views surrounded by trees) atop one of the four summits comprising Neahkahnie Mountain.

Walk across the road from the saddle to the visible trail heading W for ½ mi on a pleasant traverse N of two of the pinnacles to a smaller saddle. There are a few more tree roots here as well to force your focus, which is a theme of the entire trail actually,

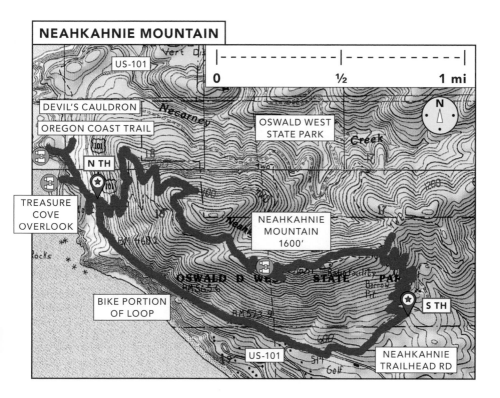

NEAHKAHNIE MOUNTAIN

US-101

Vert

0   ½   1 mi

N

DEVIL'S CAULDRON

OREGON COAST TRAIL

OSWALD WEST
STATE PARK

Creek

N TH

TREASURE
COVE
OVERLOOK

NEAHKAHNIE
MOUNTAIN
1600'

Rocks

OSWALD D WEST STATE PAR

BIKE PORTION
OF LOOP

S TH

US-101

NEAHKAHNIE
TRAILHEAD RD

Golf

Nehalem Bay from Neahkahnie Mountain.

making you happier with a loop instead of hiking up and back by the same route (especially if muddy)! Halfway is a small bench on the trail with partial views to the coast among the ancient pines. Then you have 1 steeper switchback to the small saddle between high points. Point 1631 is left (E) 100 ft and is the tallest of the three southern pinnacles but rarely visited, while your goal is right (W) from the saddle up the rocky knob. Point 1700 is the highest of the mostly tree-covered points and is located NW of the three southern pinnacles (reached by an unfriendly steep bushwhack path, if at all).

Be careful with younger ones as you must scramble the final 50 ft rather steeply to reach the fabulous vistas from the very top of the rocky hill (with wildflowers June into July) poking above most of the trees. Fortunately the rock and boulders are fairly solid on the highest ridge where there are a few quality picnic spots, but the very top near the marker is the crème de la crème! You've got the whole Nehalem River valley with Nehalem Bay and Manzanita directly below you to the S, and of course there's that rather large body of blue water to the W adding to the quality of most backdrops at many times of the day.

To descend to the N TH at the brown sign and pullout for the Oregon Coast Trail return steeply to the nearby tiny saddle, then turn right (W) 2 mi to the highway, but it's not all downhill just yet. Head down 3 solid switchbacks into the forest before a level stretch, then hike NW up less than ¼ mi before undulating more subtly for the remainder. There are more tree roots to remind you that you are in the rugged Pacific Northwest, but they aren't unbearable as you work past more giant spruce, fir, and cedar with ferns dominating the flora in a couple distinct sections. The trail narrows and becomes slightly overgrown at times especially near the bottom. Coastal birds are heard singing from the tall pines through the breeze. At almost a mile from the summit viewpoint is the first of 6 gentle switchbacks before rising a few feet, crossing a tiny creek on the narrowing trail, and coming to 2 more quick switchbacks. The ocean views and coastal cliffs come into play as the trees thin and the flora with wildflowers blooming thickens next to the trail in the steep meadow for the final 3 switchbacks down to the N TH. Be very cautious crossing the highway.

As a bonus from the N TH you are able to take a worthwhile spur more than ¼ mi to the Treasure Cove Overlook. Follow the narrow Oregon Coast Trail down steeply from the center of the pullout toward the ocean forking right almost immediately. Then left at the next fork into the woods to a bench and safety fence. The view is impeccable far down into the active cove and up the coast. Use care with children close to the cliff, especially if you bushwhack around to the opposite side of the cove from the main trail for another vantage point. The overgrown bushwhack path that continues to loop around the nearby little tree- and rhododendron-covered bump to scarce views of nearby Devil's Cauldron is dangerous and not worth it. Return back up to the N TH and continue with care walking or riding along the highway to your vehicle finishing steeply ½ mi up the gravel road if you parked at the S TH.

83 ROGERS PEAK

ELEVATION: 3706 ft, with 1100 ft vertical gain

DISTANCE: 2¼–2½ mi up, 4½–5 mi round-trip

DURATION: 1 hour up, 2 hours round-trip

DIFFICULTY: Mix of moderate for the main route (mostly old road walk, partial bushwhack to summit, route-finding, no signs, never too steep) and strenuous for the ridge scramble option (wooded, partial bushwhack, small fallen trees, steep, straightforward)

TRIP REPORT: Highest point in Tillamook County and, in fact, all of the Northern Coastal Range is Rogers Peak. For this reason it's on many folks' bucket lists, but it doesn't mean by any means that you will see anyone else besides the company you bring for this peaceful peak. Peaceful except for the drive the final 7½ mi on active logging roads (except on weekends/holidays) that are quite steep and very narrow (AWD vehicle preferred) with sharp curves and only a few safe pullouts. Yield to uphill drivers of other vehicles and yield to logging and other trucks at all times, being

Forested Rogers Peak up the ridge from older logging roads.

extremely careful (radio and windows down to hear approaching trucks), although it's not as confusing as it seems. No pass or restroom.

TRAILHEAD: Rogers Peak TH. Take US-26 W from Portland around 20 mi to the exit left for OR-6 W (Tillamook/Banks) almost 30 mi, turn right 1 mi past Lee's Camp Store (between mileposts 22/23) at a big brown sign for Jones Creek CG, Smith Homestead Day Use Area, and Diamond Mill OHV Area. Cross over the bridge on N Fork Road which turns to gravel ¼ mi to the end, turn right opposite Jones Creek Park on N Fork Wilson River Road (Cedar Creek Road/CB-18) N for 3 mi along the W side of Wilson River (stay right at a fork just past Diamond Mill OHV Area and ½ mi farther as well). Fork left 1 mi on W Fork N Fork Road (with rougher gravel, watching for logging trucks) where the right fork crosses a bridge over the river. Turn right ½ mi over the bridge and river on FR-Fb8n (no sign) as the road steepens and curves to the right turning into W Fork Road (no sign) to another fork. Drive left at the fork for the main route on W Fork Road (Gilmore Road) 3 mi very steeply, narrowly (2WD okay, AWD better), and fairly unnervingly on weekdays with huge semitrucks barreling up and down the gravel roads unaware of your presence (¾ mi from last major fork the road mellows somewhat for ¼ mi, becomes very steep again more than ½ mi, eases more than ½ mi going down a bit, and then becomes quite steep up to the TH). Carefully turn around or drive through the big yellow gate (if open) and then turn around at the nearby saddle. But park below the gate (may be locked at any time) about 100 ft to a tiny pullout or farther down where the road is wider (60 mi, 1½ hours from Portland).

ROUTE: Begin up the logging road across from a large clear-cut slope past the big yellow gate 50 ft to a little saddle with views of more clear-cut hillsides amongst the local mountains. Head steeply up to the right (N) at the fork on the wide, old gravel road to a second little saddle at less than ½ mi from the TH.

Here you will have the more difficult direct bushwhack option left of the road ½ mi steeply N up the ridgeline through the trees (watch for elk). Both ends of this ridge trail option are obscured by trees, some fallen, but it widens quite nicely with only a few little trees and branches to cross over (long pants may be preferred to avoid getting cut up). There is a small hill to descend a few feet from the road near the top of the scramble route.

The easier option, with better views SE to Kings and Elk Mountains, follows the road right (E) from the optional fork almost ½ mi to an odd four-way intersection. Turn left up the main route less than ½ mi, steeper back to the ridgeline at the top of the hidden bushwhack juncture perhaps best saved for the descent.

From the bushwhack juncture, follow the old road up the ridge ½ mi to a small fork where you walk right, down about 100 ft toward your forested goal and another saddle below the summit block with good views left (N) to Tillamook State Forest.

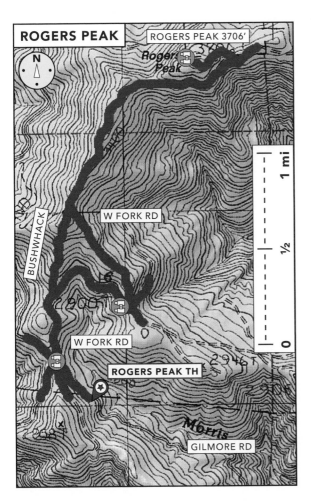

Continue S of the summit less than ½ mi on a super-easy traverse and turn sharply to the left (W) onto a faded old wide trail (no sign) before the main road begins to descend. Work your way up ¼ mi without any trouble past a few small trees and branches across the path to a tiny green meadow. Some views exist past the end of the meadow, but you should turn right just before that to scramble up a few feet, finding the summit path for the final feet, past a large anthill, to the mossy boulders and rocks that comprise the peak area within the tight pines.

84   KINGS MOUNTAIN LOOP

ELEVATION: 3226 ft, with vertical gains of 2600 ft directly, 3300 ft on a loop with Elk Mountain, 3500 ft if mountain biking up Elk Creek Trail (then hiking)

DISTANCE: More than 2½ mi up, 5¼ mi round-trip; more than 8 mi round-trip loop with Elk Mountain plus 3½ mi without a shuttle for the additional hike; 13 mi round-trip bike-n-hike Kings Mountain only (no loop, using Elk Creek Trail)

DURATION: 1–2 hours up directly or biking from Elk Creek Trail, 2–3 hours round-trip; 5–6 hours hiking loop with Elk Mountain; 4–5 hours round-trip bike-n-hike Kings Mountain

DIFFICULTY: Very challenging. Extremely steep from all approaches, fewer switchbacks, a few drop-offs, quiet during the week, not possible when wet, more difficult with snow

---

TRIP REPORT: The Kings Mountain to Elk Mountain loop is an Oregon Coast Range classic. It also just happens to be one of the most difficult short hikes in the entire state! This is because of the unreasonably steep terrain that surrounds this summit and continues up and down along the ridge to Elk Mountain and beyond in merciless fashion completely indifferent to those gasping for breath on their mission to complete the loop. There are very few opportunities to see the hidden horseshoe of summits and forested high points from the highway, and most first-time hikers here have no idea what they're signing up for.

Kings Mountain alone is "easiest" taken straight on, then quickly returning the same way from the main TH. You can also mountain bike or hike almost 5 mi up Elk Creek then W Elk Creek, and then hike from the high ridge saddle between summits to the top. For the clockwise hiking loop with a bike as your shuttle, lock your bike at Elk Creek TH and park at Kings Mountain TH to ride downhill later (carefully on/near the highway). The Wilson River Trail is adjacent the highway and covers roughly the same distance to close the loop on the bottom portion without too much trouble. No fee required at either TH, and restrooms are present at both THs.

TRAILHEAD: Kings Mountain TH. Take US-26 W from Portland around 20 mi to the exit left for OR-6 W (Tillamook/Banks) 23 mi, turn right for Elk Creek Campground (and TH, milepost 28) less than ½ mi to parking near the gated road, past the concrete bridge (extra gate closed closer to highway in winter). Begin here for the longer hike or bike up Elk Creek Trail. Lock up a bike as a shuttle if you are hiking

Kings Mountain Loop to Elk Mountain and drive almost 3½ mi farther on OR-6 W to the signed Kings Mountain TH (milepost 25) and small lot on the right (50 mi, 1 hour from Portland).

ROUTE: From Kings Mountain TH take the only trail past the signage briefly up to the juncture at the end of the loop (without a shuttle bike or vehicle) on Wilson River Trail (right, NE to Elk Creek TH). Stay straight (NNW) on Kings Mountain Trail through alder, ferns, and fir with wildflowers throughout, and with mostly Douglas fir on the higher slopes. The wide trail steepens after a mile as you ascend a couple gullies with creeks.

There are no real switchbacks to speak of on this direct route up, but keep in mind that as punishingly steep as it may be, the direct route up to Elk Mountain is even steeper! After 2 mi or so (ignoring side trails) is a micro-break as an old road meets the trail; continue on Kings Mountain Trail to rise up meadows on the SW ridge with views of your goal and the surrounding Tillamook State Forest. Resume clawing away to the NE over bumps, using hands at times, as you scramble loose, rocky steps

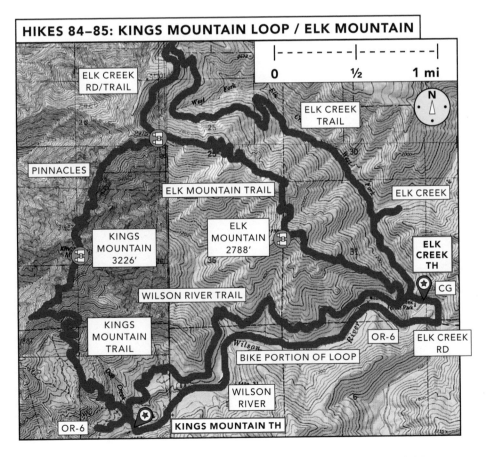

HIKES 84–85: KINGS MOUNTAIN LOOP / ELK MOUNTAIN

ELK CREEK RD/TRAIL

0   ½   1 mi

N

ELK CREEK TRAIL

PINNACLES

ELK MOUNTAIN TRAIL

ELK CREEK

KINGS MOUNTAIN 3226'

ELK MOUNTAIN 2788'

ELK CREEK TH

WILSON RIVER TRAIL

CG

KINGS MOUNTAIN TRAIL

OR-6

ELK CREEK RD

BIKE PORTION OF LOOP

WILSON RIVER

OR-6

KINGS MOUNTAIN TH

on a traverse below the summit block. Enjoy paintbrush, phlox, bear grass, and others as the trees and flora thin to the tiny peak and highest point of the loop.

Even with some trees at the top, there are a few decent picnic spots with views of the Coast Range and SW back down the narrow Lester Creek canyon, WNW over to N Fork Wilson River canyon, and S to the Wilson River valley. And nearing Kings Mountain you see Mount Hood and Mount Adams, as well as Elk Mountain down across the cirque. Return by the same route from the top or continue, as it's just beginning to get good!

The next section of high ridge known as the Pinnacles for almost 1¾ mi to the flat saddle at the intersection with Elk Creek Trail and Elk Mountain Trail is quite challenging and exquisitely beautiful at the same time. Head down N on

Super-steep pitch complete with rope just NW of Kings Mountain.

Kings Mountain Trail from the summit sign and register box without much trouble, then up almost immediately to a mostly open and rounded little fake summit (at more than 3200 ft) with a good shot back to Kings Mountain before the grind.

Summit marker in funkyvision!

Leave the ridgeline to the W side for an intimidating stretch as you descend super-steep and tight switchbacks. Then traverse below sheer rock through high brush (below 2800 ft) on the thin path. There is a tiny bit of exposure so watch your step (as well as the wildflowers and views). Use the fixed rope if you like to climb the steep dirt slope (hopefully sans mud, snow, or ice) for part of the route very steeply back to the nearby ridge between pinnacles. Hike the ridge N up, down, and up over another high point (3050 ft), and then move down before traversing NE up the wider old road steadily to the signed three-way intersection at the wide saddle (almost 3000 ft).

Either take Elk Creek Trail (N then SE) less than 5 mi down easier to Elk Creek TH, or stay en route 2 mi on Elk Mountain Trail to that summit, then about 1½ mi more to the Elk Creek TH.

For Elk Mountain, walk SE from the horseshoe ridge easy for the moment on the wide old road. Don't get used to it! There are countless little bumps along the high ridge with extra steep drops and scrambles up between each one. Hike E down 9 switchbacks and turns without much difficulty continuing down (around 2600 ft), and then it's up and down with an annoyingly steep pitch to the S, becoming ultra-steep the final ½ mi to the highest point on the ridge.

See Kings Mountain through bear grass and scattered trees across the steep and lush green valley (without any clear-cutting visible) from several locales as well as the summit. There you find another wooden sign and register box into a tree. You would think by looking down Elk Mountain's precipitous SE ridge that it would be all downhill from the summit to the TH. Not so fast. Climb up and down twice before continuing very steeply down the rocky hogback on the slender ridge using hands, and everything else you've got, for much of it. Taking the loop clockwise from Kings Mountain finally makes sense. Enjoy views for most of the descent on Elk Mountain Trail, moving into thicker alders steeply S to the juncture with Wilson River Trail.

For Elk Creek TH turn left (E) on Wilson River Trail more than ¼ mi to the campground. For the loop without a shuttle turn right (W) on Wilson River Trail 3½ mi down to Kings Mountain TH. With a shuttle you would bike or take the shuttle vehicle from Elk Creek TH down OR-6 W to Kings Mountain TH as in the trailhead directions. Although much easier than the rest of the loop, there are still a few ups and downs on Wilson River Trail before mellowing and crossing several little creeks and bridges. It's quite lovely in fact, a bit overgrown at times, and not at all crowded to the juncture with Kings Mountain Trail. Turn left at the signage briefly down to the TH.

For the bike (or hike) up Elk Creek Trail, take the old road straight past the gate (NW) from Elk Creek TH instead of heading left (W) on Wilson River Trail. Ride up steadily as Elk Creek splits off to the right and you follow W Fork Elk Creek to the NW on its left side before climbing steeper switchbacks more narrowly. The single track gets a bit monotonous and overgrown but will be well worth the downhill when the time comes. At about 4 mi from the TH is a juncture near a small saddle. Turn left (S) on Elk Creek Trail almost a mile somewhat easier on a wider traverse up to the main flat saddle between summits. For the summit of Elk Mountain and the loop down that peak, follow the description on the previous page with the paragraph that starts "For Elk Mountain…" as you head left (SE) from the horseshoe ridge. See above that for the description right (SW) to Kings Mountain (reversing the route from the saddle to the summit).

85 | ELK MOUNTAIN

ELEVATION: 2788 ft, with vertical gains of 2000 ft directly, and more than 2500 ft with a bike-n-hike or hiking loop with Elk Creek Trail

DISTANCE: More than 1½ mi up, 3¼ mi round-trip; 8½ mi hiking loop with Elk Creek Trail; 14 mi round-trip bike-n-hike with Elk Creek Trail (no loop)

DURATION: 1–1½ hours up directly, 2–4 hours round-trip; 2–3 hours biking/hiking up Elk Creek Trail, 4–6 hours round-trip

DIFFICULTY: Very challenging. Ultra-steep from both approaches, positively steep ups/downs, not for novices, scrambling, well-traveled, difficult when wet or snowy, narrow SE ridge

TRIP REPORT: Fortunately, next-door neighbor Kings Mountain gets most of the hype, so you should have most of the trail to yourself, except for those completing the loop with that mountain. See Kings Mountain (hike 84) for the bike or hike up Elk Creek Trail to Elk Mountain Trail. This great scramble must arguably be among the shortest and steepest hikes in the state from the TH! There is no fee required, and restrooms are present.

TRAILHEAD: Elk Creek TH. Take US-26 W from Portland around 20 mi to the exit left for OR-6 W (Tillamook/Banks) 23 mi, turn right for Elk Creek Campground (and

Navigating the intensely steep hogback ridge up the only way possible using hands, feet, and everything in between!

TH, milepost 28) less than ½ mi to parking near the gated road, past the concrete bridge (extra gate closed closer to highway in winter but trail still open; 50 mi, 1 hour from Portland).

ROUTE: Begin past Elk Creek Campground left (W) from the parking area easily on the very long Wilson River Trail, but you will only be taking it ¼ mi or so to the signed climber's path on the right. Head N following the signage on Elk Mountain Trail, steeper then much steeper NW less than 1½ mi to the miniscule, but notable, summit. Travel through the old forest as it thins to the ridgeline, and then you must scramble, using hands much of the time, up the very steep trail and rocky hogback closer to the top. Clearly this would be even more difficult with adverse weather conditions.

Views of the valleys, Coast Range, and Kings Mountain improve with every painful step up. Hiking gloves may come in handy. There are a couple little points on the high ridge to hike up and down before the final push to the narrow summit (and marker). Well worth the effort! Reverse the description from hike 84 for the rough route 2 mi to the flat saddle juncture, then on to Kings Mountain, or down almost 5 mi more on Elk Creek Trail. Otherwise return the same way for the most expedient route.

ELEVATION: 4097 ft, with vertical gains of 325 ft from Marys Peak Summit TH (Observation Point), 535 ft from Marys Peak Campground TH (Meadow Edge Loop), 1520 ft from Conner's Camp TH (E Ridge Trail), and 2300 ft from N Ridge TH (North Ridge Trail, also called Marys Peak Trail)

DISTANCE: ¾ mi up from Marys Peak Summit TH; 1¼ mi up from Marys Peak Campground TH; 3¼ mi up from Conner's Camp TH, 6¾ mi round-trip loop with Tie Trail; 5 mi up from N Ridge TH

DURATION: 1 hour more or less for jaunts near the peak; 1½ hours up from Conner's Camp TH, 3–4 hours round-trip loop with Tie Trail; 2-plus hours up from N Ridge TH, 3–5 hours round-trip

DIFFICULTY: Mix of moderate near the peak (brief directly, but somewhat steep, gravel road, loop options, route-finding) and strenuous for the two main hiking routes (steady grades, only steeper briefly, narrow at times, long from N Ridge TH)

TRIP REPORT: The highest summit on the Oregon Coast Range and in Benton County is also quite popular year-round even when the road can be gated in winter near the bottom forcing people to hike, snowshoe, and ski the road or numerous trails to the top. The primary reason is that unlike many Oregon summits, this rare, well-rounded summit block, although surrounded by beautiful, old growth noble and Douglas fir, has only a few trees near the top with wide-open meadows and wide-open views in all directions! The most popular times are June through August when several rounds of wildflower displays blanket the rolling meadows. Many seek the top or Observation Point at the highest drivable parking lot for sunset over the Pacific with the lights of the Willamette Valley in glow. Mountain biking is permitted on Summit Road, North Ridge Trail, Tie Trail, and East Ridge Trail mid-May through mid-October. Northwest Forest Pass required at all THs except N Ridge TH, and restrooms present at all THs except N Ridge TH.

The evolving forest floor near the summit in the clouds.

TRAILHEAD: Take I-5 S from Portland to exit 228 (Corvallis), turn right on OR-34 W 9 mi, turn left on OR-34 Bypass W 1¼ mi into US-20 W 5½ mi through Philomath, turn left on OR-34 W (Waldport) 8½ mi (last 3 mi winding), turn right at a small sign for Marys Peak Road (also twisting and turning) more than 5¼ mi to the nondescript Conner's Camp TH on the right down a brief driveway (all paved, no camping here; alternate parking a few feet farther in the pullout on the left of Marys Peak Road opposite gated FR-2005). The first gate on Marys Peak Road is right there on the corner and may be closed in winter. Continue 3¼ mi up the road for Marys Peak Campground TH to the right with a quick left into the parking lot. Drive ½ mi more to the end of the road into the parking lot at the Summit/Observation Point TH. For N Ridge TH continue 2 mi on US-20 W past the left turn for OR-34 W in Philomath, turn left on Woods Creek Road 7½ mi to the pullout on the left before the gate (around 110 mi, more than 2 hours from Portland).

ROUTE: For Marys Peak Campground TH (Meadow Edge Loop) and the Summit TH (Observation Point) see below. For the longest route from N Ridge TH, see the last paragraph.

For the primary hiking route from Conner's Camp TH up the

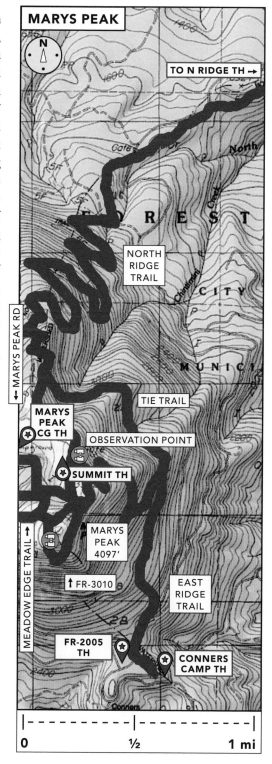

Wildflower-emblazoned meadow before the final push past a few trees to the summit of Marys Peak.

East Ridge Trail, begin across the driveway from the outhouse to the trail 200 ft through the woods to the main trail past FR-2005. From the alternate TH across from Marys Peak Road walk 40 ft E along the wide gravel road and turn left (NW then N) on the trail after the brown sign for Marys Peak Municipal Watershed. Hike 1 mi up the wide trail with a pleasant grade through the thick forest with big Douglas firs. Blue diamond markers posted high on trees help keep folks on track for winter travel. The views open somewhat to the right for a short time revealing snow-capped summits in the distance including Mount Jefferson, Three Fingered Jack, Mount Washington, and Three Sisters.

Turn left at the intersection/switchback (sign at the bench points back toward Conner's Camp) 1½ mi W and 3 switchbacks more to the Summit TH/Observation Point for the direct route to the peak. The continuing traverse (toward North Ridge Trail) is the return route for the only slightly longer clockwise loop variation on the Tie Trail. Head steadily up East Ridge Trail and the second switchback surrounded by ferns and fir. The trail becomes a bit steeper and narrower at times near the third switchback 1 mi from the intersection below. You cross the saddle of the NE ridge of Marys Peak again and begin an easier traverse WNW ½ mi breaking out of the large trees at the signed upper TH with an info kiosk present.

From Marys Peak Summit TH (Observation Point—with okay views of the Cascades but not nearly as good as from the top), either hike up the wide gravel road (FR-3010) from the gate or take the trail to the left close to the forest somewhat steeper up the wildflower-covered meadow; both routes meet in ¼ mi at an odd six-way intersection. If you came up the road, hard left is the return trail to the Summit TH, next left is a closed trail with downed trees clogging the route to East Ridge Trail, straight ahead is the road continuing ½ mi to the summit, right leads briefly to a 2 mi loop on Meadow Edge Trail, and a few feet farther up the dirt road to the right is the steeper shortcut through the trees directly to the summit for a brief loop to save for the descent perhaps.

Continue up the road, winding steeper to the summit's radio towers (fenced off) as you break out above all the trees to the large peak enveloped with a dazzling display of wildflowers late May into June. You have unobstructed views from the picnic table to the ocean and Willamette Valley to Salem with all of the big Cascade volcanoes visible in Oregon on a clear day and even Mount St. Helens and Mount Rainier in Washington! Return to the Summit TH for East or North Ridge Trails on a brief loop by taking the trail from the picnic table 50 ft NE toward the trees to a fork. Left is Meadow Edge Trail (summit spur), which very soon dives down right to the trees where it intersects that loop or continues briefly to the summit road. Head right at the fork instead through the trees steeply ¼ mi to the summit road near the six-way intersection and take the road or meadow trail briefly to the Summit TH.

From Marys Peak Campground TH, walk the camping loop on the left to find the spur trail shortly up through old growth noble fir to the 2 mi loop that is Meadow Edge Trail. Walk left for a clockwise loop and after a couple switchbacks reach a juncture where turning left would take you to the summit road briefly. Take the next left for the spur more than ¼ mi to Marys Peak and return, or continue to where the trail breaks out of the woods with views of the summit (and much more) before quickly reentering the big trees with thriving flora. Move down turns on the loop to cross colorful Parker Creek over the footbridge, and then return up a few feet to the end of the loop where you walk left down to your vehicle.

For a nice variation, try the Tie Trail loop to Conner's Camp TH from Marys Peak Summit TH. Find North Ridge Trail to the right, across from the parking lot and top of Marys Peak Road. Parallel the road W a ways before leaving it for the occasionally steeper and rockier trail N with more noble firs (even down on the trail at times but easy to cross) to a three-way juncture almost ¾ mi from Observation Point. The sign near another bench shows Woods Creek Road is left (N) down the N Ridge and Conner's Camp is right 3 mi, but it's actually closer to 2 mi.

Hike to the right (SE) a mile on Tie Trail by Doug fir, noble fir, and spruce, along a steep slope but on a friendly traverse as the trail becomes narrow and slightly overgrown in spots; there's a tiny seasonal creek to cross at one point. The final ¼ mi up to meet the East Ridge Trail at the end of the loop suddenly becomes the steepest part of the entire hike. Then continue left at the intersection on East Ridge Trail easier a mile S down to the TH.

From the tranquil N Ridge TH, walk past the gate across Woods Creek Road a couple hundred feet to the apparent trail on the right. Work S without difficulty through the ancient forest (without much for views) 3½ mi up about a dozen enjoyably graded switchbacks and turns to the three-way juncture with Tie Trail heading left (SE). Continue straight (S) on N Ridge Trail at the bench up the steepening ridge; see above for clues 1½ mi to Marys Peak, if you like, as it's never terribly difficult.

EASTERN OREGON

WALLOWAS

87 Painted Hills 267
88 Aneroid Mountain 273
89 Glacier Lake 276
90 Eagle Cap 279

87 PAINTED HILLS

ELEVATION: 2920 ft within Sheep Rock Unit; 2450 ft within Painted Hills Unit; 1800 ft within Clarno Unit, with vertical gains of around 2000 ft total including all walks listed

DISTANCE: 10 mi total round-trip including all walks listed

DURATION: Most of the day or 2 days to visit all three units and the museum

DIFFICULTY: Mix of easiest to moderate. Partially paved paths, gravel, only steep momentarily on longer hikes, well-traveled, best in late winter/spring, slippery when wet or muddy, rattlesnakes possible in summer

---

TRIP REPORT: With so many stupendous hiking choices for Oregonians the often-overlooked Painted Hills region (within the John Day Fossil Beds National Monument) makes people work a little longer in the car to get to the THs. The area pays itself off and then some, so not to worry! Note that the Thomas Condon Paleontology Center is the only visitor center and "green" museum in all of Painted Hills and contains thousands of fossils collected from the local ecosystems dating back around 50 million years. None of the hikes in this section are day hikes from Portland, although it's possible, so you got me! Follow this tour as described below for the preeminent car and camping clockwise loop route if coming from the Columbia Gorge area or Portland.

Rock layers of red, gold, green, and blue radiate to some degree within the knolls, mounds, and pinnacles that were formed long ago in an ancient river floodplain. Most people camp with plenty of options between Fossil and Mitchell. The perfect time would be right after a rain under blue skies at dusk in spring or fall with the greens of the grasses and surrounding mountains in their prime, but anytime is fine. Please be respectful and stay on designated trails at all times. No fee required at any TH, and restrooms are present at all THs.

TRAILHEAD: Take I-84 E from Portland 95 mi to exit 104 (Yakima/Bend), turn right on US-97 S 8 mi to the exit right for OR-206 E (Condon), turn left 1 mi to Wasco, turn right on OR-206 E (Clark Street briefly) 40 mi, turn right in Condon on OR-19 S (Main Street briefly) 72 mi. Turn left almost ½ mi into the small parking circle for Foree TH in the Sheep Rock Unit (225 mi, 4 hours from Portland). Look for campgrounds from Fossil to Spray (or farther in Mitchell or just N of Painted Hills Unit), reservation-only camping closest to this TH. Alternately from Portland directly to Painted Hills Unit take US-26 E 175 mi, turn left on Burnt Ranch Road into Bridge Creek Road 5½ mi total, turn left on Bear Creek Road (gravel, washboard, slow) 1 mi to the crest of a saddle with <u>Painted Hills Overlook</u> on the left ¼ mi up to <u>Painted Hills TH</u> (200 mi, less than 4 hours from Portland).

Turn left exiting the <u>Foree TH</u> within <u>Sheep Rock Unit</u> to resume the clockwise loop route and drive 4½ mi on OR-19 S, turn left into the small lot for <u>Blue Basin TH</u> (small brown sign) for an actual hike.

Then continue on OR-19 S 3 mi and perhaps visit Thomas Condon Paleontology Center on the right (open 10–5 except holidays). Continue 2 mi more on OR-19 S, turn right on US-26 W 30 mi to the small town of Mitchell with limited accommodations and a campground E of town on FR-12 (Buck Point Road). Continue 3½ mi from Mitchell on US-26 W, turn right on Burnt Ranch Road into Bridge Creek Road 5½ mi total, turn left on Bear Creek Road (gravel, washboard, slow) 1 mi to the crest of a saddle with <u>Painted Hills Overlook</u> on the left ¼ mi up to <u>Painted Hills TH</u> (with parking along the circle, but save the overlook for sunset or later in the day to visit at least three other areas in <u>Painted Hills Unit</u> first). Continue almost 2½ mi from the saddle on Bear Creek Road around to <u>Red Hill TH</u> (small sign) immediately on the left with much parking.

Drive back the same way 1½ mi after the brief walk, turn left at the corner ½ mi for <u>Painted Cove TH</u> on the left in the square lot.

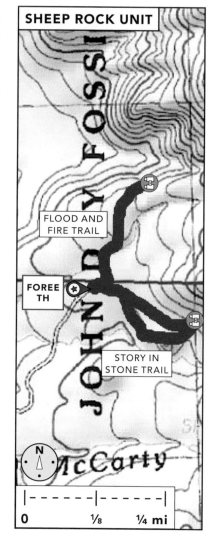

Then drive back to <u>Painted Hills Overlook</u> with limited parking at the bottom of the drive nearest Bear Creek Road for <u>Carroll Rim TH</u> and more of a hike to the top of a hill with 360-degree views. Finish with <u>Painted Hills TH</u> at the overlook for a brief walk.

For the quickest drive to <u>Clarno Unit</u> return to Mitchell, turn left on OR-207 N 24 mi, turn left almost 20 mi to Fossil, turn left on OR-218 W 16 mi. Turn right into <u>Palisades Picnic Area</u> and park in the circle or the very first parking on the right for Geologic Time Trail, Arch Trail, and the Trail of Fossils. Or cheat and drive ¼ mi more on OR-218 W to the small paved pullout on the right (alternate TH, no restroom). For the longer but more scenic drive from <u>Painted Hills Unit</u> to Fossil and then <u>Clarno Unit</u> from the beginning of Bear Creek Road, turn left on gravel Burnt Ranch Road 3¼ mi, turn right on gravel Twickenham-Bridge Creek Cutoff Road 2 mi to a small fork (semiprimitive camping at Priest Hole down fairly steep and rough to the left 1½ mi, keeping right to campsites near the river), then 7 mi more enjoying the sights, turn left over the constricted bridge above the John Day River on Rowe Creek Road (N Twickenham Road) 15 mi (slow, winding, narrowing), the last 7 mi of which are paved. Turn left on OR-19 N 10 mi to Fossil and decide whether or not to extend the day with a side trip to Clarno Unit to complete the triad (some people skip this unit if any) or continue on OR-19 N to I-84 W near the Columbia Gorge. For Clarno Unit turn left on OR-218 W in Fossil and follow like above. From Clarno Unit check the maps and return to Fossil, then N to the Columbia Gorge for Portland or stay on OR-218 W to visit White River Falls toward The Dalles (see *Day Hikes in the Columbia River Gorge* by Don J. Scarmuzzi for hikes near The Dalles).

ROUTE: From Foree TH within the Sheep Rock Unit there are two quick trails at ½ mi each round-trip. Begin left of the outhouse on the wide Flood of Fire Trail heading N up open terrain. Easily climb built-in steps en route to the end at a cliff edge viewpoint. Enjoy the layered rock with a lot of white and slight greenish hues to bright red on top and down the sides to the valley. Begin right (E) from the parking circle for the Story in Stone Trail on a simple traverse (partly paved) and stay high and left at the fork (right is the end of the short clockwise loop). Pass several mounds of different

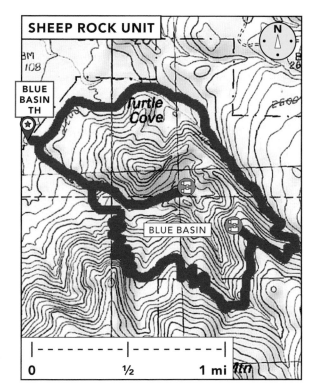

sizes with most being pink to brilliant turquoise. Rest at benches along the loop as you walk down from the climax and follow the path closer to the main blue-green fin back to end the loop, turning left to the TH.

From Blue Basin TH enjoy a clockwise loop hike with an interesting spur trail (4½ mi round-trip total, 1½ hours) with eye candy on the entire excursion. Begin left (N) at the immediate fork (right is the end of the loop) up the valley with very few trees around but with sage, larkspur, dandelion, and prairie star instead, and a larger

Painted Hills glowing at sunset, showing Oregon's splendidly diverse geology.

hill appearing to the right with charming rock formations and eroding cliffs. The wide dirt trail steepens a bit near the top as you wind up and cross a saddle on a little shoulder at the apex of the hike with a sign indicating the path down to the right about 100 ft. Take it to a better overlook of the mostly light green canyon below (that holds the main spur), the grass-covered slopes that border the hike, the valley floor, and the colorful mountains on the other side.

Walk back up from the overlook and turn right for the loop moving down a short series of narrow switchbacks after a brief traverse around a little alcove. Then traverse a few feet before descending more than a dozen steeper tight switchbacks NNW with great views into the canyon and the trail below with its many steel bridges. The trail eases to the signed juncture with the spur trail. Take it to the right (E) over gravel more than ½ mi to the end with a gradual gain up the beautiful and slender rocky canyon with 12 grated metal bridges (bad for dogs) and a babbling green brook (unless dry) to match the blue-green rock around it. There are even informative dinosaur fossil replica displays scattered about. Enjoy the wonderful setting from the end near a bench and respect closed areas while returning down. Finish more than ¼ mi NW without difficulty from the end of the loop to the TH.

From Red Hill TH for Red Scar Knoll (¼ mi round-trip) in Painted Hills Unit begin SSE on Red Hill Trail in the flats (just W of a bright red cone with white and gold becoming more prominent to the end) on the established path. The route ends up at a sign reminding you to proceed no farther. Return the same way.

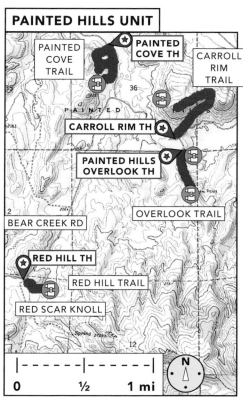

PAINTED HILLS UNIT

PAINTED COVE TRAIL

PAINTED COVE TH

CARROLL RIM TRAIL

CARROLL RIM TH

PAINTED HILLS OVERLOOK TH

OVERLOOK TRAIL

BEAR CREEK RD

RED HILL TH

RED HILL TRAIL

RED SCAR KNOLL

0   ½   1 mi

N

From <u>Painted Cove TH</u> on an adorable little counterclockwise loop, begin the less than ½ mi walk SW from the parking square on the wide Painted Cove Trail opposite the boardwalk (left) that is the end of the loop. Easily walk W of a long, red hill turning sharply left (E) up to the S end of the mound. At a clear juncture take the brief spur to the right less than 100 ft curving up to the best viewpoint on the walk that many people miss. See the entire bright red and gold knoll, the boardwalk, and Painted Hills Reservoir. Walk down to the more level boardwalk for a close-up view between red mounds and finish with more gold mixing in toward the TH.

From <u>Carroll Rim TH</u> at the saddle near the overlook, cross Bear Creek Road to the rocky and somewhat steeper Carroll Rim Trail (less than 2 mi round-trip) NNE as you begin to traverse above the Painted Hills valley. Again, not much for trees in the region, exposing more of the wildly colorful rocky hills, valleys, and mountains. Head steeper up a small alcove to a saddle on the high ridge with really cool rock formations. Cross to the E side off the thin ridge for a moment before joining it and ambling SW over more level ground past more sage and grasses to the end at a small plateau. The 360-degree view of the area from the highest point of all the walks and hikes in Painted Hills Unit is unsurpassed and relatively quiet!

From Painted Hills Overlook take the Overlook Trail uphill steadily more than ¼ mi S to the end marked by a sign. There is one brief spur partway up that hugs the edge of the rise E of the main path a few feet. Most pictures you see of Painted Hills are from this rise under various lighting and best after a recent shower, which shows the layers of vibrant rock at their best. See black, red, pink, gold, yellow, and blue-green rock like no other place in Oregon. It really is quite inspiring!

From Clarno Unit (1¼ mi round-trip total for three trails) take the Geologic Time Trail farthest left (W) from the parking and picnic area easily ¼ mi along the highway past the Palisades (tall rocky spires) over level ground to a juncture with the Trail of Fossils loop. Take this to the right, less than ¼ mi on a steep, rocky brief loop hike through time with several sites and turns through big boulders back down to a larger boulder near the alternate TH. From the alternate TH pullout off OR-218 where all paths meet, take the Arch Trail left (½ mi round-trip) W to begin up a few switchbacks, then NE steeper and rockier to the end. The arch (seen from below) is there at the top of a narrow volcanically-formed funnel after first passing a steep chute en route with fossilized logs embedded. The astute will see another arch in the Palisades above you on the way down. Return to either TH and drive home safely.

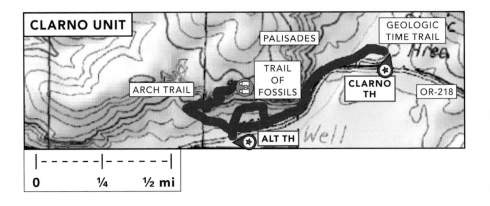

88 ANEROID MOUNTAIN

ELEVATION: 9702 ft, with around 1900 ft vertical gain total from the top of the Wallowa Lake Tramway

DISTANCE: Almost 5 mi up, nearly 10 mi round-trip

DURATION: 2½–3½ hours up, 5–7 hours round-trip

DIFFICULTY: Very challenging. Ups/downs, no trail on traverses at times, very steep terrain, scree, scrambling, high altitude, route-locating, steep, ice axe and traction devices with snow, mountain goat encounters possible, time-restricted because of somewhat limited hours to ride the Wallowa Lake Tramway

---

TRIP REPORT: Fantastic look at the Eagle Cap Wilderness in the Wallowa National Forest without having to commit to hauling camping gear for multiple days like most hikes in the region command. Either works, but for a nice, economical alternative to Wallowa Lake State Park for accommodations near the TH, try Hurricane Creek Campground from Enterprise or Joseph. Even though you begin at 8150 ft the hike is still demanding, just less so without adding East and Hidden Peaks along the high ridge to Aneroid Mountain. Best in late summer without snow/ice concerns. No fee required, and a restroom is present.

TRAILHEAD: Wallowa Lake Tramway (wallowalaketramway.com). Take I-84 E from Portland to exit 261 (La Grande/Elgin), turn right on OR-82 E 70 mi (with a couple turns) to Joseph (watch your speed through town). Continue 6 mi into OR-351 S around Wallowa Lake watching for wildlife, fork left in the woods (opposite Wallowa Lake State Park) ¼ mi to the narrow gravel driveway and parking on the left signed for the Mount Howard Tramway (330 mi, 5–5½ hours from Portland).

ROUTE: Pay the exorbitant fee ($33 or so each) to ride the rickety old tram round-trip; arrive early if time is a concern as several minutes pass before each tiny gondola car is released to rise an astounding 3650 ft in just 12 minutes! After great views of Wallowa Lake and the nearby mountains, arrive at the top where there is an informative kiosk, a small restaurant, a restroom, and several brief hiking trails with an unmarked one being our goal, taking folks to East Peak and Aneroid Mountain. Some folks bushwhack much easier down, then back up, the brief wide-open slope more directly to and from the trees and more solid path after summiting nearby Mount Howard. For both choices walk left from the tram station, then a quick right

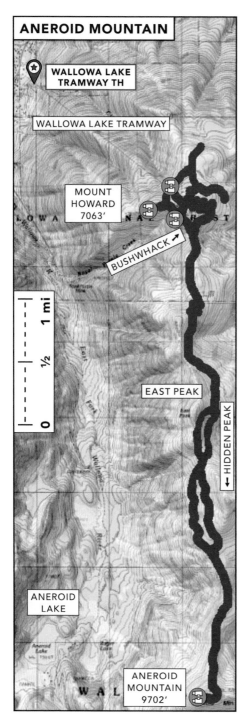

ANEROID MOUNTAIN

WALLOWA LAKE TRAMWAY TH

WALLOWA LAKE TRAMWAY

MOUNT HOWARD 7063'

BUSHWHACK

1 mi

½

0

EAST PEAK

← HIDDEN PEAK

ANEROID LAKE

ANEROID MOUNTAIN 9702'

(SE) up the hill past wooden steps a few hundred feet to a signed juncture. For the more solid path and slightly longer option turn left (E) toward the Valley Overlook/Loop very briefly to a four-way junction. Left is Valley Overlook/Loop, right is Summit Overlook/Loop, and straight is the unsigned, narrow path for Aneroid Mountain that quickly becomes a rather steep downhill track, moving E then easier SSW up gradually to the trees on the ridgeline under Mount Howard (¾ mi in).

For Mount Howard, from the first signed juncture turn right (SSW) less than ¼ mi without trouble to the unassuming Summit Overlook/Mount Howard with great views of the main ridge S up past a couple bumps to East Peak. Then following the skyline is Cusick Mountain, Sentinel Peak, Pete's Point, Eagle Cap, Craig Mountain, Matterhorn Peak, Sacajawea Peak, and Point Joseph to name a few. Loop clockwise down to more viewpoints en route to the tram tower or continue the adventure. Come back a few feet from Mount Howard for the steep bush-whack 150 yards and about 150 ft down in elevation without a trail directly to the solid path nearest the trees, then follow it right, up very steeply through the woods and open slope W of a little ridge bump as the traverse becomes easier to a wide saddle.

Hike up steeper turns with a few small cairns on the open ridge before you move left (E) of a larger ridge obstacle to an intersection with the right fork leading to the nearby saddle and route up the N ridge of East

Sentinel Peak, Pete's Point, and Eagle Cap above Aneroid Lake in the Wallowas.

Peak (1½ mi from the tram). Head left instead 1¼ mi contouring well below and E of the summit to the East Peak–Hidden Peak saddle. The first stretch is simple (unless snow-covered) to a faint juncture at a rockier, cliffy area where you can finally see Aneroid Mountain with Hidden Peak cloaked in between. Small stones may lead some right at the fork to the upper trail traveling in the same direction SSW about 30 ft higher and slightly more difficult than the lower path that traverses at around 8900 ft. Both thin paths move across a very steep slope that becomes a bit rougher near the East Peak–Hidden Peak saddle where you ascend the larger rocks to the wide saddle watching for cairns.

Like the S ridge of East Peak, Hidden Peak's S ridge is a rougher scramble than its N ridge and neither of these mountains are necessary to summit (although alluring) in attempting Aneroid Mountain. Cross the rocky saddle to the other side finding the most solid path S ¾ mi on a traverse W of and well below Hidden Peak to the Aneroid Mountain–Hidden Peak saddle. Very quickly this path too splits into at least two paths more suited for mountain goats across the steep slope at a weird angle. The higher one at about 8850 ft is a tad more difficult than the lower traverse at about 8800 ft as both cross marshy areas and steeper terrain with scree and with little to no trails to the saddle. The upper route moves down to the saddle near the end, while the lower one heads up somewhat (as a hint). As a consolation for your efforts you will be rewarded with a fantastic backdrop of the beautiful Aneroid Lake, Eagle Cap behind Pete's Point, Aneroid Mountain, Hidden Peak, and more, along the tough section!

At around 3½ mi from the tram at the long saddle between Hidden Peak and Aneroid Mountain you can finally see the remainder of the rocky and ethereal route S; it appears longer than it really is and is indeed the most fun of the entire hike! Ascend the wide granite-filled ridge to a tiny bump ½ mi away as the first goal without trouble, and then aim just to the right of a small rock band blocking the ridgeline ahead. It's much steeper, but you'll find a somewhat solid path that heads back toward the ridge crest and semisolid to loose rock to the top from there. A few (Class 2/3) options are nearest the peak depending on snow coverage. A slightly simpler one takes you a bit left, then bouldering right very briefly up the summit block, finishing a few feet easier SW to the top where it's completely breathtaking (in more ways than one)! Mind the clock as there's not much time for lingering during periods of shortened tram hours and there will be a whole lot more hiking down if you miss it!

<table>
<tr><td>**89**</td><td>**GLACIER LAKE**</td></tr>
</table>

ELEVATION: 8200 ft, with about 3700 ft vertical gain

DISTANCE: 12 mi up, 25–28 mi round-trip

DURATION: 6–8 hours up, 4–5 hours down; 2 days minimum

DIFFICULTY: Very challenging. Mandatory camp-in, very long, never too steep, solitude, much terrain above tree line, cold with snow coverage early/late in season (spring into August and from October on), mosquitoes until autumn

---

TRIP REPORT: While the surrounding treks can be accomplished as long day hikes from the THs, this one is best suited as a multi-day camping trip unless you are a serious trail runner. The chilly, beautiful lake with a few little islands lies in a prodigious, rocky basin carved out by the last of the glaciers during the Pleistocene Epoch. You'll have a front-row campsite from the banks of the water up to Glacier Peak and Eagle Cap. Unlike the Enchantments of Washington and other wilderness areas, Eagle Cap Wilderness within the Wallowa Mountains is a little more rustic providing no privy at camping areas. No pass required for the TH, and restrooms are present.

TRAILHEAD: Wallowa Lake TH. Take I-84 E from Portland to exit 261 (La Grande/Elgin), turn right on OR-82 E 70 mi (with a couple turns) to Joseph (watch your speed through town). Continue 6 mi into OR-351 S around Wallowa Lake, watching for wildlife; fork left in the woods (opposite Wallowa Lake State Park) 1 mi more to the end with a long pullout on the right opposite the trail before the turnaround (330 mi, 5–5½ hours from Portland).

ROUTE: Begin past the signage and free self-issue Wilderness Permit kiosk to an immediate juncture. Stay right (W) ¼ mi for West Fork Wallowa River Trail 1820 around the hydro-plant to another fork and continue left up the wide and well-trodden path shared with equestrians. The going is a bit steep and rocky ½ mi before undulating mildly upwards (slightly annoying with larger backpacks coming down) with great views through the trees and small clearings to the rugged mountains and ridges above on both sides. Hike S up the valley with the West Fork Wallowa River below as you pass boulder fields, tiny creeks, tons of flora, Ponderosa pine, fir, larch, and spruce. Rise up 2 switchbacks at less than 2½ mi from the TH and continue ½ mi through the thinning woods to a signed intersection.

To the right is the more crowded Ice Lake Trail 1808 that moves steeply around

Every turn at Glacier Lake holds another sensational surprise!

5 mi up to Ice Lake where many camp and even climb Matterhorn or Sacajawea Peaks. Stay straight (S) instead on Trail 1820 past the sign with a typo ("Trail 1920"). It's more than 3¼ mi of easy walking to the next major intersection in Six Mile Meadow (Lakes Basin Trail 1810). On the way to Six Mile Meadow you'll pass predominant Craig Mountain towering up to the right and cross nearly a couple dozen more petite creeks and seepages rolling along the dusty, gentle, wide trail to the juncture in the woods. From there some folks hike about 6½ mi W up Lakes Basin Trail past several subalpine lakes within the core of the Lakes Basin to Glacier Lake Trail 1806 at the isthmus on Moccasin Lake.

Continue straight (S) instead on West Fork Wallowa River Trail 1820 for 2¼ mi to the next junction. You will enjoy more sun than trees as you cross a couple small creeks on the narrower path, then head a bit steeper at times up the left side of the meadow through a clearing between forest groves. Enjoy views in all directions including Cusick Mountain at the S end of the valley and the rocky W face of nearby Sentinel Peak up to the left (SE). The sometimes-rocky trail heads up 2 switchbacks to a signless junction in a steep, rocky, and dry gully with a cairn present. Instead of switching back left stay straight 15 ft across the rocky bed and continue to traverse S back into the trees on Trail 1820 with wildflowers popping up everywhere August into September.

After crossing the rocky bed and hiking into the trees, you will round a turn left in about ¼ mi. This brings you into a scenic, narrow chasm with the river just to the right of Trail 1820 below. The hike morphs into a rather wild and spectacular alpine setting for the remainder up to Glacier Lake and beyond! Easily stroll ½ mi through the center of the next widening valley S with imposing granite cliffs above. Walk past white rock, boulders, and wildflowers, then rock hop or cross logs over the river at about 6800 ft (difficult earlier in the summer). See the long cascade coming down as you climb 4 switchbacks steeper to the right of it (with some decent rock formations). Turn right (W) around the corner easier and down a bit to the shallow and emerald Frazier Lake (10 mi from the TH). There are a few flat areas to camp for those who have had enough with carrying a heavier pack for one day.

About ¼ mi past Frazier Lake (careful not to step on baby frogs), you come upon a fork with a faded signpost within a pile of rocks. To the left is the rest of Trail 1808 up steeply to Little Frazier Lake and then Hawkins Pass. Hike right (NW) instead 2 mi more, now on Glacier Lake Trail 1806 to Glacier Lake. Look back to see Frazier Lake and notice a long, narrow, deeper blue lake tucked in behind Frazier Lake against the steep mountain. Head up a switchback, a turn, and 2 more switchbacks through boulder fields as the route becomes a bit steeper NW up the right side of the river in the next grand valley. There are virtually no trees for shade or protection including at the large lake (the few pines there drip sap at times). See Oregon's Glacier Peak between the mountains, then Eagle Cap as well, before you reach the top of the widening valley. The last ½ mi or so is relatively easier than below as you turn left (WSW) through the rocks and scree more narrowly to the outlet of Glacier Lake (more than 12¼ mi from the TH).

From the lake, Trail 1806 continues ¾ mi and a few hundred feet N up to Glacier Pass, then steadily steeply 2¾ mi NW down directly to the isthmus at Moccasin Lake in the Lakes Basin. Camping areas are located along the main trail as you continue right, around the lake dotted with a few small islands. Smaller paths head to the left in the boulder-filled meadow next to the lake before the trail steepens somewhat to the pass. Glacier Lake basin at the foot of Glacier Peak (with a sawtooth ridge on the right and glaciers under the summit to the lake) and Eagle Cap look great from the pass, but the other side is slightly underwhelming (outside of the glimpse of the Matterhorn) as the lakes in the core are out of sight until you continue down to the N.

Investigate the path at Glacier Lake on both sides of the outlet stream if you like and even take a frigid plunge into the striking blue-green water. Cross the outlet stream over logs without difficulty and follow the path SE for the perfect reflection of Glacier Peak and Eagle Cap's summit. See the long cascade coming down under Eagle Cap as well as all the granite cliffs and steep scree slopes into the lake. More camp spots are plausible here. It's also feasible to continue ½ mi around to discover another colorful, much smaller lake after scrambling the steep, wide rocky shelf 40 ft above the lake, then walking down a bit. Take advantage while camping to enjoy the sunset, the starry night's light show, and then sunrise as well! Return by the same long route to Wallowa Lake TH.

ELEVATION: 9572 ft, with 4120 ft vertical gain to the summit including a side trip to nearby Mirror and Moccasin Lakes

DISTANCE: 11½ mi up including a 2 mi side trip, 21 mi round-trip

DURATION: 5–6 hours up including the side trip, 10–12 hours round-trip

DIFFICULTY: Mix of very challenging as a multi-day trip camping within Lakes Basin, and expert only to Eagle Cap from the TH as a day hike. Extremely long, rougher trail (especially for horses to the lakes), steeper in places, signed, switchbacks, high altitude, rocky, steeper snow slopes to rise or cross above Upper Lake changes Class 1 hike to Class 3 early in season (until late July or August) with traction devices and ice axe mandatory, wildlife may include pikas, deer, elk, black bear, mountain lion, bighorn sheep, mountain goats, hawks, falcons, eagles, and finches

---

TRIP REPORT: The masterpiece of the Wallowas within the Eagle Cap Wilderness is in the very center and is, in fact, Eagle Cap itself. This summit holds one of the very finest views from any high point in Oregon. At least eight sizable valleys dotted with high alpine lakes radiate out from the summit in mind-blowing fashion where it's evident why so many people spend several days camping within the many picturesque basins. It's like The Enchantments within Alpine Lakes Wilderness (of Washington) met Yosemite National Park! The abundant rock and granite here contain slate, quartzite, limestone, marble, and basalt. By all means camp near Mirror Lake or Upper Lake as others do, but for this trek we cheat by cramming a lot into one very long day with a lighter backpack and a stay at one of many campsites near or at the busy TH. Expect more snow, wildlife, and bugs before late July or August and less of those (and also fewer people) in

Isthmus on Moccasin Lake to Glacier Pass.

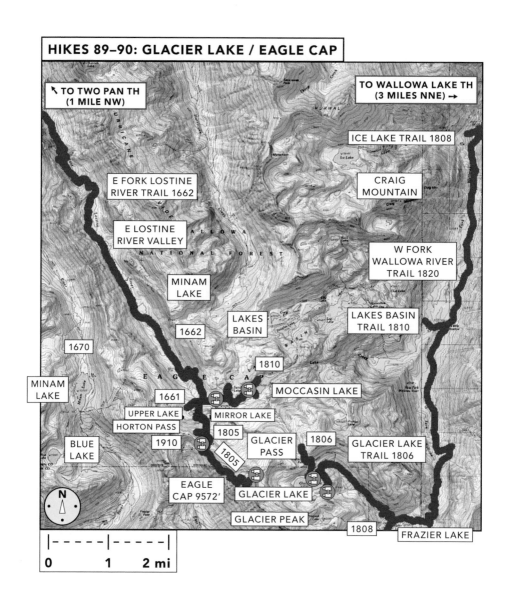

TO TWO PAN TH
(1 MILE NW)

TO WALLOWA LAKE TH
(3 MILES NNE) →

ICE LAKE TRAIL 1808

E FORK LOSTINE
RIVER TRAIL 1662

CRAIG
MOUNTAIN

E LOSTINE
RIVER VALLEY

W FORK
WALLOWA RIVER
TRAIL 1820

MINAM
LAKE

LAKES
BASIN

LAKES BASIN
TRAIL 1810

1662

1670

1810

MINAM
LAKE

1661

MOCCASIN LAKE

UPPER LAKE
HORTON PASS

MIRROR LAKE

1805

1910

GLACIER
PASS

1806

GLACIER LAKE
TRAIL 1806

BLUE
LAKE

1805

N

EAGLE
CAP 9572'

GLACIER LAKE

GLACIER PEAK

1808

FRAZIER LAKE

0   1   2 mi

September where cooler temperatures and different colors prevail. Northwest Forest
Pass required, and an outhouse is present.

TRAILHEAD: Two Pan TH. Take I-84 E from Portland to exit 261 (La Grande/
Elgin); turn right on OR-82 E 53 mi (with a couple turns); fork right in Lostine on
Lostine River Road 6¾ mi where it turns into gravel FR-8210 for almost 5 mi; then
narrower, rougher gravel (from the Guard Station), but not steep, 5¾ mi to the end at
a spacious parking area for cars, trucks, and equestrians (330 mi, 5½–6 hours driving
from Portland).

ROUTE: Between the equestrian parking lot and the auto parking areas (including on the side along the road) is the Two Pan TH with kiosks and signage for the Lostine River trails. Hikers should fill out the free self-issue Wilderness Permit and head right ¼ mi easily to a signed intersection. To the right is the trail for the W Fork Lostine's longer parallel valley to Minam and Blue Lakes (almost 3 mi before the trail eases somewhat through the long upper valley). Stay left (SE) instead on E Fork Lostine River Trail 1662 and ascend 6 steeper turns over rocks to the flatter dirt trail and a fork before a footbridge at 1 mi from the TH. Turn right on

East Fork Lostine River valley to Eagle Cap.

Trail 1662 to the W side over the E Lostine River, which is more of a beautiful creek or stream at best, but whatever.

Watching for horses and horse manure, hike up steadily ¾ mi SE to the first of 11 rocky, steep switchbacks before the route levels through the forest over the wide and dusty trail. Hear, then see, a nice little cascade before the route steepens again less than ½ mi to the upper valley where you have your first look at Eagle Cap. See Lost Lake and ponds through a few trees on the left, which are really just widening expanses in the river. The trail is flatter but not exactly a cakewalk making you pay attention 2 mi SE through the vast glacier-carved valley to another bridge crossing the waterway. Stay on the right (W) side above the river to the crossing through several large rock fields with wildflowers, tiny creeks, and developing views of Eagle Cap and the steep canyon walls surrounding you.

Move over the meadow on the trail to the left (E) side and walk across a bridge around 5½ mi and almost 2 hours from the TH. In less than ½ mi ascend 2 switchbacks through the woods, then in ¾ mi climb E up 8 steeper switchbacks before the easier traverse SE briefly to the Lakes Basin. Pass the first sign ("Lakes Basin Mgmt" and "Fires prohibited beyond this point") to another signpost for "Horton Pass, Minam Lake, Ivan Carper Tr 1661, Lakes Basin Tr 1810, E Fk Lostine Tr 1662, and East Eagle Tr 1910" at a major intersection 7¼ mi and 3 hours from the TH. The view from the basin is intensified as you see Mirror Lake left and are drawn in all scintillating directions. For Eagle Cap directly walk right (S) on East Eagle Trail 1920 and for the Lakes Basin side trip put your jaw back in your mouth and stroll left (E) on Lakes Basin Trail 1810 much easier.

Pass Mirror Lake noting the steep, rocky walls and cliffs on the far side, which add to the drama. There are many great angles with reflections of the mountains above and especially of Eagle Cap. Stay off revegetating areas as you reach a signpost within a rather large rocky cairn less than ½ mi from the previous juncture. Stay right for Moccasin Lake (opposite the trail to nearby Sunshine Lake or Hurricane Creek) passing huge, sloped and flat rock. See Eagle Cap more clearly and with even better reflections from Moccasin Lake as you walk down 4 quick switchbacks on the rocky path. Turn right (SE) at the sign toward Glacier Pass a few feet to the isthmus connecting land masses between the smaller and much larger lake with only a few well-placed rocks and boulders. The visceral experience is memorizing from this area! And you are only 1 mi from juncture with E Fork Lostine River Trail 1662. Investigate further on either trail around the lake and return back up to the major intersection past (W of) Mirror Lake.

For Eagle Cap (2¼ mi to summit) walk straight (W) from the juncture with Trail 1662 on East Eagle Trail 1920 a few feet to another signed junction. Right (Trail 1661) leads to camping at nearby Upper Lake or steeply up, then down, over Carper Pass to Minam Lake in the W Fork Lostine. Walk left (S) instead toward Horton Pass on East Eagle Trail 1910 through a lovely meadow using the rocks and logs to hop over the nearby creek. Arrive quickly above scenic Upper Lake (and waterfall behind) with a fork down to the water but stay left on the rockier trail as you ascend 12 steeper switchbacks. After the fourth switchback you see the tip of Matterhorn Peak (9826 ft), a magnificent and precipitous marble and limestone mountain, which soon defines part of the view to the N.

Hike Trail 1910 up a steep gully that retains snow until late in summer. Walk up the snow or rocky sides without difficulty to the top at a small sign and juncture (1 mi from the major intersection in Lakes Basin). See the long E Fork Lostine River valley you ascended to the NW. Right moves SW to Horton Pass and E Fork Eagle Creek on Trail 1910. Walk left (S) instead on Eagle Cap Summit Trail 1805 and soon up the 6 steepest and rockiest switchbacks of the day to the high ridge less than ½ mi away. Lingering snow may require traction devices and route-finding early, but it's usually fairly navigable. And while descending much of this section it's possible for more experienced hikers to sort of glissade down (while standing up) to the solid rocky trail. High altitude sickness, known as hypoxia, affects everyone differently. If you feel nauseous, headachy, dehydrated, or experience vertigo, consider descending immediately and rehydrating as a partial cure. If not, press on.

Once on the high ridge, the Eagle Cap Wilderness truly unfolds as you appreciate the untold grandeur before you! Jagged mountaintops, grandiose valleys,

Dreamy gaze to Eagle Cap reflected from the Lakes Basin.

and high alpine lakes too many to number will be some of the focus to the peak. Turn left (SE) steeply up the high ridge for a moment before traversing steadily very carefully on the right (S) side of the ridgeline around a bump. Not paying attention on the traverse across the super-steep slope and falling off the trail would certainly be treacherous; otherwise the route remains one of the longest Class 1 hikes to a major Pacific Northwest summit. Arrive at a small, partially (short) tree-covered saddle before the final push up the summit block.

Climb steadily and steeply NE up the final 8 rocky switchbacks through mostly wide-open terrain with a few stunted pines. Finish easier over rocks between the pines on the widening and rounded summit of Eagle Cap. Without a doubt this sought-after locale holds one of the very best 360-degree panoramas for a peak anywhere! Continuing E you see the large deep blue Glacier Lake below for the first time in its own grand basin. Just ENE is Glacier Pass N of the lake. Past the lake E is Sentinel Peak with Pete's Point and Aneroid Mountain NE. And due N between the Hurricane Divide and Hurwal Divide are Matterhorn and Sacajawea Peaks towering above countless colorful lakes. Return to the Mirror Lake area or hike the long slog 9½ mi NW to the Two Pan TH (which seems at least 3 mi too long for most sane individuals on a day hike). Cheers!

INDEX

Page locators in **bold** indicate maps; page locators in *italics* indicate photographs.

Abiqua Falls, Butte Creek Falls to Abiqua Falls, 155–57, *156*, **157**
Adams Glacier, 85
Aiken Lava Bed, 79
Alec Creek, *13*
Aneroid Mountain, 273–75, **274**, *275*, 283
Angry Mountain, 57, 59, 60
Ape Cave Loop, 31–33, **32**, *33*
asters, *122*, *125*

Bald Mountain, 126, 144
Barlow Butte, 106, 107
Barrett Spur Summit, **143**, 147, 148–49, *149*
Barrett's penstemon, *202*
Battle Ax Creek, **174**, 176
Battle Ax Mountain, 169, *175*, 179
Bays Lake, 206, *208*, 209
Bear Creek Mountain, 65–67, *65*, **66**, *67*, 70
Bear Lake, **17**, 19
Bear Point, 202–3, *202*, **203**
Belknap Crater, 219–21, *219*, **220**
Big Lake, 212, **212**
Big Slide Mountain to Bull of the Woods Loop, 180–82, *180*, **181**, *182*
Bird Mountain, 16, **17**, 18–19
Black Butte, 169, 191, 196
Black Crater, 220, 221–22, **221**, *222*
Blue Lake, 37–38, **38**
Booth Lake, 191, 192, **193**
Broken Hand, 224, 225
Broken Saddle, 224, **227**
Broken Top, 88, 175, 190, 223–25, *225*, 226–29, **227**, *228–29*
Buck Peak, **136**, 139–41, *140*, *141*
Bull of the Woods Lookout, 180, 181, *182*
Bull of the Woods Wilderness, Big Slide Mountain to Bull of the Woods Loop, 180–82, *180*, **181**, *182*
Bull Run Lake, 141, *141*

Butte Creek Falls to Abiqua Falls, 155–57, *156*, **157**

Cairn Basin, Vista Ridge to Cairn Basin Loop, **143**, 146–47
Canada thistle, *195*
Cannon Beach to Silver Point, 248–49, **248**, *249*
Canyon Creek Meadows, **193**, 194–96
caves: Ape Cave Loop, 31–33, **32**, *33*; Kazumura Cave, 32
Cirque Lake, Porcupine Rock to Cirque Lake Loop, **193**, 194–96
Clark's Mountain (Tillamook Head Summit), 245–47, *245*, **246**
Clatsop Spit Loop, 241–42, *241*, **242**
Clear Lake, **17**, 19, 64
Cloud Cap Inn, 112, **113**, 114, 116
Coe Glacier, 149
Coffin Mountain, 175, *178*, 179
Cold Spring Creek (Tamanawas Falls), 110, 111
Coldwater Peak, 35, 40–42, *40*, *41*, *42*, 45
Cone Peak, Iron Mountain Lookout to Cone Peak Loop, 185–88, **186**, *187*
Conrad Glacier, *65*
Cool Creek, **96**, 97
Cool Creek Trail 794, **96**, 99
Cooper Spur, **113**, 115–17, 149
Cooper Spur Shelter, **113**, 114, 117, *117*
Copper Creek Falls, 14
Craig Mountain, 274, 277
Crater Lake, 232, 233, 234–39, **235**, *236*, *238*
Crescent Glacier, 87, *87*, 89
Crescent Ridge, 39, *39*
Crook Glacier, 223
Crooked Creek Falls, 79
Cultus Lake, **17**, 18
Curly Creek Falls, 11, 14
Cusick Mountain, 274

Detroit Lake, **177**, 178
Devil's Cauldron, **251**, 253
Devil's Horn, 67, 70
Devil's Peak, 95
Devil's Peak Lookout, **96**, 99–100, *100*
Devil's Pulpit, **136**, 141
Devil's Tooth, 100
Diamond Peak, 190, 202, 228
Dickey Lake, 182
Dinah-Mo Peak, 203, 209
The Dome, 42, 47
Dome Rock, 177–79, *177*, *178*, *179*
Double Falls, 154
Downing Creek, Upper Downing Creek
    Falls, 197–98, **197**, *198*
Drake Falls, 154
Dryer Glacier, **51**, 55

Eagle Cap, 274, *275*, 279–83, **280**, *281*, *283*
East Fork Lostine River, *281*
East Peak, 274–75, **274**
East Soda Peak, Soda Peaks Lake to West
    Soda Peak, 22–25, *23*, **25**
Ecola State Park, 245–47, **246**, *247*
Eden Park, Vista Ridge to Cairn Basin Loop,
    143, 146–47, *147*
Elephant Rock, 179
Eliot Glacier, **113**, 115, 116
elk, *63*
Elk Cove, 148–49
Elk Lake, 19
Elk Meadows, 118–19, **119**
Elk Mountain, 256, 257–60, **257**, 260–61,
    261
Elkhorn Falls, 165
Equestria Lake, 83, 85

Falls Creek Falls, 20–21, **20**, *21*
Fort Stevens State Park, 241, **241**
Frazier Lake, 278
Fret Creek Trail 456A, **108**, 109
Frog Lake Buttes, 106

Garfield Peak, 234, **235**, *236*, 237
Gilbert Peak, 60, 64, *65*, 66–67, 68, 69, 70,
    73
Ginnette Lake, **62**, 63, *64*
Glacier Lake (Eagle Cap Wilderness),
    276–78, *277*, **280**

Glacier Lake (Johnson Peak), **58**, 59
Glacier Peak, 88
Glisan Glacier, 145
Gnar Gnar Trail, 103, **103**
Gnarl Ridge Trail 652, 119, **119**, 121
Goat Creek, 73, 75
Goat Lake, 60, **71**, 74, 76
Goat Lake Loop to Hawkeye Point, **71**,
    72–74, *73*, *74*
Goat Mountain, 34–36, **36**
Goat Rocks Wilderness: Bear Creek
    Mountain, 65–67, *65*, **66**, *67*; from
    Coldwater Peak, 42; Goat Lake Loop to
    Hawkeye Point, **71**, 72–74, *73*, *74*; from
    High Camp/Adams Glacier Meadows, 83;
    Hogback Mountain, 62; Johnson Peak, 57,
    58, 60; from Lemei Rock Loop, 18; from
    McClellan Viewpoint, 11; from Mount
    Adams, 88; Nannie Ridge to Cispus Pass,
    68–70, **71**; Old Snowy Mountain, **71**,
    75–76, *76*; from West Soda Peak, 24
Great Pyramid, **96**, 98
Green Knob, 95, **95**
Green Lakes basin, 226–28, **227**
Grizzly Lake, 46, **48**
Grizzly Peak, 199–200, *199*, *200*

Hawkeye Point, 57, 60, 64, 67, **71**, 72–74,
    73, *74*
Haystack Rock, 249, *249*
Heart Lake, 57, **58**, 60
Hellroaring Canyon Viewpoint to Iceberg
    Lake Overlook, 77–80, *77*, **78**, *79*
Hellroaring Falls, *79*, 80
Henline Mountain and Henline Falls, 165,
    166, 167–70, *169*
Hidden Peak, 275
High Camp/Adams Glacier Meadows to
    Equestria Lake, 83–85, **84**, *85*
High Prairie, **108**, 109
hiking: information and safety, 7–8;
    overview map, **2–3**; trailheads and
    parking, 7
Hogback Mountain, 61–64, **62**, *64*
Hole-in-the-Wall Arch, **41**, 42
Horseshoe Meadows, 80, 82, **82**
Huckleberry Mountain, 93
Huffman Peak, Siouxon Peak to Huffman
    Peak, 28–30, **29**, *30*

Humbug Mountain, 243, **243**, 244
Hunchback Mountain, **96**, 97–98, *99*
Hunchback Trail 793, **96**, 100

Iceberg Lake, 77, *77*, **78**, 80, 88, *88*
Illumination Rock, 123, **124**, *128*, *130*, 135
Illumination Saddle, **124**, 128–30, *128*, *130*
Indian Heaven Wilderness, Lemei Rock
  Loop, 16, **17**, 18–19, *19*
Iron Mountain Lookout to Cone Peak Loop,
  185–88, **186**, *187*
Ives Peak, 60, 64, *65*, 67, 68, 69, 70

Jawbone Flats, 171, **174**, 176
Jefferson Park to Park Ridge Summit, 207–9,
  208, **209**
John Day Fossil Beds National Monument,
  267
Johnson Peak, 57–61, *58*, 64, 67, 73
Johnston, David, 40
Junction Lake, 16, **17**, 19

Kings Mountain Loop, 256–60, **257**, *258*,
  259, 260–61
Klickitat Glacier, 80
Knob Peak, *180*, 181
Koosah Falls, Sahalie–Koosah Falls Loop,
  214–16, *214*, **215**

Ladd Creek, 147
Ladd Glacier, 149
Lake Lenore, *180*, 181
Lake Wapiki overlook, 16, **17**, 18, *18*
Lakes Basin, Eagle Cap Wilderness, **280**,
  281–83, *283*
Lamberson Butte to Newton Creek Canyon
  Loop, 118–21, **119**, *120*
lavender, *65*
Leech Lake, **62**, 63, 64
Lemei Rock Loop, 16–19, **17**, *19*
Lewis and Clark Discover Trail, 246–47
Lewis Glacier, 231
Lewis River Falls, 11–15, **12**, *14*
Lily Basin, 57, *58*, 59–60, *59*
Little Belknap Crater, 219–20, **220**
Little Frazier Lake, 278
Little Mount Adams, 80
Little North Santiam Falls, 166

Little North Santiam Loop to Three Pools,
  163–67, *165*, **166**
Little Zigzag Canyon Loop, 121–23, **124**
Lookingglass Lake, 81, *81*, 82
Lookout Mountain, 108–9, **108**
Loowit Trail 216, 38, 39, **51**, 52
Lost Lake, **136**, 137, 139, *140*, 141, 145
Lost Lake Butte, **136**, 137–39, *138*
Lostine River, 281, *281*
Lower Copper Creek Falls, 14–15
Lower Soda Creek Falls, 183–84, *183*, **184**
Lunch Counter, 86, 87–89, **87**
lupine, *73*, *126*, *191*

Martin Lake, 192, **193**
Marys Peak, 169, 179, 262–65, *262*, **263**, *264*
Matterhorn Peak, 274, 277, 283
Maxwell Butte, 189–90, *189*, 192, **193**
Mazama Glacier, 80, **87**, 88
McCall Glacier, *65*
McIntyre Ridge, 91, 92, **92**, 93
McKenzie River: Sahalie–Koosah Fall Loop,
  214–16, *214*, **215**; Tamolitch (Blue) Pool,
  216–18, **217**, *218*
McNeil Point, 142–45, *142*, **143**, 147
Meade Glacier, *65*
Meta Lake, 44, **44**
Middle Falls Creek Falls, *21*, **21**
Middle Sister, *219*, 220
Miller Creek Falls, 14
Mirror Lake, 101–2, *102*, **103**
Mississippi Head, 122, *123*, **124**, 125–27,
  130
Moccasin Lake, 278, *279*, **280**
Moraine Lake, **227**, 230
Mother Lode Mountain, 181
Mount Adams: from Bear Creek Mountain,
  66, *67*; from Buck Peak, 141; from Cooper
  Spur, 116, *117*; from Devil's Peak
  Lookout, 100; from East Soda Peak, 24;
  from Eden Park, 147; from Goat Lake
  Loop, 73; from Goat Mountain, 35; from
  Harry's Ridge Trail, 41; from Hogback
  Mountain, 64; from Johnson Peak, 60;
  from Lemei Rock Loop, 19, *19*; from
  Lookout Mountain, *109*; from Lost Lake
  Butte, 139; from McNeil Point, 145; from
  Mount St. Helens, *54*, 55; from Nannie
  Ridge, 69; from Newton Creek Canyon,

120; from Old Snowy Mountain, 76, *76*; from Rooster Rock Viewpoint, 162; from Siouxon Peak, 29; from Sister Rocks, 28; Stagman Ridge Loop, 80–82, *81*, **82**; Suksdorf Ridge route, 86–89, **87**, *88*; from Table Rock, 160; from Tamanawas Falls, 111; from Yocum Ridge, *135*

Mount Bachelor, 224, 228, *231*

Mount Bailey, 233

Mount Baker, 88

Mount Defiance, 141

Mount Hood: from Aiken Lava Bed, 79; from Barrett Spur, *149*; from Big Slide Mountain, 181, *182*; from Buck Peak, *141*; Cooper Spur route, **113**, 115–17; from Devil's Peak Lookout, *99*, 100; from Dome Rock, 179; from Eden Park, 147; from Harry's Ridge Trail, 41; from Henline Mountain, 169; Illumination Saddle, **124**, 128–30, *128*, *130*; from Iron Mountain, 188; Little Zigzag Canyon Loop, 121–23, **124**; from Lookout Mountain, 109; from Lost Lake, *140*; from Lost Lake Butte, 138, *138*; from Maxwell Butte, 190; from McNeil Point, 144, 145; from Mount Adams, 87; from Palmateer Point, 107; from Ramona Falls Loop, 132; Ramona Falls Loop, 131–33, **131**, *132*; from Rockpile, 98; from Rooster Rock Viewpoint, 162; from Salmon Butte, 95; Salmon Butte, 94; from Sister Rocks, *26*, 28; from Stagman Ridge Loop, 82; from Table Rock, 160; from Trillium Lake Snowshoe Loop, 105; from West Soda Peak, 24; from Whetstone Mountain, 175; from Wildcat Mountain, 91, 92–93, *93*; Yocum Ridge, 130, 133, 134–35, **134**, *135*

Mount Howard, 274, **274**

Mount Jefferson: from Bear Point, 203; from Big Slide Mountain, 181; from Broken Top, 229; from Buck Peak, 141; from Cooper Spur, 117; from Devil's Peak Lookout, 100; from Dome Rock, 177, *178*, 179; from Grizzly Peak, 200, *200*; from Henline Mountain, 168, 169; from Illumination Saddle, 129; from Iron Mountain, 187, 188; from Little Zigzag Canyon Loop, 122; from Lookout Mountain, 109; from Marys Peak, 264; from Maxwell Butte, 190; from Mount Adams, 87; from Mount St. Helens, 55; from Newton Creek Canyon, 119, 120; from Paradise Park/Mississippi Head, 127; from Sister Rocks, 28; from Table Rock, 160; from Tom Dick and Harry Mountain, 102; from Triangulation Peak, 202, *202*; from Whetstone Mountain, 175, *175*; from Wildcat Mountain, 93; from Yocum Ridge, 135

Mount Margaret, 42, 45, 46–47, *47*, **48**, 49

Mount Rainier: from Bear Creek Mountain, 66; from Buck Peak, 141; from Cooper Spur, 116, *117*; from East Soda Peak, 24; from Eden Park, 147; from Goat Lake Loop, 73; from Goat Mountain, 35; from Harry's Ridge Trail, 42; from High Camp/Adams Glacier Meadows, 85; from Hogback Mountain, 64; from Johnson Peak, 59, *59*, 60; Lemei Rock Loop, 18, 19; from Lookout Mountain, 108; from McNeil Point, 145; from Mount Adams, 88; from Mount St. Helens, *53*, 55; from Nannie Peak lookout, 69; from Old Snowy Mountain, 76; from Rooster Rock Viewpoint, 162; from Salmon Butte, 95; from Siouxon Peak, 29, *30*; from Sister Rocks, 28; from Table Rock, 160; from White Pass Ski Area, *61*, 63; from Yocum Ridge, *135*

Mount St. Helens: from Ape Cave Loop, 32; from Cooper Spur, 116; from East Soda Peak, 24; from Eden Park, 147; from Goat Mountain, 35; from High Camp/Adams Glacier Meadows, 85; from Hogback Mountain, 64; from Illumination Saddle, 130; from Iron Mountain, 188; from Johnson Peak, 60; from McClellan Viewpoint, 11; from McNeil Point, 145; Monitor Ridge Route, 50–55, *50*, **51**, *52–53*, *54–55*; from Mount Adams, 87; from Mount Margaret, 46–47, *47*; from Nannie Ridge, 69; from Old Snowy Mountain, 76; from Rooster Rock Viewpoint, 162; from Siouxon Peak, 29, 30, *30*; from Stagman Ridge Loop, 81; from Table Rock, 160; from Wildcat Mountain, 91; from Yocum Ridge, *135*

Mount Shasta, 160

Mount Stuart, 67
Mount Thielsen, 228, 232–33, *233*, **233**
Mount Washington: from Belknap Crater, 220; from Big Slide Mountain, 181; from Dome Rock, 178, 179; from Henline Mountain, 169; from Iron Mountain, 188; from Marys Peak, 264; from Maxwell Butte, *189*, 190; north ridge route, 211–13, **212**, *213*; from Rooster Rock Viewpoint, 162; from Table Rock, 160; from Three Fingered Jack Loop, 192
Mount Whittier, 42, 45, 46, 47, **48**, 49
Mountaineer Trail, Mount Hood, 123, **124**, 127, 128, 129, 130

Nannie Peak, 68, 69, **71**
Nannie Ridge to Cispus Pass, 68–70, *69*, *70*, **71**
Neahkahnie Mountain, 250–53, *250*, **251**, *252*
Needle Rock, **177**, 178
Newton Clark Glacier, 115, 120
Newton Creek, 118–19, 121
Newton Creek Canyon, 119–20, **119**
No Name Lake to Broken Saddle, 223–25, *225*, **227**
North Falls, 152, 154
Norway Pass and Harmony Falls, 43–45, *44*, **44**, *45*, 46

Observation Peak to Sister Rocks, 26–28, *26*, **27**
Observation Peak Trail 132, 23, 27–28, **27**
Olallie Butte, 135, 169, 175, 179, 204, 206
Old Snowy Mountain, 60, 64, 67, 68, 69, **71**, 73–74, *74*, 75–76, *76*
Opal Creek, 170–72, **171**, *172*, 176
Opal Creek Wilderness, **2**, 168, 173
Oswald West State Park, 250–51, **251**

Pacific Crest Trail: Belknap Crater, 219–20, **220**; Buck Peak, **136**, 140–41; Crater Lake, **235**, 236–37; High Camp/Adams Glacier Meadows, **84**, 85; Hogback Mountain, 61, **62**, 63–64; Illumination Saddle, 129, 130; Lemei Rock Loop, **17**, 19; Little Zigzag Canyon Loop, 122, **124**; McNeil Point, **143**, 144; Mount Thielsen, 232–33, **233**;

Mount Washington, 211–12, **212**; Old Snowy Mountain, 75; Pacific Crest Trail to Park Ridge Summit, 204–6, **205**, *206*; Palmateer Point, 106–7, **107**; Paradise Park to Mississippi Head Loop, **124**, 125–26; Porcupine Rock to Cirque Lake Loop, **193**, 196; Ramona Falls Loop, **131**, 132–33; Sheep Lake intersection, 70; Three Fingered Jack Loop, 191–92, **193**
Packwood Lake, 59, *59*, 76
paintbrush, *69*, *125*, *147*
Painted Hills, 267–72, **268**, **269**, *270–71*, **271**, **272**
Palisade Point, 109
Palmateer Point, 106–7, *106*, **107**
Pamelia Lake, **199**, 200, *200*
Paradise Park to Mississippi Head Loop, **124**, 125–27, *125*, *126*
Pechuck Lookout, **159**, *162*, 163
Peter Iredale Wreck, 242, *242*
Pete's Point, 274, **275**, 283
Pigtail Peak, **62**, 63, 64
Piker's Peak, **77**, 80, 88, 89
Point Joseph, 274
Porcupine Rock to Cirque Lake Loop, **193**, 194–96
Preacher's Peak, **136**, 141
Prouty Glacier, 230
Pulpit Rock, 149
Pyramid Butte, 204

Ramona Falls, 126, **131**, 134, **134**, 135
Ramona Falls Loop, 131–33, **131**, *132*
Reid Glacier, **124**, 128, 130, 135
rhododendrons, 91, 92, 93, 94, 95, 99, *99*, 102, 111, 178
Rockpile, **96**, 97–98, *98*
Rogers Peak, 253–55, *254*, **255**
Rooster Rock to Pechuck Lookout, **159**, 160–63, *161*, *162*
Round-the-Mountain Trail, Mount Adams, 77, **78**, 79, 81–82, **82**, 87, **87**

Sacajawea Peak, 274, 277, 283
Saddle Mountain, 243–44, **243**, *244*
Sahalie–Koosah Falls Loop, 214–16, *214*, **215**
St. Helens Lake, 42, *42*
Salmon Butte, 94–95, *94*, **95**

Salmon-Huckleberry Wilderness: Devil's Peak Lookout, **96**, 99–100, *100*; Hunchback Mountain, **96**, 97–98, *98*; Salmon Butte, 94–95, *94*, **95**; from Tom Dick and Harry Mountain, 102; Wildcat Mountain, 91–93, **92**, *93*
Salmon Lake, 95
Salmon River, 97
Sandy Glacier, 144, 145
Sandy River, 131–33, **131**, *133*, 135
Santiam River, Little North Santiam Loop to Three Pools, 163–67, *165*, **166**
Sardine Mountain, 179
Sawmill Falls, 171, **171**, *172*
Schreiner Peak, 181
scree: Cispus Pass, 70; East Soda Peak, 24; Mount Hood, 116; Mount Washington, 212; Park Ridge, 205; Table Rock, 160
Senecal Spring, **108**, 109
Sentinel Peak (Eagle Cap Wilderness), 274, *275*, 283
Sentinel Peak (Lost Lake), *140*
Sheep Canyon Loop, 37–39, *37*, **38**, *39*
Sheep Canyon Trail 240, 38, **38**, 39
Sheep Lake, 68, 69, 70, *70*, **71**
Silcox Hut, 122, 123, **124**, 129
Silver Falls State Park, 151–54, *151*, **152**, *153*
Silver Point, Cannon Beach to Silver Point, 248–49, **248**, *249*
Siouxon Peak to Huffman Peak, 28–30, **29**, *30*
Snowgrass Flats, 70, **71**, 74, *74*, 75
Soda Creek, Lower Soda Creek Falls, 183–84, **183**, *184*
Soda Peaks Lake, 24, 25, **25**
Soda Peaks Lake to West Soda Peak, 22–25, *23*, **25**, *26*
South Falls, 153–54, *154*
South Sister: from Belknap Crater, *219*, 220; from Broken Top, 228–29, *228–29*; south ridge route, **227**, 230–31, *231*
Spire Rock, **201**, 202
spirea, *192*
Spirit Lake, *40*, 41, 42, 43, *44*, **44**, 45, *45*, *52*
Square Lake, 191, **193**
Stagman Ridge Loop, 80–82, *81*, **82**
Suksdorf Ridge, Mount Adams, 86–89, **87**, *88*
Swift Glacier, **51**, 53

Swift Reservoir, 29, *30*

Table Rock, 158–60, *158*, **159**, 162
Taitnapum Falls, 15
Takhlakh Lake, 83, *85*
Tamanawas Falls, 110–11, *111*, **113**
Tamolitch (Blue) Pool, 216–18, **217**, *218*
Teardrop Pool, **227**, 230
Thomas Condon Paleontology Center, 267, 268
Thor's Playroom, *165*
Three Fingered Jack: from Dome Rock, *178*, 179; from Henline Mountain, 169; from Iron Mountain, 188; from Marys Peak, 264; from Maxwell Butte, 190; from Porcupine Rock/Cirque Lake Loop, 194; Three Fingered Jack Loop, 190–92, **193**; from Whetstone Mountain, 175
Three Pools, Little North Santiam Loop to Three Pools, 163–67, *165*, **166**
Three Sisters: from Big Slide Mountain, 181; from Broken Top, 228–29, *228–29*; from Dome Rock, 178–79; from Henline Mountain, 169; from Illumination Saddle, 129; from Iron Mountain, 188; from Little Zigzag Canyon Loop, 122; from Marys Peak, 264; from Maxwell Butte, 190; from Mount Washington, 213; from Newton Creek Canyon, 120; from Rooster Rock Viewpoint, 162; from Three Fingered Jack, 192; from Yocum Ridge, 135
Tieton Peak, *65*, 67, 70
Tillamook Head, Clark's Mountain (Tillamook Head Summit), 245–47, *245*, **246**
Tillamook Lighthouse, 245, *245*, 246
Tilly Jane Snowshoe Loop, 112–14, **113**, *114*, *115*, 117
Timberline Lodge, 122, 123, **124**, 125, 128, 129
Timberline Trail 600, 120–21, **124**, 125–27, 129, 130, **131**, 132–33, 144
Tom Dick and Harry Mountain, 101–3, **103**, 123
Tombstone Pass, Iron Mountain Lookout to Cone Peak Loop, 185–88, **186**, *187*
Toutle Trail 238, 34–35, 38, **38**
Trail 133, 23–25, **25**
Trail of the Flowers, 78, **78**, 79

Trapper Creek Wilderness, 21, 22–24, *26*
Treasure Cove Overlook, 250, *250*, **251**, 252
Triangulation Peak, 201–2, **201**, *202*
Trillium Lake Snowshoe Loop, **103**, 104–5, *105*
trilliums, *46*
Triple Falls, 166
Tumble Falls, 179
Tumble Lake, 177, 178, 179, *179*
Twin Falls, 154
Twin Lakes, 106–7, *106*, **107**
Twin Peaks, 63, 64

Upper Downing Creek Falls, 197–98, **197**, *198*
Upper Falls Creek Falls, 21, **21**
Upper Sheep Canyon Falls, *37*, 38, **38**

Vidae Falls, 238
Vista Ridge to Cairn Basin Loop, **143**, 146–47

Walupt Lake, 70, **71**
Wasco Lake, **193**, 195, 196
Watchman Peak Lookout, 234, **235**, 236–38
waterfalls: Butte Creek Falls to Abiqua Falls, 155–57, *156*, **157**; Copper Creek Falls, 14; Crooked Creek Falls, 79; Curly Creek Falls, 11, 14; Double Falls, 154; Drake Falls, 154; Elkhorn Falls, 165; Falls Creek Falls, 20–21, *20*, **21**; Harmony Falls Viewpoint, 45; Hellroaring Falls, *79*, 80; Henline Falls, 169–70, *169*; Lewis River Falls, **12**, 13–15, *14*; Little North Santiam Falls, 166; Lower Copper Creek Falls, 14–15; Lower Soda Creek Falls, 183–84, **183**, *184*; Middle Falls Creek Falls, *21*, **21**; Miller Creek Falls, 14; North Falls, 152, 154; Ramona Falls, 126; Ramona Falls Loop, 131–33, **131**, *132*; Sahalie–Koosah Falls Loop, 214–16, *214*, **215**; Sawmill Falls, 171, **171**, *172*; Silver Falls State Park, 151–54, *151*, **152**, *153*; South Falls, 153–54, *154*; Taitnapum Falls, 15; Tamanawas Falls, 110–11, *111*, **113**; Triple Falls, 166; Tumble Falls, 179; Twin Falls, 154; Upper Downing Creek Falls, 197–98, **197**, *198*; Upper Falls Creek Falls, 21, **21**; Upper Sheep Canyon Falls,

37, 38, **38**; Vidae Falls, 238; Winter Falls, *151*, 152
West Soda Peak, Soda Peaks Lake to West Soda Peak, 22–25, *23*, **25**
Western pasqueflower, *145*
Whetstone Mountain, 169, 173–76, **174**, *175*
Wildcat Mountain, 91–93, **92**, *93*
wildflowers: Barrett's penstemon, *202*; Bear Creek Mountain, *65*; Canada thistle, *195*; Cispus Pass, *69*; Elk Meadows, 119; Goat Lake, 74; Hawkeye Point, *73*; High Camp/Adams Glacier Meadows, 83; Lily Basin, 57, 59–60, *59*; lupine, *73*, *126*, *191*; Marys Peak, 262, 265; McNeil Point, 144, 145, *145*; Mount Hood, *122*, *125*, *126*; Mount Washington, *211*; Mount Whittier, 49; Neahkahnie Mountain, 252; Old Snowy Mountain, 75; paintbrush, *69*, *125*, *147*; Palmateer Point, 107; Salmon Butte, 94; spirea, *192*; trilliums, *46*; Western pasqueflower, *145*; Wildcat Mountain, 91, 92, 93, *93*
Winter Falls, *151*, 152
Wizard Island, **235**, 236, *236*
Wy'East Basin, **143**, 147

Yocum Ridge, 130, 133, 134–35, **134**, *135*, 145, 149

Zigzag Canyon Overlook, 121, 122, **124**
Zigzag Glacier, **124**, 127, 128, 129, 130

DEDICATION

A very special thank you to first responders, EMTs, local and distant firefighters, Oregon State Fire Fighters Council, Oregon Volunteer Firefighters Association, National Guard, National Interagency Fire Center, Washington State Fire Fighters' Association, U.S. Forest Service, and any others mistakenly overlooked for their dangerous and tireless work year after year saving people and keeping our trails and natural places pristine for generations to come!

ACKNOWLEDGMENTS

Northwest Waterfall Survey, United States Geological Survey Map Database, my Graphic Arts Books/Westwinds Press edit and design team Rachel Lopez Metzger, Olivia Ngai, and others.

Library of Congress Control Number: 2017956811

ISBN 9781513261423 (paperback)
ISBN 9781513261430 (hardbound)
ISBN 9781513261096 (e-book)

Printed in China
22 21 20 2 3 4 5

Edited by Michelle Blair
Indexed by Sheila Ryan
Overview Map by Lohnes+Wright

Cover photo by Don J. Scarmuzzi. The preeminent perch from Park Ridge to Mount Jefferson above Jefferson Park is so worthy a goal that not one but two hikes here are dedicated to reaching it. Happy hiking!

Proudly distributed by Ingram Publisher Services

WestWinds Press®
An imprint of

WEST
MARGIN
PRESS

WestMarginPress.com

WEST MARGIN PRESS
Publishing Director: Jennifer Newens
Marketing Manager: Angela Zbornik
Editor: Olivia Ngai
Design & Production: Rachel Lopez Metzger